Mark Twain's

Letters from Hawaii

Mark Twain's
Letters from Hawaii

Edited and with an Introduction
by A. Grove Day

University of Hawaii Press

Honolulu

PUBLISHED ORIGINALLY BY APPLETON-CENTURY

UNIVERSITY OF HAWAII PRESS EDITION 1975

01 02 03 04 05   16 15 14 13

Library of Congress Cataloging-in-Publication Data

Clemens, Samuel Langhorne, 1835–1910.
    Mark Twain's letters from Hawaii.

    Reprint of the ed. published by Appleton-Century,
New York.
    1. Clemens Samuel Langhorne, 1835–1910—Journeys.
2.   Hawaii–Description and travel—To 1950.I.   Day,
Arthur Grove, 1904–   ed.II.   Title.
PS1331.A3D3   1975   919.69'03'2   74–31359
ISBN 0–8248–0288–8

University of Hawai'i Press books are printed on acid-free
paper and meet the guidelines for permanence and
durability of the Council on Library Resources.

Introduction

Why should anyone today want to read the travel letters written by Mark Twain from the Hawaiian Islands more than a hundred years ago?

To answer that question, the reader ought to know a few facts—when Mark Twain came to the islands, what he did there, what he considered worth writing about, and what effect this adventure had on his later, more celebrated career.

Mark Twain's lifelong love affair with the future fiftieth state began when the steamer *Ajax* arrived in Honolulu on Sunday, March 18, 1866. This beloved American author, Samuel Langhorne Clemens (1835–1910), later to be termed "the Lincoln of our literature," had only recently begun to use the pseudonym "Mark Twain," which was later to become the most famous one in the world. He came as a newspaper correspondent to write a series of travel letters, and spent only four months and a day in the Sandwich Islands, as they were then called, but he never forgot his adventures there.

Weary of journalism in Nevada and California, and not yet the author of a single published book, Mark Twain was to discover that this first excursion out of his native United

States would bring him pleasure and fame. It furnished him with a much-needed period of refreshment; gave him a start on a new and lucrative profession—that of lecturer; and provided material for a series of popular travel accounts anticipating those later made into his first important book, *The Innocents Abroad*. One of his Hawaiian letters was a notable "scoop" on a famous Pacific sea disaster that made the author a "literary personage," so that when Mark Twain returned to California after his Sandwich Islands odyssey he was "about the best-known honest man on the Pacific Coast." Some of the finest descriptions of the islands, including his celebrated "prose poem," came from his pen. Perhaps the most often quoted remark in Hawaiian literature is Mark Twain's characterization of the future Aloha State as "the loveliest fleet of islands that lies anchored in any ocean." And as late as 1884 he began to write a novel with a Hawaiian setting.

The arrival of the man who signed himself "Mark Twain" on the passenger list of the *Ajax* was not noted in the local press. A tireless sightseer, Twain began at once his reportorial duties, riding around the capital island of Oahu on a spavined horse. The young man from Missouri, with drooping moustache and flaming red hair, was usually garbed in a starched brown linen duster reaching to his ankles, and he talked and gesticulated so much that people who did not know him thought he was always drunk. After a tour of the neighboring island of Maui, where he climbed to the summit of the giant crater of Haleakala and viewed Iao Valley, he took a schooner to the Kona Coast, voyaged around the southern end of the Big Island (where at Waiohinu he is reputed to have planted a monkeypod tree which grew to immense size before it blew down in a windstorm in 1957), and then climbed around the Kilauea Volcano district. After visiting the sugar plantations of the Hamakua region he rode along the deep gash of Waipio Valley, crossed the Waimea tableland, and caught the little steamer *Kilauea* at Kawaihae for his return to Honolulu.

Most important of Mark Twain's contributions to Hawaiian literature is the series of twenty-five picturesque letters he wrote as a roving reporter for the Sacramento *Union,* most powerful and popular newspaper on the West Coast. These were printed in both the daily and weekly editions. The letters are excellent reportage by a keen-eyed man who all his life was a shrewd observer of the universe around him. They cover not only the sugar and whaling industries, which were of interest to American businessmen of the time, but also the Hawaiian trade, whose exports brought high fees to the United States Customs. One can learn from the letters such useful facts as that, a century ago, the chief market for Hawaiian oranges was California. Much of their material deals with scenery and climate, politics, social conditions, history and legends, Polynesian lore, the monarchy, religious affairs, horse traders, and even the "millions of cats" of Honolulu. No mention is made of leprosy, brought into the kingdom of Hawaii before 1854, probably because Twain did not wish to frighten off the businessmen who would be his main readers. The fabulous future of California and the Pacific is prophesied in Letter 23.

As might be expected of the writer who became America's greatest comic genius, the letters are sprinkled with humor. A good example is the "equestrian excursion" on the sleepy steed Oahu, recounted in the sixth and seventh letters, or in the naïve and sometimes vulgar comments of

Mark's invented traveling companion, Mr. Brown. The letters are laden also with dozens of descriptions of scenic features of the islands that are still landmarks today. If we make proper allowance for the calculated exaggerations for which Twain was famous, one can recommend a close reading of these Sandwich Island letters to anyone who wishes a frank and sometimes violent view of Hawaii in the reign of the fifth Kamehameha.

Aside from sketches of travel, the letters reveal a number of personal attitudes. Included is an admiring portrait of Matthew Kekuanaoa, president of the legislative assembly and father of the ruling monarch, Kamehameha V. The king himself appears in a highly favorable light in letters 13 and 17. Later, in a letter appearing in the New York *Daily Tribune* of January 9, 1873, in which he favored annexation of the islands by the United States, Twain recalled, "There was no trivial royal nonsense about him; he dressed plainly, poked about Honolulu, night and day, on his old horse, unattended; he was popular, greatly respected, and even beloved." The letters also discuss the possible successors to the throne, Prince William C. Lunalilo and David Kalakaua. (Both of them were later elected kings, "Prince Bill" in 1873 and Kalakaua in 1874.) The month-long funeral ceremonies and rites of national mourning at the death of Princess Victoria Kamamalu are described.

Missionary activities are also discussed. Although he remarked in his *Notebook,* "More missionaries and more row about saving these 60,000 people than would take to convert hell itself," it is clear that Twain felt the Christian, democratic order in the islands was infinitely better than the old pagan feudalism that it had endeavored to replace.

He had a good word to say also for the Roman Catholic mission under Bishop L. D. Maigret. But he felt that the incursion of the Church of England, founded in Honolulu in 1862 under royal British auspices, was unnecessary. He reserved his most choice invective for Bishop T. N. Staley and the lanky American finance minister, C. C. Harris, who, said Twain, belonged "body and soul, and boots, to the King of the Sandwich Islands and the 'Lord Bishop of Honolulu.' "

Perhaps the most famous single letter is the fifteenth. It was a news story headlined "Burning of the Clipper Ship *Hornet* at Sea," and was dated at Honolulu on June 25, 1866. To Mark Twain had come a chance to report one of the most amazing incidents in the chronicles of the sea. The ship *Hornet*, commanded by Captain Josiah A. Mitchell, caught fire near the equator south of Hawaii, from an explosion which resulted when one of the mates, against orders, went below with an open light to draw a can of varnish. The crew abandoned the ship in such haste that holes were staved in the boats in which they had to embark on a bitter voyage from which half of them did not return.

Captain Mitchell and fourteen of his men arrived in the longboat at Laupahoehoe, a village on the shore of the island of Hawaii, after a forty-three-day, open-boat ordeal in which they voyaged four thousand miles. Lack of food and tight rationing of water had caused a conspiracy, intent on cannibalism, against the captain, who dared not sleep for fear of mutiny. James Norman Hall, in a footnote to his *The Tale of a Shipwreck,* calls the achievement of Captain Mitchell "fully as heroic as that performed by Captain Bligh and the *Bounty*'s men, and, in some respects, even more remarkable."

When some of the rescued seamen were brought to a hospital in Honolulu, Mark Twain himself was laid up in his lodgings with saddle boils as a result of his strenuous ride around Hawaii. But his recent acquaintance, Anson Burlingame, on his way to serve as United States Minister to China, arranged to have Twain carried in his cot to the hospital. There Burlingame questioned the survivors and Twain took notes for the article which he sat up all night to write. Next morning the manuscript of this longest of the letters to the *Union* was tossed aboard a schooner which had already cast off for San Francisco.

This front-page story was the first full report of the disaster to reach the United States and was widely reprinted. On his return to California, Twain boldly billed the newspaper for three hundred dollars, a sum fifteen times the usual amount of twenty dollars for his letters. He later used the *Hornet* material for two other articles: "Forty-three Days in an Open Boat" (*Harper's Magazine*, December 1866) and "My Debut as a Literary Person" (*Century Magazine*, November 1899).

Dates given at the heads of the letters cannot always be fully trusted. The last eight letters were published after Mark's return to California, and some of them were written after his return and dated earlier. Letter 23 was dated "Honolulu, September 10," nearly a month after he was back in San Francisco. The last letter, dated "Volcano House, June 3d—Midnight," was published on November 16, and gave the date of his stay at the volcano rather than the date he wrote the letter that wound up the series.

Some years later, when Mark Twain needed to fill out his book of western travel, *Roughing It* (1872), he wrote chapters 74 through 78 by drawing upon the ninety thousand words of his *Union* letters about Hawaii. The chapters in *Roughing It* (omitted in most later reprints) used thirty thousand words from the letters and added some five thousand words of new material, describing how he got down the volcano and back home, since Letter 25 leaves him perched in the famed Volcano House at Kilauea. Some of the material in the letters was left out because it was too spirited, for when part of it was reprinted in the Honolulu newspapers, a great stir resulted. Twain never printed, however, the material he jotted down in his dog-eared notebook, and another stir is to be expected in Hawaii when the forthcoming unexpurgated edition of Twain's *Notebook* is published.

The shorter, later version of the Hawaiian adventures in *Roughing It* is smoothly written and artfully told, and the crude Mr. Brown does not appear. A good sample of this style is found in the passage about Mark's explorations in the volcano region. Although the fire pit of Halemaumau was not in violent eruption at the time, Twain's account states that Vesuvius was "a mere toy, a child's volcano, a soup kettle" by comparison. He also describes a harrowing hike in darkness, lighted only by eruptive flares, across the bottom of the pit, when straying a few inches off the invisible path might plunge the reporter and his comrade into chasms below the rotten lava crust.

Mark Twain left the islands on July 19 on the sailing vessel *Smyrniote*. Arriving in San Francisco without funds, he was persuaded to earn some money by giving a lecture at the Academy of Music in that city on October 2, 1866. The announcement ended: "Doors open at 7 o'clock; the trouble to begin at 8." The topic—one that was to be his sole platform subject for a year and a half and a staple of his repertory for seven—he often billed as "Our Fellow Savages of the Sandwich Islands." Almost collapsing with stage fright, Mark nevertheless put on a performance that was greeted with uproarious enthusiasm. Thereafter, as he said, "I have always been able to gain my living without dong any work." Lecturing—expanded to include readings from his works and after-dinner speaking—became a profession for him second only to that of authorship.

Many times during his life Mark Twain yearned to revisit the islands to which, as Albert Bigelow Paine claimed, Twain always planned "to return some day, to stay there until he died." In a letter of October 26, 1881, to his friend Charles Warren Stoddard in Hawaii, Mark wrote:

> If the house would only burn down, we would pack up the cubs and fly to the isles of the blest, and shut ourselves up in the healing solitudes of Haleakala and get a good rest; for the mails do not intrude there, nor yet the telephone and the telegraph. And after resting, we would come down the mountain a piece and board with a godly, breech-clouted native, and eat poi and dirt and give thanks to whom all thanks belong, for those privileges, and never house-keep any more. . . . What I have always longed for was the privilege of living forever away up on one of those mountains in the Sandwich Islands overlooking the sea.

Many admirers of Mark Twain do not know that in 1884 he was at work on a novel about Hawaii. The Mark Twain Collection in the University of California Library at Berkeley contains seventeen pages of this manuscript. Part of the story, according to a letter written by Twain to his friend William Dean Howells on October 7, would deal with the leper colony on the island of Molokai. Like other visiting writers to Hawaii, such as Robert Louis Stevenson,

Jack London, and James A. Michener, Twain was fascinated by the drama of exile to the gray peninsula where Father Damien labored and died.

The novel was apparently never completed. The reason may be, as suggested by Fred W. Lorch in *American Literature* for March 1958, that Twain incorporated much of his material, and not a few main ideas, into a novel with a quite different setting—*A Connecticut Yankee in King Arthur's Court* (1889). "It will be seen," remarks Professor Lorch, "that Mark Twain's indictment of the social, political, and religious practices in the Islands is strikingly similar to his indictment of these same practices in King Arthur's England. And no less remarkable is the similarity between the role of the American missionaries who destroyed the old order in the Sandwich Islands and the role of the Connecticut Yankee who sought to free King Arthur's serfs in much the same way." Moreover, there are similarities between King Arthur and King Kamehameha V, the first reigning monarch that Mark Twain ever saw.

Mark Twain dreamed for almost thirty years of returning to the paradise he had remembered. He was destined to get a tantalizing glimpse of Honolulu again in 1895, when he was on a globe-girdling lecture trip designed to repay the creditors who had lost money in Twain's financial collapse. First stop in the Pacific was Hawaii, and from the deck of the steamer *Warrimoo* the author once more sighted Diamond Head and Honolulu, but was not allowed to go ashore, because cholera had broken out in the capital of what was now the Republic of Hawaii. The third chapter of *Following the Equator* tells of this disappointment and is an additional bit of Hawaiiana by Twain.

The first publication of the celebrated "prose poem" had come in the New York *Sun* for April 9, 1889, reporting an extemporaneous tribute by Mark Twain to his lovely islands. According to Paine's biography of Twain, "In April, '89, he made an address at a dinner given to a victorious baseball team returning from a tour of the world by way of the Sandwich Islands. . . . He told of the curious island habits for his hearers' amusement, but at the close the poetry of his memories once more possessed him." This passage always comes to mind when thinking of Mark Twain and Hawaii:

> No alien land in all the world has any deep strong charm for me but that one, no other land could so longingly and so beseechingly haunt me, sleeping and waking, through half a lifetime, as that one has done. Other things leave me, but it abides; other things change, but it remains the same. For me its balmy airs are always blowing, its summer seas flashing in the sun; the pulsing of its surfbeat is in my ear; I can see its garlanded crags, its leaping cascades, its plumy palms drowsing by the shore, its remote summits floating like islands above the cloud wrack; I can feel the spirit of its woodland solitudes, I can hear the plash of its brooks; in my nostrils still lives the breath of flowers that perished twenty years ago.

Now, what do Mark Twain's letters from Hawaii have to say to readers in the final quarter of the twentieth century?

First, many among the millions of visitors to the islands in recent years will appreciate the historical and social reports that this keen observer gives of influential events and local customs. Many of the scenes he described are little changed. His accounts of the Kona Coast and the Kilauea

Volcano region are still reliable guides. Flora and fauna are much the same. Honolulu still has "millions of cats." The legislature, it is feared, is still "like all other legislatures." The whaling ships have disappeared, but the tassels of sugarcane still wave over the smiling landscape.

Again, lovers of adventure can enjoy the adventures of Mark Twain, the Huckleberry Finn among foreign correspondents. He it was, be it noted, who first reported the story of the survivors of the ill-fated clipper ship *Hornet*, a great Pacific odyssey.

Moreover, students of the career of Samuel Langhorne Clemens can note herein the skill and development of a young author whose earliest fame resulted from the writing of amusing travel accounts. Mark Twain's first real book, *The Innocents Abroad* (1869), was also based on letters of travel. Had his correspondence from Hawaii been collected and bound at the time, however, his first book would have been *Letters from Hawaii*. The Sandwich Islands experience also provided Mark with material for a lifelong career as lecturer, and gave him a variety of subjects that appeared in later works.

Likewise, the present volume can be examined for its literary values. The humor, for example, is less polished than that found in more celebrated works, but some of the descriptive passages are hard to equal elsewhere. Twain, along with Herman Melville (who also visited Hawaii), is one of the two American authors most frequently analyzed in scholarly publications in recent years. Students might find in the Hawaii volume further material for sources and critiques.

Finally, the millions of latter-day "innocents" who follow Mark Twain's footsteps around the fiftieth American state might to worse than imitate the spirit in which he sojourned in the islands. Wherever he went, he found— among residents and foreigners alike—the hospitable spirit of aloha that is still a treasured quality of life in Hawaii. Mark might even be the patron of those who want to unwind and to enjoy the simple art of living. He was the prototype of the beachcomber, the dropout. As he admitted, he went to the island of Maui to stay a week—he stayed five, and never touched a pen. "I only got back yesterday," he wrote in Letter 12. "I never spent so pleasant a month before, or bade any place good-bye so regretfully. I had a jolly time. I would not have fooled away any of it writing letters under any consideration whatever." Mark Twain knew when to work hard, and when to relax!

A. GROVE DAY
Senior Professor of
    English, Emeritus
University of Hawaii

A NOTE ON THIS EDITION

Although often reprinted separately, Mark Twain's letters from Hawaii were never collected in book form until 1937, when the Grabhorn Press in San Francisco published, with an introduction and conclusion by G. Ezra Dane, a limited edition of 550 copies, entitled *Letters from the Sandwich Islands* and illustrated by Dorothy Grover. The following year a photo-offset reprint was issued by the Stanford University Press. The Dane volume omitted part of Letter 3 on Hawaiian trade and all of letters 10 (whaling), 15 (the *Hornet* disaster), and 23 (the sugar industry). These four letters were published in 1939 by Thomas Nickerson of Honolulu, with an introduction by John W. Vandercook; the volume, entitled *Letters from Honolulu*, was limited to one thousand copies and was printed by the Lakeside Press of Chicago. The first complete reprinting appeared as Appendix C of *Mark Twain and Hawaii* (1947), the excellent study by the late Walter Francis Frear, well-known judge and third governor of the Territory of Hawaii. Frear's book was also published by the Lakeside Press and limited to one thousand autographed copies. The first complete general edition, edited and with an introduction by A. Grove Day, was published in 1966 by Appleton-Century, New York. It is hoped that this reprinting of that edition, with a revised introduction, will win new readers for these charming letters by one of America's greatest writers.

Mark Twain's

Letters from Hawaii

1❀

CLIMATIC

We arrived here today at noon, and while I spent an hour or so talking, the other passengers exhausted all the lodging accommodations of Honolulu. So I must remain on board the ship tonight. It is very warm in the stateroom, no air enters the ports. Therefore, have dressed in a way which seems best calculated to suit the exigencies of the case. A description of this dress is not necessary. I may observe, however, that I bought the chief article of it at "Ward's."

There are a good many mosquitoes around tonight and they are rather troublesome; but it is a source of unalloyed satisfaction to me to know that the two millions I sat down on a minute ago will never sing again.

SEA-GOING OUTFIT

I will "bunch" the first four or five days of my "log" of this voyage and make up a few paragraphs therefrom.

We backed out from San Francisco at 4 P.M., all full—some full of tender regrets for severed associations, others full of buoyant anticipations of a pleasant voyage and a revivifying change of scene, and yet others full of schemes

3

for extending their business relations and making larger profits. The balance were full of whiskey. All except Brown. Brown had had a couple of peanuts for lunch, and therefore one could not say he was full of whiskey, solely, without shamefully transcending the limits of truth.

Our little band of passengers were as well and thoughtfully cared for by the friends they left weeping upon the wharf as ever were any similar party of pilgrims. The traveling outfit conferred upon me began with a naval uniform, continued with a case of wine, a small assortment of medicinal liquors and brandy, several boxes of cigars, a bunch of matches, a fine-tooth comb and a cake of soap, and ended with a pair of socks. (N.B. I gave the soap to Brown, who bit into it, and then shook his head and said that "as a general thing, he liked to prospect curious foreign dishes and find out what they were like, but he couldn't go that"—and threw it overboard.) This outfit is a fair sample of what our friends did for all of us. Three of our passengers—old sea captains, whalers—Captain Cuttle, Captain Phelps, and Captain Fitch (fictitious names)—had bought eight gallons of whiskey, and their friends sent them eleven gallons more. (N.B. Owing to head winds and a rough sea, this outfit did not hold out; the nineteen gallons were ample for the proposed eight-day voyage, but we were out upwards of ten days, you see. The whalers were all dry and unhappy this morning.)

"MAKING SAIL"

Leaving all care and trouble and business behind in the city, now swinging gently around the hills and passing house by house and street by street out of view, we swept down through the Golden Gate and stretched away toward the shoreless horizon. It was a pleasant, breezy afternoon, and the strange new sense of entire and perfect emancipation from labor and responsibility coming strong upon me, I went up on the hurricane deck so that I could have room to enjoy it. I sat down on a bench, and for an hour I took a tranquil delight in that kind of labor which is such a luxury to the enlightened Christian—to wit, the labor of other people. Captain Godfrey was "making sail," and he was moving the men around briskly. He made short work of the job, and his orders were marked by a felicity of language which challenged my admiration. Said he:

"Let go the main-hatch. Belay! Haul away on your tops'l jib! Belay! Clew up your top-gallants'l spanker-boom halliards! Belay! Port your gaff-tops'l sky-scrapers! Belay! Lively, you lubbers! Take a reef in the lee scuppers! Belay! Mr. Baxter, it's coming on to blow at about four bells in the hog-watch; have everything taut and trim for it. Belay!"

The ship was rolling fearfully. At this point I got up and started over to ask the captain if it wouldn't be a good idea to belay a little for a change, but I fell down. I then resumed my former seat. For twenty minutes after this I took careful note of how the captain leaned his body to port when the ship lurched to starboard, and hard to larboard when she lurched to port, and then got up to practice a little. I only met with moderate success, though, and after a few extraordinary evolutions, fetched up against the mainmast. The concussion did not injure the mast perceptibly, but if it had been a brick house the case might have been very different. I proceeded below, rather discouraged.

SEVERAL EFFECTS OF THE TURBULENT SEA

I found twenty-two passengers leaning over the bulwarks vomiting and remarking, "Oh, my God!" and then vomiting again. Brown was there, ever kind and thoughtful, passing from one to another and saying, "That's all right—that's all right, you know—it'll clean you out like a jug, and then you won't feel so onery and smell so ridiculous."

The sea was very rough for several days and nights, and the vessel rolled and pitched heavily. All but six or eight of us took their meals in bed constantly, and remained shut up in the staterooms day and night. The saloons and decks looked deserted and lonesome. But gradually the seasick unfortunates convalesced until our dinner complement was augmented to fifteen or twenty. There were frames or "racks" on the tables to keep the dishes in their places, but they did not always succeed in doing it. An occasional heavy lurch would hoist out a dozen and start them prospecting for the deck. Brown was bitterly opposed to the racks, and said he "wasn't raised to eat out of them brick molds." No rack would answer for soup. The soup plate had to be held in the hand and nicely tilted from side to side to accommodate the fluid to the pitching of the ship. The chairs were not fastened to the floor, and it was fun to see a procession of gentlemen go sliding backwards to the bulkhead, holding their soup plates on a level with their breasts, and giving their whole attention to preventing the contents from splashing out. They would come back with the flowtide and sail away again on the ebb. It would not do to set a glass of water down. The attentive waiters kept bringing water to Brown, who was always talking, and would not see the glass set down in time to make his remark heard: "Frank, don't bring me any water; have to drink it at a gulp to keep it from spilling, and I've had more'n enough already." And yet about once every two minutes some passenger opposite would put up his hands and shrink behind them and exclaim, "Your water, Mr. Brown! your water! Look out for your water!" and lo, the suffering Brown would find his glass once more replenished and canting dangerously to leeward. It would be instantly seized and emptied. At the end of a quarter of an hour Brown had accomplished nothing in the way of dinner, on account of these incessant watery interruptions. The boy Frank brought another glass of water, and said, "Will you have some beefsteak, Mr. Brown?" "Take that water and go to blazes with it! Beefsteak! no! I've drank eleven gallons of water in fifteen minutes, and there ain't room enough in me for a sirloin steak off'm a sand fly!"

JOURNAL

Heaving my "log," I find the following entries on my tablets:

Wednesday, 7th—left San Francisco at 4 P.M.; rough night.

Thursday—weather still rough. Passengers nearly all sick; only half a dozen at breakfast out of thirty.

Friday—strong gale all night; heavy sea on this evening; black overhead.

Saturday—weather same, or more so.

You can take that four-days dose of your infamous "Pacific," Mr. Balboa, and digest it, and you may consider it well for your reputation in California that we had pretty fair weather the balance of the voyage. If we hadn't, I would have given you a blast in this letter that would have made your old dry bones rattle in your coffin—you shameless old foreign humbug!

Mark Twain

2❀

HONOLULU, MARCH 19, 1866.

THE AJAX VOYAGE CONTINUED—

THE "OLD NOR'WEST SWELL"

On the Sunday following our departure we had a fine day, and no wind scarcely, yet the sea ran high and the ship rolled a good deal. Upon inquiry, I learned that this was caused by the "old nor'west swell," which resembles any Broadway "swell" in that it puts on a good many airs and conducts itself pretentiously even when it is not able to "raise the wind." The old nor'west swell, produced by the prevailing wind from that quarter, is always present in these seas, ever drifting on its eternal journey across the waters of the Pacific, year after year—and century after century as well, no doubt—and piling its billows aloft, careless whether it be storm or calm. The wind and the swell both die out just above the equator. Another wind and another swell come up around Cape Horn from the opposite direction, and these die out just below the equator —so that a windless, waveless belt is left at the center of the earth, which marks the equator as distinctly as does the little black line on the map. Ships drift idly on that glassy sea, under the flaming sun of the tropics, for weeks

together, without a breath of wind to flutter the drooping sails or fan the sweltering and blasphemous sailors.

A BLAST FOR BALBOA, THE DISCOVERER

We hear all our lives about the "gentle, stormless
Pacific," and about the "smooth and delightful route to
the Sandwich Islands," and about the "steady blowing
trades" that never vary, never change, never "chop
around," and all the days of our boyhood we read how
that infatuated old ass, Balboa, looked out from the top
of a high rock upon a broad sea as calm and peaceful as a
sylvan lake, and went into an ecstasy of delight, like any
other greaser over any other trifle, and shouted in his foreign tongue and waved his country's banner, and named
his great discovery "Pacific"—thus uttering a lie which
will go on deceiving generation after generation of students while the old ocean lasts. If I had been there, with
my experience, I would have said to this man Balboa,
"Now, if you think you have made a sufficient display of
yourself, cavorting around on this conspicuous rock, you
had better fold up your old rag and get back into the
woods again, because you have jumped to a conclusion,
and christened this sleeping boy-baby by a girl's name,
without stopping to inquire into the sex of it."

From all I can discover, if this foreign person had named
this ocean the "Four Months Pacific," he would have come
nearer the mark. My information is to the effect that the
summer months give fine weather, smooth seas, and steady
winds, with a month and a few days good weather at the
fag end of spring and the beginning of autumn; and that
for the other seven or eight months of the year one can
calculate pretty regularly on head winds and stern winds,

and winds on the quarter, and winds several points abaft the beam, and winds that blow straight up from the bottom, and still other winds that come so straight down from above that the fore-stuns'l-spanker-jib-boom makes a hole through them as clean as a telescope. And the sea rolls and leaps and chops and surges "thortships" and up and down and fore-and-aft by turns, when the gales are blowing; and when they die out, the old nor'west swell comes in and takes a hand, and stands a watch, and keeps up the marine earthquake until the winds are rested and ready to make trouble again.

In a word, the Pacific is "rough" for seven or eight months in the year—not stormy, understand me; not what one could justly call stormy, but contrary, baffling, and very "rough." Therefore, if that Balboa-constrictor had constructed a name for it that had "Wild" or "Untamed" to it, there would have been a majority of two months in the year in favor and in support of it.

A WORD TO THE COMMERCIALLY WISE

If the Pacific were always pacific and its "trades" blew steadily the year around, there would never be any necessity for steamers between Honolulu and San Francisco; but as it is, a trade is building up between the two ports, a considerable share of which is going to consist of fast freight and passengers, and only steamers can extend and develop this and conduct it successfully. You see we plowed through the tangled seas and against the head winds this trip in a fraction over ten days, arriving a day after one of the fast clippers which left San Francisco a matter of three weeks before. The passage back, at this rate, is about five to seven days longer for the clipper; but not more than a day and a half or two days longer for the *Ajax*. You can rest assured that in the tremendous trade that is to spring up between California and the Islands during the next few years, the fast freight and passengers must be carried by steamers for seven or eight months in the year.

I will remark here that my information about the character of this ocean route is obtained from old ship captains, one of whom has commanded in the packet trade for many years, and who has sailed these seas, whaling and otherwise, for forty-six years.

But the main argument in favor of a line of fast steamers is this: They would soon populate these islands with Americans, and loosen that French and English grip which is gradually closing around them, and which will result in a contest before many years as to which of the two shall seize and hold them. I leave America out of this contest, for her influence and her share in it have fallen gradually away until she is out in the cold now, and does not even play third fiddle to this European element.

But if California can send capitalists down here in seven or eight days time and take them back in nine or ten, she can fill these islands full of Americans and regain her lost foothold. Hawaii is too far away now, though, when it takes a man twenty days to come here and twenty-five or thirty to get back again in a sailing vessel.

The steamer line ought to be established, even if it should lose money for two years. Your state has never paid one single dollar of profit to the United States—you are nothing but a burden and an expense to the country—but the kingdom of Hawaii, without costing the United States a cent, has paid her, in customs, $400,000 in a single year.

California's profits from this section can be made greater

and far more lasting than those from Montana. Therefore let your Merchants' Exchange look after the former just as earnestly as they are doing with the latter.

PASSING AWAY THE WEARY TIME

In writing about sea voyages it is customary to state, with the blandest air of conveying information of rare freshness and originality, that anything, however trivial, that promises to spice the weary monotony of the voyage with a new sensation, is eagerly seized upon and the most made of it by the passengers. I decline to insult your intelligence by making this threadbare statement, preferring to believe you would easily divine the existence of the fact without having to be told it.

We had a bullock tied up on the forecastle, and a box nearby with two sheep and a pig in it. These animals afforded a trifling amusement for us on our fair days, and when the opportunity offered we used to go forward and worry them. The bullock was always down on his beamends. If he ever dared to get up on his feet for a second in stormy weather, the next lurch of the ship would "snatch him bald-headed," as Mr. Brown expressed it, and flop him flat on the deck; and in fair weather he was seldom able to get up, on account of his sore bones, acquired through the bangs and bruises of his foul weather experiences. So the bullock lay down pretty much all the time from San Francisco to Honolulu—and ever as his wandering gaze rested upon reeling men, and plunging ship and towering billow, his eloquent eye damned the weather.

Said Mr. Brown once: "Let's go forward and twist the captain's tail."

"Who? Captain Godfrey?"

"Thunder! no; Captain Gordon."

"Who?"

"Why, the bullock—Captain Gordon. We call him Captain Gordon because he lays down so much."

I recognized the point of Mr. Brown's facetiousness then. Captain Gordon, a not undistinguished officer of the Eastern armies, had kept his room all the way, but as he was unwell enough to prefer that course to staggering about the tossing decks, and had a right to do as he pleased anyway, I reprimanded Brown on the spot for his inconsiderate levity.

The pig was pulled and hauled and cuffed for the amusement of the idle passengers, but unknown to himself he had his revenge; for he imparted such a villainous odor of the sty to the hands and clothing of any man who meddled with him, that that man could never drift to windward of a lady passenger without suffering disgrace and humiliation under the rebuke of her offended upturned nose. The pig had no name. This was a source of ceaseless regret to Mr. Brown, and he often spoke of it. At last one of the sailors named it, and Brown happened to be passing by and overheard him. The sailor was feeding the animals, and the pig kept crowding the sheep away and monopolizing the slop pail. The sailor rapped him on the nose and said:

"Oh, go way wid you, Dennis."

To have heard the passengers go into explosions of laughter when Brown rushed in, in a state of wild excitement, and related this circumstance, one might have supposed that this ship had been sailing round and round the world for dreary ages, and that this was the first funny circumstance that had ever blessed with a gleam of cheerfulness the dismal voyage. But, as other writers have said before, even so diluted a thing as this can send a thrill of delight through minds and bodies growing torpid under the dull sameness of a long sea voyage.

From that day forward it was Dennis here, and Dennis there, and Dennis everywhere. Dennis was in everybody's mouth; Dennis was mentioned twice where the everlasting wonder, "how many miles we made yesterday," was expressed once. A stranger's curiosity would have been excited to the last degree to know who this rival to General Grant in notoriety was, that had so suddenly sprung up—this so thoroughly canvassed, discussed, and popular "Dennis." But on the 16th of March Dennis was secretly executed by order of the steward, and Brown said that when the fact became generally known, there was not a dry eye in the ship. He fully believed what he said, too. He has a generous heart and a fervent imagination, and a capacity for creating impossible facts and then implicitly believing them himself, which is perfectly marvelous.

Dennis was served up on the 17th for our St. Patrick's dinner, and gave me a stomach-ache that lasted twenty-four hours. In life he was lovely, and behold, he was powerful in death. Peace to his ashes!

The most steady-going amusement the gentlemen had on the trip was euchre, and the most steady-going the ladies had was being seasick. For days and nights together we used to sit in the smoking room and play euchre on the same table so sacredly devoted to "seven-up" by the livelier set of passengers who traveled last voyage in the

Ajax. It took me some little time to learn to play euchre with those old sea captains, because they brought in so many terms that are neither in Hoyle nor the dictionary. Hear how they talked:

Captain Fitch: "Who hove that ace on there?"

Captain Phelps: "Why, I did."

Captain Cuttle: "No, you didn't, either; I hove it myself."

Captain Phelps: "You didn't, by the Eternal!—you hove the king."

Captain Fitch: "Well, now, that's just the way—always jawin' about who hove this and who hove that—always sailin' on a taut bowlin'. Why can't you go slow? You keep heavin' on 'em down so fast that a man can't tell nothing about it."

Captain Phelps: "Well, I don't care—let it go—I can stand it, I cal'late. Here goes for a euchre!" (Here the captain played an odd-suit ace.) "Swing your bower if you've got it, but I'll take them three last tricks or break a rope yarn."

(I, as partner to Captain Phelps, get bewildered, and make a bad play.)

Captain Phelps: "Now what did you trump my ace for? That ain't any way to do; you're always a-sailin' too close to the wind."

(In a moment or two I make another bad play.)

Captain Phelps: "Ger-reat Scotland! What in the nation you dumpin' that blubber at such a time as this for? Rip! I knowed it! took with a nine-spot! royals, stuns'ls—everything, gone to smash, and nobody euchred!"

It is necessary to explain that those ancient, incomprehensible whalers always called worthless odd-suit cards "blubber."

AT HOME

We passengers are all at home now—taking meals at the American Hotel, and sleeping in neat white cottages, buried in noble shade trees and enchanting tropical flowers and shrubbery.

Mark Twain

3❀

STILL AT SEA

I have been here a day or two now, but I do not know enough concerning the country yet to commence writing about it with confidence, so I will drift back to sea again.

THE AJAX—HER OFFICERS

The *Ajax* is a two-thousand-ton propeller, and one of the strongest built vessels afloat. All her timberwork is very heavy and fastened and bolted together as if to hold for a century. She was intended for a warship, and this accounts for her extraordinary strength. She has excellent cabin accommodations for sixty passengers, without crowding, and bunks for forty more. She has room for over twelve hundred tons of freight after her coal and stores for the round trip are all in; and when a coal depot is established for her hereafter at Honolulu, so that she need carry only fuel enough for half the voyage, she can take two or three hundred tons more. Her principal officers all served in the war. Captain Godfrey and the chief mate, Baxter, were both in our Navy, and Sanford, the chief engineer, has seen a great deal of service. He held his commission as chief engineer in the Navy for sixteen years, and was in seven battles in the Mexican War, and six during the Rebellion—a very good record. Hite, the purser, served under General Sherman, in the paymaster's department, with the rank of captain.

THE STEAMER'S ENGINES

The *Ajax* has a "harp" engine, laid horizontally, so as to be entirely below the water line—a judicious arrangement, in view of the ship's intended duty originally, in a service where cannon balls and shells would pelt her, instead of the rain showers of the Pacific. The horizontal engine takes up much less room than when placed in an upright position; it packs as closely as sardines in a box and gives the ship a good deal of extra space for freight and passengers. Every portion of the *Ajax's* engine and firerooms is kept in perfect neatness and good order by the chief's crew of eighteen men.

In this place I would drop a hint of caution to all romantic young people who yearn to become bold sailor boys and ship as firemen on a steamer. Such a berth has its little drawbacks—inconveniences which not all the romance in the world can reconcile one to. The principal of these is the sultry temperature of the furnace room, where the fireman, far below the surface of the sea and away from the fresh air and the light of day, stands in a narrow space between two rows of furnaces that flame and glare like the fires of hell, and shovels coal four hours at a stretch in an unvarying temperature of 148 degrees Fahrenheit! And yet how the people of Honolulu growl and sweat on an uncommonly warm day, with the mercury at 82 degrees in the shade and somewhere in the neighbor-

hood of 100 degrees in the sun! Steamer firemen do not
live, on an average, over five years.

THE IMPORTANCE OF THE HAWAIIAN TRADE

It is a matter of the utmost importance to the United
States that her trade with these islands should be carefully
fostered and augmented. Because—it pays. There can be
no better reason than that. In actual revenue California is
a burden to the country; she always falls behind; she always leaves a deficit at the end of the year to be made up
by the nation; she never yields revenue enough to support
the government establishments within her borders. In contrast with this, the Sandwich Islands, which cost the United
States but little, have paid her, in customs, as high as
$400,000 in gold coin in a single year! duties paid upon
sugar, etc., received in American ports and subtracted
from the profits of the producer here. I will give the figures. They were compiled by the late N. Lombard Ingals,
Secretary of the San Francisco Board of Brokers, regarded
as one of the best accountants and financial statisticians
that ever visited these islands. The following estimate is
for 1864:

Coffee—14,854 lbs.; duty: 5¢ per lb.	$ 742.70
Molasses—259,469 gals.; duty: 8¢ per gal.	23,757.52 *
Pulu—664,600 lbs. (at 7¢ per lb., $46,522); at 20 percent	9,304.40
Salt—308,000 lbs.; at 18¢ per 100 lbs.	554.40
Sugar—885,957 lbs.; at 3¢ average duty	265,558.71 *
Rice—337,978 lbs.; at 2½¢ per lb.	9,449.45 *
Unenumerated—at least	2,000.00
Being for San Francisco alone, fully	$311,367.18

* [*Sic*]

Mr. Ingals then adds sugar and molasses sent to Portland,
Oregon, the same year, on which forty thousand dollars

duties were paid, making over $350,000 paid in revenues to the United States for Sandwich Island products on the Pacific coast alone.

Mr. Ingals then says: "The Eastern vessels' cargoes consist mostly of oil transshipped from American whalers, and therefore duty free; the balance of their cargoes are hides, wool, and sundries. I think it would be safe to estimate that the whole of them did not pay over fifty thousand dollars to the customhouse."

You will acknowledge that a trade which pays so well, albeit with no risk and small expense to the United States, ought to be encouraged, extended, and irrevocably secured. There are two ways of doing this: Let Congress moderate the high duties somewhat; secondly—let the Islands be populated with Americans. To accomplish the latter, a steamer is indispensable. The sailing vessels can carry freight easily enough, but they [are] too slow and uncertain to build up the passenger trade from which immigration and permanent settlement here must naturally result. In California people are always pressed for time; it is only a few scattering idlers and pleasure seekers who can look serenely upon such an appalling sacrifice of precious hours as a tedious voyage of three weeks hither in a baffled and buffeted sailing vessel and a return trip occupying four or five weeks. But business men and capitalists would run down here by the steamer when they knew the sea voyage could be ciphered down to days and hours before starting —and a short number of days at that. And with the influx of capital would come population, and then I could not ride over mile after mile of fertile soil (as I did yesterday) without seeing half a dozen human habitations.

HOW OUR TRADE MUST BE EXTENDED, IF IT IS DONE AT ALL

An important question to be considered is how a steamer is to be made to pay during the year or two that she is populating the islands, doubling their productions and establishing a profitable trade for herself (for more than one half of the export trade is now in the hands of the sailing vessels, secured to them by joint ownership in ships and plantations, by long-time contracts for transportation, and by advance money to planters), and will remain so for some time. The legitimate way to establish a steamer on a paying basis from the first is to give her a government subsidy of fifty or a hundred thousand dollars a year for carrying the mails, and subtract it from the $500,000 a year appropriated for the China Mail Company, which is to begin business the first of next January. The latter company will either let a subcontract to the *Ajax*, or else put a small steamer of their own into the Honolulu trade—probably the former.

The China steamer will be a five thousand ton vessel; the *Ajax* is two thousand tons burden. Neither of them can enter here except in broad daylight, so narrow and crooked and shallow is the channel. The harbor is so small that it cannot accommodate more than two hundred vessels comfortably, and so narrow that a large ship cannot be handled freely in it. It is not much wider than the river at Sacramento—a section of your river a mile and a half long opposite Sacramento would afford an ampler harbor than this. For half a mile a ship coming in winds about through a channel as crooked as a dog's hind leg, and marked by long lines of upright posts on either side, and in this channel there is not good room enough for two ships to pass abreast.

The great China mail steamer cannot enter this port. She will draw too much water—there is only about twenty-two feet on the bar. If she arrived here at dusk she would have to lie at anchor outside the harbor all night and exchange mails by small boats in the morning—that is, in fair weather. In the stormy season—in the season of the terrible kona—she might have to lie there for five or six days. The China mail steamer will be at sea from thirty-five to forty days on a round trip. With her provisions and sixty or seventy tons of coal a day, and other expenses, if she gets off with an outlay of fifteen hundred dollars a day, while under way, she will do well. Honolulu is clear out of her way, both going and coming. Leaving San Francisco she would naturally come down until a little below the thirtieth parallel, to get the benefit of "the trades," but from thence to Honolulu, nine degrees further south, would be all lost time to her. Returning, she would leave Shanghae [*sic*] and bend around north till above the fortieth parallel, to get the west winds, and then if she had no destination but San Francisco she could go straight across with a spanking breeze all the way—but that not being the case she would make use of the west wind a great part of the voyage, I suppose, and then take in a lot of no longer useful canvas and come straight down south a matter of twenty degrees, land at Honolulu, and then sail north again about seventeen, to get to San Francisco. Thus, you see she will come out of her course, outward bound, over five hundred miles, to strike Honolulu; returning, she will come out of her course twelve hundred—altogether, full seventeen hundred miles every trip more than she would have to make if she left the islands out of her voyage. The *Ajax* is considered fast; the greatest day's run she made this trip, with the wind exactly right and every rag of canvas set and drawing, was about three hundred miles. On several other occasions she did not make over two hundred. So, to allow the China ship the very liberal average speed of 275 miles a day (250 would be nearer right), she must lose over six days every voyage if she comes to Honolulu; she will fool away at least one day here, each way—eight days altogether; expense for a year, $144,000. It cannot be done any cheaper by the China mail steamer.

The *Ajax* can do it for a great deal less, and the China company would make money by subletting the contract to her. The China steamer will certainly never perform the Sandwich Island part of her contract with the Government; that portion will unquestionably be executed by some other steamer, and so, why not turn it over to the *Ajax,* and thus secure to the country the benefits that must accrue to it from the permanent establishment of a San Francisco and Honolulu steamship line?

I am not particular whether the *Ajax* owners continue her in this trade or not, but I would like to see some steamer line established on this route, and I only speak of the *Ajax* in this connection because she has already gained a good footing, and because she is owned by a company which has the confidence of the public and is financially able to carry out a project of this kind in a good and satisfactory manner, and because, further, if the China company put a small steamer of their own in this trade they will not be likely to do it for a year to come, and a twelve-month is a good deal of time to lose.

MARK TWAIN

4✿

OUR ARRIVAL ELABORATED A LITTLE MORE

We came in sight of two of this group of islands, Oahu and Molokai (pronounced O-waw-hoo and Mollo-*ki*), on the morning of the 18th, and soon exchanged the dark blue waters of the deep sea for the brilliant light blue of "sounding." The fat, ugly birds (said to be a species of albatross) which had skimmed after us on tireless wings clear across the ocean, left us, and an occasional flying fish went skimming over the water in their stead. Oahu loomed high, rugged, treeless, barren, black and dreary, out of the sea, and in the distance Molokai lay like a homely sway-backed whale on the water.

THE HAWAIIAN FLAG

As we rounded the promontory of Diamond Head (bringing into view a grove of coconut trees, first ocular proof that we were in the tropics), we ran up the Stars and Stripes at the main spencer gaff, and the Hawaiian flag at the fore. The latter is suggestive of the prominent political elements of the Islands. It is part French, part English, part American, and is Hawaiian in general. The union is the English cross; the remainder of the flag (horizontal stripes) looks American, but has a blue French stripe in addition to our red and white ones. The flag was gotten up by foreign legations in council with the Hawaiian Government. The eight stripes refer to the eight islands which are inhabited; the other four are barren rocks incapable of supporting a population.

REFLECTIONS

As we came in sight we fired a gun, and a good part of Honolulu turned out to welcome the steamer. It was Sunday morning, and about church time, and we steamed through the narrow channel to the music of six different church bells, which sent their mellow tones far and wide, over hills and valleys, which were peopled by naked, savage, thundering barbarians only fifty years ago! Six Christian churches within five miles of the ruins of a pagan temple, where human sacrifices were daily offered up to hideous idols in the last century! We were within pistol shot of one of a group of islands whose ferocious inhabitants closed in upon the doomed and helpless Captain Cook and murdered him, eighty-seven years ago; and lo! their descendants were at church! Behold what the missionaries have wrought!

THE CROWD ON THE PIER

By the time we had worked our slow way up to the wharf, under the guidance of McIntyre, the pilot, a mixed crowd of four or five hundred people had assembled: Chinamen, in the costume of their country; foreigners and the better class of natives, and "half whites" in carriages and dressed in Sacramento summer fashion; other native men on foot, some in the cast-off clothing of white folks, and a few wearing a battered hat, an old ragged vest, and nothing else—at least nothing but an unnecessarily slender rag passed between the legs; native women clad in a single garment—a bright colored robe or wrapper as voluminous as a balloon, with full sleeves. This robe is "gathered" from shoulder to shoulder, before and behind, and then descends in ample folds to the feet—seldom a chemise or any other undergarment—fits like a circus tent fits the tent pole, and no hoops. These robes were bright yellow, or bright crimson, or pure black occasionally, or gleaming white; but "solid colors" and "stunning" ones were the rule. They wore little hats such as the sex wear in your cities, and some of the younger women had very pretty faces and splendid black eyes and heavy masses of long black hair, occasionally put up in a "net"; some of these dark, gingerbread colored beauties were on foot—generally on bare foot, I may add—and others were on horseback—astraddle; they never ride any other way, and they ought to know which way is best, for there are no more accomplished horsewomen in the world, it is said. The balance of the crowd consisted chiefly of little half-naked native boys and girls. All were chattering in the catchy, chopped-up Kanaka language; but what they were chattering about will always remain a mystery to me.

THE KING

Captain Fitch said, "There's the King! that's him in the buggy! I know him far as I can see him."

I had never seen a king in my life, and I naturally took out my notebook and put him down: "Tall, slender, dark; full-bearded; green frock coat, with lapels and collar bordered with gold band an inch wide; plug hat—broad gold band around it; royal costume looks too much like a livery; this man isn't as fleshy as I thought he was."

I had just got these notes entered when Captain Fitch discovered that he had got hold of the wrong King—or, rather, that he had got hold of the King's driver or a carriage-driver of one of the nobility. The King was not present at all. It was a great disappointment to me. I heard afterward that the comfortable, easy-going King Kamehameha (pronounced Ka-may-ah-may-ah) V had been seen sitting on a barrel on the wharf, the day before, fishing; but there was no consolation in that; that did not restore to me my lost King.

HONOLULU

The town of Honolulu (said to contain between twelve thousand and fifteen thousand inhabitants) is spread over a dead level; has streets from twenty to thirty feet wide, solid and level as a floor, most of them straight as a line and a few as crooked as a corkscrew; houses one and two stories high, built of wood, straw, 'dobes, and dull cream-colored pebble-and-shell-conglomerated coral cut into oblong square blocks and laid in cement, but no brick houses; there are great yards, more like plazas, about a large number of the dwelling houses, and these are carpeted with bright green grass, into which your foot sinks out of sight; and they are ornamented by a hundred species of beautiful flowers and blossoming shrubs, and shaded by noble tamarind trees and the "Pride of India," with its fragrant flower, and by the "Umbrella Tree," and I do not know how many more. I had rather smell Honolulu at sunset than the old police courtroom in San Francisco.

ALMOST A KING

I had not shaved since I left San Francisco—ten days. As soon as I got ashore, I hunted for a striped pole, and shortly found one. I always had a yearning to be a king. This may never be, I suppose. But at any rate it will always be a satisfaction to me to know that if I am not a king, I am the next thing to it—I have been shaved by the King's barber.

LANDSMEN ON "SEA LEGS"

Walking about on shore was very uncomfortable at first; there was no spring to the solid ground, and I missed the heaving and rolling of the ship's deck; it was unpleasant to lean unconsciously to an anticipated lurch of the world and find that the world did not lurch, as it should have done. And there was something else missed—something gone—something wanting, I could not tell what—a dismal vacuum of some kind or other—a sense of emptiness. But I found out what it was presently. It was the absence of the ceaseless dull hum of beating waves and whipping sails and fluttering of the propeller, and creaking of the ship—sounds I had become so accustomed to that I had ceased to notice them and had become unaware of their existence until the deep Sunday stillness on shore made me vaguely conscious that a familiar spirit of some kind or other was gone from me. Walking on the solid earth with legs used to the "giving" of the decks under his tread made Brown sick, and he went off to bed and left me to wander alone about this odd-looking city of the tropics.

NEW SCENES AND STRONG CONTRASTS

The further I traveled through the town the better I liked it. Every step revealed a new contrast—disclosed something I was unaccustomed to. In place of the grand mud-colored brown stone fronts of San Francisco, I saw neat white cottages, with green window shutters; in place of front yards like billiard tables with iron fences around them, I saw those cottages surrounded by ample yards, about like Portsmouth Square (as to size), thickly clad with green grass, and shaded by tall trees, through whose dense foliage the sun could scarcely penetrate; in place of the customary infernal geranium languishing in dust and general debility on tin-roofed rear additions or in bedroom windows, I saw luxurious banks and thickets of flowers, fresh as a meadow after a rain, and glowing with the richest dyes; in place of the dingy horrors of the "Willows," and the painful sharp-pointed shrubbery of that funny caricature of nature which they call "South Park," I saw huge-bodied, wide-spreading forest trees, with strange names and stranger appearance—trees that cast a shadow like a thundercloud, and were able to stand alone without being tied to green poles; in place of those vile, tiresome, stupid, everlasting goldfish, wiggling around in glass globes and assuming all shades and degrees of distortion through the magnifying and diminishing qualities of their transparent prison houses, I saw cats—Tom cats, Mary Ann cats, long-tailed cats, bobtail cats, blind cats, one-eyed cats, walleyed cats, cross-eyed cats, gray cats, black cats, white cats, yellow cats, striped cats, spotted cats, tame cats, wild cats, singed cats, individual cats, groups of cats, platoons of cats, companies of cats, regiments of cats, armies of cats, multitudes of cats, millions of cats, and all of them sleek, fat, lazy, and sound asleep; in place of roughs and rowdies staring and blackguarding on the corners, I saw long-haired, saddle-colored Sandwich Island maidens sitting on the ground in the shade of corner houses, gazing indolently at whatever or whoever happened along; instead of that wretched cobblestone pavement nuisance, I walked on a firm foundation of coral, built up from the bottom of the sea by the absurd but persevering insect of that name, with a light layer of lava and cinders overlying the coral, belched up out of fathomless hell long ago through the seared and blackened crater that stands dead and cold and harmless yonder in the distance now; instead of cramped and crowded streetcars, I met dusky native women sweeping by, free as the wind, on fleet horses and astraddle, with gaudy riding sashes streaming like banners behind them; instead of the combined stenches of Sacramento Street, Chinadom, and Brannan Street slaughterhouses, I breathed the balmy fragrance of jessamine, oleander, and the Pride of India; in place of the hurry and bustle and noisy confusion of San Francisco, I moved in the midst of a summer calm as tranquil as dawn in the Garden of Eden; in place of our familiar skirting sand hills and the placid bay, I saw on the one side a framework of tall, precipitous mountains close at hand, clad in refreshing green, and cleft by deep, cool, chasmlike valleys—and in front the grand sweep of the ocean; a brilliant, transparent green near the shore, bound and bordered by a long white line of foamy spray dashing against the reef, and further out the dead blue water of the deep sea, flecked with "white caps," and in the far horizon a single, lonely sail—

At this moment, this man Brown, who has no better manners than to read over one's shoulder, observes:

"Yes, and hot. Oh, I reckon not (only 82 in the shade)! Go on, now, and put it all down, now that you've begun; just say, 'And more "santipedes," and cockroaches, and fleas, and lizards, and red ants, and scorpions, and spiders, and mosquitoes and missionaries'—oh, blame my cats if I'd live here two months, not if I was High-You-Muck-a-Muck and King of Wawhoo, and had a harem full of hyenas!" (Wahine, most generally pronounced Wyheeny, seems to answer for wife, woman, and female of questionable character, indifferently. I never can get this man Brown to understand that "hyena" is not the proper pronunciation. He says "It ain't any odds; it describes some of 'em, anyway.")

I remarked: "But, Mr. Brown, these are trifles."

"Trifles be—blowed! You get nipped by one of them scorpions once, and see how you like it! There was Mrs. Jones, swabbing her face with a sponge; she felt something grab her cheek; she dropped the sponge and out popped a scorpion an inch and a half long! Well, she just got up and danced the Highland fling for two hours and a half—and yell!—why, you could have heard her from Lu-wow to Hoolahoola, with the wind fair! and for three days she soaked her cheek in brandy and salt, and it swelled up as big as your two fists. And you want to know what made me light out of bed so sudden last night? Only a 'santipede' —nothing, only a 'santipede,' with forty-two legs on a side, and every foot hot enough to burn a hole through a rawhide. Don't you know one of them things grabbed Miss Boone's foot when she was riding one day? He was hid in the stirrup, and just clamped himself around her foot and sunk his fangs plum through her shoe; and she just throwed her whole soul into one war whoop and then fainted. And she didn't get out of bed nor set that foot on the floor again for three weeks. And how did Captain Godfrey always get off so easy? Why, because he always carried a bottle full of scorpions and santipedes soaked in alcohol, and whenever he got bit he bathed the place with that devilish mixture or took a drink out of it, I don't recollect which. And how did he have to do once, when he hadn't his bottle along? He had to cut out the bite with his knife and fill up the hole with arnica, and then prop his mouth open with the bootjack to keep from getting the lockjaw. Oh, fill me up about this lovely country! You can go on writing that slop about balmy breezes and fragrant flowers, and all that sort of truck, but you're not going to leave out them santipedes and things for want of being reminded of it, you know."

I said mildly: "But, Mr. Brown, these are the mere—"

"Mere—your grandmother! they ain't the mere anything! What's the use of you telling me they're the mere —mere—whatever it was you was going to call it? You look at them raw splotches all over my face—all over my arms—all over my body! Mosquito bites! Don't tell me about mere—mere things! You can't get around them mosquito bites. I took and brushed out my bar [mosquito net] good night before last, and tucked it in all around, and before morning I was eternally chawed up, anyhow. And the night before I fastened her up all right, and got in bed and smoked that old strong pipe until I got strangled and smothered and couldn't get out, and then they swarmed in there and jammed their bills through my shirt and sucked me as dry as a life preserver before I got my breath again. And how did that deadfall work? I was two days making it, and sweated two buckets full of brine, and blame the mosquito even went under it; and sloshing around in my sleep I ketched my foot in it and got it flattened out so that it wouldn't go into a green turtle shell forty-four inches across the back. Jim Ayers grinding out seven double verses of poetry about Waw-*hoo!* and crying about leaving the blasted place in the two last verses; and you slobbering here about—there you are! Now—*now*, what do you say? That yellow spider could straddle over a saucer just like nothing—and if I hadn't been here to set that spittoon on him, he would have been between your sheets in a minute—he was traveling straight for your bed—he had his eye on it. Just pull at that web that he's been stringing after him—pretty near as hard to break as sewing silk; and look at his feet sticking out all round the spittoon. Oh, confound Waw-*hoo!*"

I am glad Brown has got disgusted at that murdered spider and gone; I don't like to be interrupted when I am writing—especially by Brown, who is one of those men who always looks at the unpleasant side of everything, and I seldom do.

MARK TWAIN

5❀

BOARD AND LODGING SECURED

I did not expect to find as comfortable a hotel as the American, with its large, airy, well-furnished rooms, distinguished by perfect neatness and cleanliness, its cool, commodious verandas, its excellent table, its ample front yard, carpeted with grass and adorned with shrubbery, et cetera—and so I was agreeably disappointed. One of our lady passengers from San Francisco, who brings high recommendations, has purchased a half interest in the hotel, and she shows such a determination to earn success that I heartily wish she may achieve it—and the more so because she is an American, and if common remark can be depended upon, the foreign element here will not allow an American to succeed if a good strong struggle can prevent it.

Several of us have taken rooms in a cottage in the center of the town, and are well satisfied with our quarters. There is a grassy yard as large as Platt's Hall on each of the three sides of the premises; a number of great tamarind and algeraba trees tower above us, and their dense, wide-spreading foliage casts a shade that palls our verandas with a sort of solemn twilight, even at noonday. If I were not so fond of looking into the rich masses of green leaves that swathe the stately tamarind right before my door, I would idle less and write more, I think. The leaf of this tree is of the size and shape of that of our sickly, homely locust in the States; but the tamarind is as much more superb a tree than the locust as a beautiful white woman is more lovely than a Digger squaw who may chance to generally resemble her in shape and size.

The algeraba (my spelling is guesswork) has a gnarled and twisted trunk, as thick as a barrel, far-reaching crooked branches and a delicate, feathery foliage which would be much better suited to a garden shrub than to so large a tree.

We have got some handsome mango trees about us also, with dark green leaves, as long as a goose quill and not more than twice as broad. The trunk of this tree is about six inches through, and is very straight and smooth. Five feet from the ground it divides into three branches of equal size, which bend out with a graceful curve and then assume an upright position. From these numerous smaller branches sprout. The main branches are not always three in number, I believe; but ours have this characteristic, at any rate.

We pay from five to seven dollars a week for furnished rooms, and ten dollars for board.

FURTHER PARTICULARS IN THIS CONNECTION

Mr. Laller, an American, and well spoken of, keeps a restaurant where meals can be had at all hours. So you see that folks of both regular and eccentric habits can be accommodated in Honolulu.

Washing is done chiefly by the natives; price, a dollar a dozen. If you are not watchful, though, your shirt won't stand more than one washing, because Kanaka artists work by a most destructive method. They use only cold water—sit down by a brook, soap the garment, lay it on one rock, and "pound" it with another. This gives a shirt a handsome fringe around its borders, but it is ruinous on buttons. If your washerwoman knows you will not put up with this sort of thing, however, she will do her pounding with a bottle, or else rub your clothes clean with her hands. After the garments are washed, the artist spreads them on the green grass, and the flaming sun and the winds soon bleach them as white as snow. They are then ironed on a coco-leaf mat spread on the ground, and the job is finished. I cannot discover that anything of the nature of starch is used.

Board, lodging, clean clothes, furnished room, coal oil or whale oil lamp (dingy, greasy, villainous)—next you want water, fruit, tobacco and cigars, and possibly wines and liquors—and then you are "fixed," and ready to live in Honolulu.

WATER

The water is pure, sweet, cool, clear as crystal, and comes from a spring in the mountains, and is distributed all over the town through leaden pipes. You can find a hydrant spurting away at the bases of three or four trees in a single yard sometimes, so plenty and cheap is this excellent water. Only twenty-four dollars a year supplies a whole household with a limitless quantity of it.

FRUIT

You must have fruit. You feel the want of it here. At any rate, I do, though I cared nothing whatever for it in San Francisco. You pay about twenty-five cents ("two reals," in the language of the country, borrowed from Mexico, where a good deal of their silver money comes from) a dozen for oranges; and so delicious are they that some people frequently eat a good many at luncheon. I seldom eat more than ten or fifteen at a sitting, however, because I despise to see anybody gormandize. Even fifteen is a little surprising to me, though, for two or three oranges in succession were about as much as I could ever relish at home. Bananas are worth about a bit a dozen— enough for that rather overrated fruit. Strawberries are plenty, and as cheap as the bananas. Those which are carefully cultivated here have a far finer flavor than the California article. They are in season a good part of the year. I have a kind of a general idea that the tamarinds are rather sour this year. I had a curiosity to taste these things, and I knocked half a dozen off the tree and ate them the other day. They sharpened my teeth up like a razor, and put a "wire edge" on them that I think likely will wear off when the enamel does. My judgment now is that when it comes to sublimated sourness, persimmons will have to take a back seat and let the tamarinds come to the front. They are shaped and colored like a peanut, and about three times as large. The seeds inside of the thin pod are covered with that sour, gluey substance which I experimented on. They say tamarinds make excellent preserves (and by a wise provision of Providence, they are generally placed in sugar-growing countries), and also that a few of them placed in impure water at sea will render it palatable. Mangoes and guavas are plenty. I do not like them. The limes are excellent, but not very plenty. Most of the apples brought to this market are imported from Oregon. Those I have eaten were as good as bad turnips, but not better. They claim to raise good apples and peaches on some of these islands. I have not seen any grapes, or pears or melons here. They may be out of season, but I keep thinking it is dead summer time now.

CIGARS

The only cigars smoked here are those trifling, insipid, tasteless, flavorless things they call "Manilas"—ten for twenty-five cents; and it would take a thousand to be worth half the money. After you have smoked about thirty-five dollars worth of them in a forenoon you feel nothing but a desperate yearning to go out somewhere and take a smoke. They say high duties and a sparse population render it unprofitable to import good cigars, but I do not see why some enterprising citizen does not manufacture them from the native tobacco. A Kanaka gave me some Oahu tobacco yesterday, of fine texture, pretty good flavor, and so strong that one pipe full of it satisfied me for several hours. (This man Brown has just come in and says he has bought a couple of tons of Manilas to smoke tonight.)

WINES AND LIQUORS

Wines and liquors can be had in abundance, but not of the very best quality. The duty on brandy and whiskey amounts to about three dollars a gallon, and on wines from thirty to sixty cents a bottle, according to market value.

And just here I would caution Californians who design
visiting these islands against bringing wines or liquors with
their baggage, lest they provoke the confiscation of the
latter. They will be told that to uncork the bottles and
take a little of the contents out will compass the disabilities
of the law, but they may find it dangerous to act upon
such a suggestion, which is nothing but an unworthy eva-
sion of the law, at best. It is incumbent upon the custom
officers to open trunks and search for contraband articles,
and although I think the spirit of the law means to permit
foreigners to bring a little wine or liquor ashore for private
use, I know the letter of it allows nothing of the kind. In
addition to searching a passenger's baggage, the customhouse officer makes him swear that he has got nothing contraband with him. I will also mention, as a matter of information, that a small sum (two dollars for each person)
is exacted for permission to land baggage, and this goes to
the support of the hospitals.

I have said that the wines and liquors sold here are not
of the best quality. It could not well be otherwise, as I can
show. There seem to be no hard, regular drinkers in this
town, or at least very few; you perceive that the duties
are high; saloonkeepers pay a license of a thousand dollars
a year; they must close up at ten o'clock at night and not
open again before daylight the next morning; they are
not allowed to open on Sunday at all. These laws are very
strict, and are rigidly obeyed.

WATER AGAIN

I must come back to water again, though I thought I
had exhausted the subject. As no ice is kept here, and as
the notion that snow is brought to Honolulu from the

prodigious mountains on the island of Hawaii is a happy fiction of some imaginative writer, the water used for drinking is usually kept cool by putting it into "monkeys" and placing those animals in open windows, where the breezes of heaven may blow upon them. "Monkeys" are slender-necked, large-bodied, gourd-shaped earthenware vessels, manufactured in Germany, and are popularly supposed to keep water very cool and fresh, but I cannot indorse that supposition. If a wet blanket were wrapped around the monkey, I think the evaporation would cool the water within, but nobody seems to consider it worthwhile to go to that trouble, and I include myself among this number.

Ice is worth a hundred dollars a ton in San Francisco, and five or six hundred here, and if the steamer continues to run, a profitable trade may possibly be driven in the article hereafter. It does not pay to bring it from Sitka in sailing vessels, though. It has been tried. It proved a mutinous and demoralizing cargo, too; for the sailors drank the melted freight and got so high-toned that they refused ever afterwards to go to sea unless the captains would guarantee them ice water on the voyage. Brown got the latter fact from Captain Phelps, and says he "coppered it in consideration of the source." To "copper" a thing, he informs me, is to bet against it.

ETIQUETTE

If you get into conversation with a stranger in Honolulu, and experience that natural desire to know what sort of ground you are treading on by finding out what manner of man your stranger is, strike out boldly and address him as "Captain." Watch him narrowly, and if you see by his countenance that you are on the wrong tack, ask him where he preaches. It is a safe bet that he is either a missionary or captain of a whaler. I am now personally acquainted with seventy-two captains and ninety-six missionaries. The captains and ministers form one half of the population; the third fourth is composed of common Kanakas and mercantile foreigners and their families, and the final fourth is made up of high officers of the Hawaiian Government. And there are just about cats enough for three apiece all around.

A solemn stranger met me in the suburbs yesterday, and said:

"Good morning, your reverence. Preach in the stone church yonder, no doubt?"

"No, I don't. I'm not a preacher."

"Really, I beg your pardon, Captain. I trust you had a good season. How much oil—?"

"Oil? Why, what do you take me for? I'm not a whaler."

"Oh, I beg a thousand pardons, your Excellency. Major General in the household troops, no doubt? Minister of the Interior, likely? Secretary of War? First Gentleman of the Bedchamber? Commissioner of the Royal—?"

"Stuff! man. I'm no official. I'm not connected in any way with the Government."

"Bless my life! Then, who the mischief are you? What the mischief are you? and how the mischief did you get here, and where in thunder did you come from?"

"I'm only a private personage—an unassuming stranger —lately arrived from America."

"No? Not a missionary! not a whaler! not a member of his Majesty's Government! not even Secretary of the

Navy! Ah, Heaven! it is too blissful to be true; alas, I do but dream. And yet that noble, honest countenance—those oblique, ingenuous eyes—that massive head, incapable of—of—anything; your hand; give me your hand, bright waif. Excuse these tears. For sixteen weary years I have yearned for a moment like this, and—"

Here his feelings were too much for him, and he swooned away. I pitied this poor creature from the bottom of my heart. I was deeply moved. I shed a few tears on him and kissed him for his mother. I then took what small change he had and "shoved."

MARK TWAIN

6🌸

HONOLULU, MARCH, 1866.

COMING HOME FROM PRISON

I am probably the most sensitive man in the kingdom of Hawaii tonight—especially about sitting down in the presence of my betters. I have ridden fifteen or twenty miles on horseback since 5 P.M., and to tell the honest truth, I have a delicacy about sitting down at all. I am one of the poorest horsemen in the world, and I never mount a horse without experiencing a sort of dread that I may be setting out on that last mysterious journey which all of us must take sooner or later, and I never come back in safety from a horseback trip without thinking of my latter end for two or three days afterward. This same old regular devotional sentiment began just as soon as I sat down here five minutes ago.

An excursion to Diamond Head and the King's Cocoanut Grove was planned today—time, 4:30 P.M.—the party to consist of half a dozen gentlemen and three ladies. They all started at the appointed hour except myself. I was at the government prison, and got so interested in its examination that I did not notice how quickly the time was passing. Somebody remarked that it was twenty minutes past five o'clock, and that woke me up. It was a fortunate circumstance that Captain Phillips was there with his "turnout," as he calls a top buggy that Captain Cook brought here in 1778, and a horse that was here when Captain Cook came. Captain Phillips takes a just pride in his driving and in the speed of his horse, and to his passion for displaying them I owe it that we were only sixteen minutes coming from the prison to the American Hotel—a distance which has been estimated to be over half a mile. But it took some awful driving. The captain's whip came down fast, and the blows started so much dust out of the horse's hide that during the last half of the journey we rode through an impenetrable fog, and ran by a pocket compass in the hands of Captain Fish, a whaler captain of twenty-six years experience, who sat there through that perilous voyage as self-possessed as if he had been on the euchre-deck of his own ship, and calmly said, "Port your helm—port," from time to time, and "Hold her a little free—steady—so-o," and "Luff—hard down to starboard!" and never once lost his presence of mind or betrayed the least anxiety by voice or manner. When we came to anchor at last, and Captain Phillips looked at his watch and said, "Sixteen minutes—I told you it was in her! that's over three miles an hour!" I could see he felt entitled to a compliment, and so I said I had never seen lightning go like that horse. And I never had.

THE STEED "OAHU"

The landlord of the American said the party had been gone nearly an hour, but that he could give me my choice of several horses that could easily overtake them. I said, never mind—I preferred a safe horse to a fast one—I would like to have an excessively gentle horse—a horse with no spirit whatever—a lame one, if he had such a thing. Inside of five minutes I was mounted, and perfectly satisfied with my outfit. I had no time to label him "This is a horse," and so if the public took him for a sheep, I cannot help it. I was satisfied, and that was the main thing. I could see that he had as many fine points as any man's horse, and I just hung my hat on one of them, behind the saddle, and swabbed the perspiration from my face and started. I named him after this island, "Oahu" (pronounced O-waw-hoo). The first gate he came to he started in; I had neither whip nor spur, and so I simply argued the case with him. He firmly resisted argument, but ultimately yielded to insult and abuse. He backed out of that gate and steered for another one on the other side of the street. I triumphed by my former process. Within the next six hundred yards he crossed the street fourteen times and attempted thirteen gates, and in the meantime the tropical sun was beating down and threatening to cave the top of my head in, and I was literally dripping with perspiration and profanity. (I am only human and I was sorely aggravated. I shall behave better next time.) He quit the gate business after that and went along peaceably enough, but absorbed in meditation. I noticed this latter circumstance, and it soon began to fill me with the gravest apprehension. I said to myself, this malignant brute is planning some new outrage, some fresh deviltry or other —no horse ever thought over a subject so profoundly as this one is doing just for nothing. The more this thing preyed upon my mind, the more uneasy I became, until at last the suspense became unbearable and I dismounted to see if there was anything wild in his eye—for I had heard that the eye of this noblest of our domestic animals is very expressive. I cannot describe what a load of anxiety was lifted from my mind when I found that he was only asleep. I woke him up and started him into a faster walk, and then the inborn villainy of his nature came out again. He tried to climb over a stone wall, five or six feet high. I saw that I must apply force to this horse, and that I might as well begin first as last. I plucked a stout switch from a tamarind tree, and the moment he saw it, he gave in. He broke into a convulsive sort of a canter, which had three short steps in it and one long one, and reminded me alternately of the clattering shake of the great earthquake, and the sweeping plunging of the *Ajax* in a storm.

OUT OF PRISON, BUT IN THE STOCKS

And now it occurs to me that there can be no fitter occasion than the present to pronounce a fervent curse upon the man who invented the American saddle. There is no seat to speak of about it—one might as well sit in a shovel —and the stirrups are nothing but an ornamental nuisance. If I were to write down here all the abuse I expended on those stirrups, it would make a large book, even without pictures. Sometimes I got one foot so far through, that the stirrup partook of the nature of an anklet; sometimes both feet were through, and I was handcuffed by the legs, and sometimes my feet got clear out and left the stirrups wildly dangling about my shins. Even when I was in proper position and carefully balanced upon the balls of my feet, there was no comfort in it, on account of my nervous dread that they were going to slip one way or the other in a moment. But the subject is too exasperating to write about.

ABOUT HORSES AND KANAKA SHREWDNESS

This is a good time to drop in a paragraph of information. There is no regular livery stable in Honolulu, or, indeed, in any part of the kingdom of Hawaii; therefore, unless you are acquainted with wealthy residents (who all have good horses), you must hire animals of the vilest description from the Kanakas. Any horse you hire, even though it be from a white man, is not often of much account, because it will be brought in for you from some ranch, and has necessarily been leading a hard life. If the Kanakas who have been caring for him (inveterate riders they are) have not ridden him half to death every day themselves, you can depend upon it they have been doing the same thing by proxy, by clandestinely hiring him out. At least, so I am informed. The result is, that no horse has a chance to eat, drink, rest, recuperate, or look well or feel well, and so strangers go about in the islands mounted as I was today.

In hiring a horse from a Kanaka, you must have all your eyes about you, because you can rest satisfied that you are dealing with as shrewd a rascal as ever patronized a penitentiary. You may leave your door open and your trunk unlocked as long as you please, and he will not meddle with your property; he has no important vices and no inclination to commit robbery on a large scale; but if he can get ahead of you in the horse business, he will take a genuine delight in doing it. This trait is characteristic of horse jockeys, the world over, is it not? He will overcharge you if he can; he will hire you a fine-looking horse at night (anybody's—maybe the King's, if the royal steed be in convenient view), and bring you the mate to my

Oahu in the morning, and contend that it is the same animal. If you raise a row, he will get out by saying it was not himself who made the bargain with you, but his brother, "who went out in the country this morning." They have always got a "brother" to shift the responsibility upon. A victim said to one of these fellows one day:

"But I know I hired the horse of you, because I noticed that scar on your cheek."

The reply was not bad: "Oh, yes—yes—my brother all same—we twins!"

A friend of mine, J. Smith, hired a horse yesterday, the Kanaka warranting him to be in excellent condition. Smith had a saddle and blanket of his own, and he ordered the Kanaka to put these on the horse. The Kanaka protested that he was perfectly willing to trust the gentleman with the saddle that was already on the animal, but Smith refused to use it. The change was made; then Smith noticed that the Kanaka had only changed the saddles, and had left the original blanket on the horse; he said he forgot to change the blankets, and so, to cut the bother short, Smith mounted and rode away. The horse went lame a mile from town, and afterward got to cutting up some extraordinary capers. Smith got down and took off the saddle, but the blanket stuck fast to the horse—glued to a procession of raw sores. The Kanaka's mysterious conduct stood explained.

Another friend of mine bought a pretty good horse from a native, a day or two ago, after a tolerably thorough examination of the animal. He discovered today that the horse was as blind as a bat, in one eye. He meant to have examined that eye, and came home with a general notion that he had done it; but he remembers now that every time he made the attempt his attention was called to something else by his victimizer.

One more yarn, and then I will pass to something else. I am informed that when Leland was here he bought a pair of very respectable-looking match horses from a native. They were in a little stable with a partition through the middle of it—one horse in each apartment. Leland examined one of them critically through a window (the Kanaka's "brother" having gone to the country with the key), and then went around the house and examined the other through a window on the other side. He said it was the neatest match he had ever seen, and paid for the horses on the spot. Whereupon the Kanaka departed to join his brother in the country. The scoundrel had shamefully swindled Leland. There was only one "match" horse, and he had examined his starboard side through one window and his port side through another! I decline to believe this story, but I give it because it is worth something as a fanciful illustration of a fixed fact—namely, that the Kanaka horse jockey is fertile in invention and elastic in conscience.

HONOLULU PRICES FOR HORSEFLESH

You can buy a pretty good horse for forty or fifty dollars, and a good enough horse for all practical purposes for two dollars and a half. I estimate Oahu to be worth somewhere in the neighborhood of thirty-five cents. A good deal better animal than he is was sold here day before yesterday for a dollar and six bits, and sold again today for two dollars and twenty-five cents; Brown bought a handsome and lively little pony yesterday for ten dollars; and about the best common horse on the island (and he is a really good one) sold yesterday, with good Mexican saddle and bridle, for seventy dollars—a horse which is well and widely known, and greatly respected for his speed, good disposition, and everlasting bottom. You give your horse a little grain once a day; it comes from San Francisco, and is worth about two cents a pound; and you give him as much hay as he wants; it is cut and brought to the market by natives, and is not very good; it is baled into long, round bundles, about the size of a large man; one of them is stuck by the middle on each end of a six-foot pole, and the Kanaka shoulders the pole and walks about the streets between the upright bales in search of customers. These hay bales, thus carried, have a general resemblance to a colossal capital H.

These hay bundles cost twenty-five cents apiece, and one will last a horse about a day. You can get a horse for a song, a week's hay for another song, and you can turn your animal loose among the luxuriant grass in your neighbor's broad front yard without a song at all—you do it at midnight, and stable the beast again before morning. You have been at no expense thus far, but when you come to buy a saddle and bridle they will cost you from $20 to $35. You can hire a horse, saddle, and bridle at from $7 to $10 a week, and the owner will take care of them at his own expense.

Well, Oahu worried along over a smooth, hard road, bordered on either side by cottages, at intervals, pulu swamps at intervals, fish ponds at intervals, but through a dead level country all the time, and no trees to hide the wide Pacific Ocean on the right or the rugged, towering rampart of solid rock, called Diamond Head or Diamond Point, straight ahead.

THE KING'S GROVE, WAIKIKI

A mile and a half from town, I came to a grove of
tall coconut trees, with clean, branchless stems reaching
straight up sixty or seventy feet and topped with a spray
of green foliage sheltering clusters of coconuts—not more
picturesque than a forest of colossal ragged parasols, with
bunches of magnified grapes under them, would be. About
a dozen cottages, some frame and the others of native
grass, nestled sleepily in the shade here and there. The grass
cabins are of a grayish color, are shaped much like our
own cottages, only with higher and steeper roofs usually,
and are made of some kind of weed strongly bound together in bundles. The roofs are very thick, and so are the
walls; the latter have square holes in them for windows.
At a little distance these cabins have a furry appearance,
as if they might be made of bear skins. They are very cool
and pleasant inside. The King's flag was flying from the
roof of one of the cottages, and His Majesty was probably
within. He owns the whole concern thereabouts, and passes
his time there frequently, on sultry days "laying off." The
spot is called "the King's Grove."

RUINS OF AN ANCIENT HEATHEN TEMPLE

Nearby is an interesting ruin—the meager remains of
an ancient heathen temple—a place where human sacrifices were offered up in those old bygone days when the
simple child of nature, yielding momentarily to sin when
sorely tempted, acknowledged his error when calm reflection had shown it to him, and came forward with noble
frankness and offered up his grandmother as an atoning
sacrifice—in those old days when the luckless sinner could

keep on cleansing his conscience and achieving periodical happiness as long as his relations held out; long, long before the missionaries braved a thousand privations to come and make them permanently miserable by telling them how beautiful and how blissful a place heaven is, and how nearly impossible it is to get there; and showed the poor native how dreary a place perdition is and what unnecessarily liberal facilities there are for going to it; showed him how, in his ignorance, he had gone and fooled away all his kinfolks to no purpose; showed him what rapture it is to work all day long for fifty cents to buy food for next day with, as compared with fishing for pastime and lolling in the shade through eternal summer, and eating of the bounty that nobody labored to provide but nature. How sad it is to think of the multitudes who have gone to their graves in this beautiful island and never knew there was a hell! And it inclines right-thinking man to weep rather than to laugh when he reflects how surprised they must have been when they got there.

This ancient temple was built of rough blocks of lava, and was simply a roofless inclosure, a hundred and thirty feet long and seventy wide—nothing but naked walls, very thick but not much higher than a man's head. They will last for ages, no doubt, if left unmolested. Its three altars and other sacred appurtenances have crumbled and passed away years ago. It is said that in the old times thousands of human beings were slaughtered here, in the presence of multitudes of naked, whooping, and howling savages. If these mute stones could speak, what tales they could tell, what pictures they could describe, of fettered victims, writhing and shrieking under the knife; of dense masses of dusky forms straining forward out of the gloom,

with eager and ferocious faces lit up with the weird light
of sacrificial fires; of the vague background of ghostly
trees; of the mournful sea washing the dim shore; of the
dark pyramid of Diamond Head standing sentinel over the
dismal scene, and the peaceful moon looking calmly down
upon it through rifts in the drifting clouds!

When Kamehameha (pronounced Ka-may-ha-may-ah)
the Great—who was a very Napoleon in military genius
and uniform success—invaded this island of Oahu three
quarters of a century ago, and exterminated the army sent
to oppose him, and took full and final possession of the
country, he searched out the dead body of the king of
Oahu, and those of the principal chiefs, and impaled their
heads upon the walls of this temple.

Those were savage times when this old slaughterhouse
was in its prime. The king and the chiefs ruled the common herd with a rod of iron; made them gather all the
provisions the masters needed; build all the houses and
temples; stand all the expenses, of whatever kind; take
kicks and cuffs for thanks; drag out lives well flavored
with misery, and then suffer death for trifling offenses or
yield up their lives on the sacrificial altars to purchase
favors from the gods for their hard rulers. The missionaries have clothed them, educated them, broken up the
tyrannous authority of their chiefs, and given them free-
dom and the right to enjoy whatever the labor of their
hands and brains produces, with equal laws for all and
punishment for all alike who transgress them. The contrast is so strong—the wonderful benefit conferred upon
this people by the missionaries is so prominent, so palpable,
and so unquestionable, that the frankest compliment I can
pay them, and the best, is simply to point to the condi-

tion of the Sandwich Islanders of Captain Cook's time, and their condition today. Their work speaks for itself.

The little collection of cottages (of which I was speaking a while ago) under the coconut trees is a historical point. It is the village of Waikiki (usually pronounced Wy-kee-ky), once the capital of the kingdom and the abode of the great Kamehameha I. In 1801, while he lay encamped at this place with seven thousand men, preparing to invade the island of Kau[a]i (he had previously captured and subdued the seven other inhabited islands of the group, one after another), a pestilence broke out in Oahu and raged with great virulence. It attacked the King's army and made great havoc in it. It is said that three hundred bodies were washed out to sea in one day.

There is an opening in the coral reef at this point, and anchorage inside for a small number of vessels, though one accustomed to the great bay of San Francisco would never take this little belt of smooth water, with its border of foaming surf, to be a harbor, save for Whitehall boats or something of that kind. But harbors are scarce in these islands—open roadsteads are the rule here. The harbor of Waikiki was discovered in 1786 (seven or eight years after Captain Cook's murder) by Captains Portlock and Dixon, in the ships *King George* and *Queen Charlotte* —the first English vessels that visited the islands after that unhappy occurrence. This little bathing tub of smooth water possesses some further historical interest as being the spot where the distinguished navigator Vancouver landed when he came here in 1792.

In a conversation with a gentleman today about the scarcity of harbors among the islands (and in all the islands of the South Pacific), he said the natives of Tahiti have a theory that the reason why there are harbors wherever fresh water streams empty into the sea, and none elsewhere, is that the fresh water kills the coral insect, or so discommodes or disgusts it that it will not build its stony wall in its vicinity, and instanced what is claimed as fact, viz., that the break in the reef is always found where the fresh water passes over it, in support of this theory.

(This notable equestrian excursion will be concluded in my next, if nothing happens.)

MARK TWAIN

7❀

THE EQUESTRIAN EXCURSION CONCLUDED

I wandered along the sea beach on my steed Oahu around the base of the extinct crater of Leahi, or Diamond Head, and a quarter of a mile beyond the point I overtook the party of ladies and gentlemen and assumed my proper place—that is, in the rear, for the horse I ride always persists in remaining in the rear in spite of kicks, cuffs, and curses. I was satisfied as long as I could keep Oahu within hailing distance of the cavalcade—I knew I could accomplish nothing better even if Oahu were Norfolk himself.

We went on—on—on—a great deal too far, I thought, for people who were unaccustomed to riding on horseback, and who must expect to suffer on the morrow if they indulged too freely in this sort of exercise. Finally we got to a point which we were expecting to go around in order to strike an easy road home; but we were too late; it was full tide and the sea had closed in on the shore. Young Henry McFarlane said he knew a nice, comfortable route over the hill—a short cut—and the crowd dropped into his wake. We climbed a hill a hundred and fifty feet high, and about as straight up and down as the side of a house, and as full of rough lava blocks as it could stick—not as wide, perhaps, as the broad road that leads to destruction, but nearly as dangerous to travel, and apparently leading in the same general direction. I felt for the ladies, but I had no time to speak any words of sympathy, by reason of my attention being so much occupied by Oahu. The place was so steep that at times he stood straight up on his tiptoes and clung by his forward toenails, with his back to the Pacific Ocean and his nose close to the moon—and thus situated we formed an equestrian picture which was as uncomfortable to me as it may have been picturesque to the spectators. You may think I was afraid, but I was not. I knew I could stay on him as long as his ears did not pull out.

It was a great relief to me to know that we were all safe and sound on the summit at last, because the sun was just disappearing in the waves, night was abroad in the land, candles and lamps were already twinkling in the distant town, and we gratefully reflected that Henry had saved us from having to go back around the rocky, sandy beach. But a new trouble arose while the party were admiring the rising moon and the cool, balmy night breeze, with its odor of countless flowers, for it was discovered that we had got into a place we could not get out of— we were apparently surrounded by precipices—our pilot's chart was at fault, and he could not extricate us, and so we had the prospect before us of either spending the night in the admired night breeze, under the admired moon, or of clambering down the way we came, in the dark. However, a Kanaka came along presently and found a first-rate road for us down an almost imperceptible decline, and the party set out on a cheerful gallop again, and Oahu struck up his miraculous canter once more. The moon rose up, and flooded mountain and valley and ocean with silvery light, and I was not sorry we had lately been in trouble, because the consciousness of being safe again raised our spirits and made us more capable of enjoying the beautiful scene than we would have been otherwise. I never breathed such a soft, delicious atmosphere before, nor one freighted with such rich fragrance. A barber shop is nothing to it.

A BATTLEGROUND WHOSE HISTORY IS FORGOTTEN

Gaily laughing and talking, the party galloped on, and with set teeth and bouncing body I clung to the pommel and cantered after. Presently we came to a place where no grass grew—a wide expanse of deep sand. They said it was an old battleground. All around everywhere, not three feet apart, the bleached bones of men gleamed white in the moonlight. We picked up a lot of them for mementoes. I got quite a number of arm bones and leg bones—of great chiefs, maybe, who had fought savagely in that fearful battle in the old days, when blood flowed like wine where we now stood—and wore the choicest of them out on Oahu afterward, trying to make him go. All sorts of bones could be found except skulls; but a citizen said, irreverently, that there had been an unusual number of "skull hunters" there lately—a species of sportsmen I had never heard of before. The conversation at this point took a unique and ghastly turn. A gentleman said:

"Give me some of your bones, Miss Blank; I'll carry them for you."

Another said:

"You haven't got bones enough, Mrs. Blank; here's a good shinbone, if you want it."

Such observations as these fell from the lips of ladies with reference to their queer newly-acquired property:

"Mr. Brown, will you please hold some of my bones for me a minute?" And, "Mr. Smith, you have got some of my bones; and you have got one, too, Mr. Jones; and you have got my spine, Mr. Twain. Now don't any of you gentlemen get my bones all mixed up with yours so that you can't tell them apart."

These remarks look very irreverent on paper, but they did not sound so, being used merely in a business way and with no intention of making sport of the remains. I did not think it was just right to carry off any of these bones, but we did it, anyhow. We considered that it was at least as right as it is for the Hawaiian Government and the city of Honolulu (which is the most excessively moral and religious town that can be found on the map of the world), to permit those remains to lie decade after decade, to bleach and rot in the sun and wind and suffer desecration by careless strangers and by the beasts of the field, unprotected by even a worm fence. Call us hard names if you will, you statesmen and missionaries! but I say shame upon you, that after raising a nation from idolatry to Christianity, and from barbarism to civilization, you have not taught it the comment [*sic*] of respect for the dead. Your work is incomplete.

LEGENDARY

Nothing whatever is known about this place—its story is a secret that will never be revealed. The oldest natives make no pretense of being possessed of its history. They say these bones were here when they were children. They were here when their grandfathers were children—but how they came here, they can only conjecture. Many people believe this spot to be an ancient battleground, and it is usual to call it so; and they believe that these skeletons have lain for ages just where their proprietors fell in the great fight. Other people believe that Kamehameha I fought his first battle here. On this point, I have heard a story, which may have been taken from one of the numerous books which have been written, concerning these islands—I do not know where the narrator got it. He said that when Kamehameha (who was at first merely a subordinate chief on the island of Hawaii), landed here, he brought a large army with him, and encamped at Waikiki. The Oahuans marched against him, and so confident were they of success that they readily acceded to a demand of their priests that they should draw a line where these bones now lie, and take an oath that, if forced to retreat at all, they would never retreat beyond this boundary. The priests told them that death and everlasting punishment would overtake any who violated the oath, and the march was resumed. Kamehameha drove them back step by step; the priests fought in the front rank and exhorted them both by voice and inspiring example to remember their oath—to die, if need be, but never cross the fatal line. The struggle was manfully maintained, but at last the chief priest fell, pierced to the heart with a spear, and the unlucky omen fell like a blight upon the brave souls at his back; with a triumphant shout the invaders pressed forward—the line was crossed—the offended gods deserted the despairing army, and, accepting the doom their perjury had brought upon them, they broke and fled over the plain where Honolulu stands now—up the beautiful Nuuanu Valley—paused a moment, hemmed in by precipitous mountains on either hand and the frightful precipice of the Pari (pronounced *Pally;* intelligent natives claim that there is no *r* in the Kanaka alphabet) in front, and then were driven over—a sheer plunge of six hundred feet!

The story is pretty enough, but Mr. Jarves' excellent history says the Oahuans were intrenched in Nuuanu Valley; that Kamehameha ousted them, routed them, pursued them up the valley and drove them over the precipice. He makes no mention of our bone yard at all in his book.

There was a terrible pestilence here in 1804, which killed great numbers of the inhabitants, and the natives have legends of others that swept the islands long before that; and therefore many persons now believe that these bones belonged to victims of one of these epidemics who were hastily buried in a great pit. It is by far the most reasonable conjecture, because Jarves says that the weapons of the Islanders were so rude and inefficient that their battles were not often very bloody. If this was a battle, it was astonishingly deadly, for in spite of the depredations of "skull hunters," we rode a considerable distance over ground so thickly strewn with human bones that the horses' feet crushed them, not occasionally, but at every step.

SENTIMENT

Impressed by the profound silence and repose that rested over the beautiful landscape, and being, as usual, in the rear, I gave voice to my thought. I said:

"What a picture is here slumbering in the solemn glory

of the moon! How strong the rugged outlines of the dead volcano stand out against the clear sky! What a snowy fringe marks the bursting of the surf over the long, curved reef! How calmly the dim city sleeps yonder in the plain! How soft the shadows lie upon the stately mountains that border the dream-haunted Manoa Valley! What a grand pyramid of billowy clouds towers above the storied Pari! How the grim warriors of the past seem flocking in ghostly squadrons to their ancient battlefield again—how the wails of the dying well up from the—"

At this point the horse called Oahu deliberately sat down in the sand. Sat down to listen, I suppose. Never mind what he heard. I stopped apostrophizing and convinced him that I was not a man to allow contempt of court on the part of a horse. I broke the backbone of a chief over his rump and set out to join the cavalcade again.

Very considerably fagged out we arrived in town at nine o'clock at night, myself in the lead—for when my horse finally came to understand that he was homeward bound and hadn't far to go, he threw his legs wildly out before and behind him, depressed his head and laid his ears back, and flew by the admiring company like a telegram. In five minutes he was far away ahead of everybody.

We stopped in front of a private residence—Brown and I did—to wait for the rest and see that none were lost. I soon saw that I had attracted the attention of a comely young girl, and I felt duly flattered. Perhaps, thought I, she admires my horsemanship—and I made a savage jerk at the bridle and said, "Ho! will you!" to show how fierce and unmanageable the beast was—though, to say truly, he was leaning up against a hitching post peaceably enough at the time. I stirred Oahu up and moved him about, and went up the street a short distance to look for the party, and "loped" gallantly back again, all the while making a pretense of being unconscious that I was an object of interest. I then addressed a few "peart" remarks to Brown, to give the young lady a chance to admire my style of conversation, and was gratified to see her step up and whisper to Brown and glance furtively at me at the same time. I could see that her gentle face bore an expression of the most kindly and earnest solicitude, and I was shocked and angered to hear Brown burst into a fit of brutal laughter.

As soon as we started home, I asked with a fair show of indifference, what she had been saying.

Brown laughed again and said: "She thought from the slouchy way you rode and the way you drawled out your words, that you was drunk! She said, 'Why don't you take the poor creature home, Mr. Brown? It makes me nervous to see him galloping that horse and just hanging on that way, and he so drunk.' "

I laughed very loudly at the joke, but it was a sort of hollow, sepulchral laugh, after all. And then I took it out of Oahu.

AN OLD ACQUAINTANCE

I have found an old acquaintance here—Rev. Franklin S. Rising, of the Episcopal ministry, who has had charge of a church in Virginia [City], Nevada, for several years, and who is well known in Sacramento and San Francisco. He sprained his knee in September last, and is here for his health. He thinks he has made no progress worth mentioning towards regaining it, but I think differently. He can ride on horseback, and is able to walk a few steps without his crutches—things he could not do a week ago.

"WHILE WE WERE MARCHING THROUGH GEORGIA!"

The popular-song nuisance follows us here. In San Francisco it used to be "Just Before the Battle, Mother," every night and all night long. Then it was "When Johnny Comes Marching Home." After that it was "Wearin' of the Green." And last and most dreadful of all, came that calamity of "While We Were Marching Through Georgia." It was the last thing I heard when the ship sailed, and it gratified me to think I should hear it no more for months. And now, here at dead of night, at the very outpost and fag-end of the world, on a little rock in the middle of a limitless ocean, a pack of dark-skinned savages are tramping down the street singing it with a vim and an energy that make my hair rise!—singing it in their own barbarous tongue! They have got the tune to perfection—otherwise I never would have suspected that *"Waikiki lantani oe Kaa hooly hooly wawhoo"* means, "While We Were Marching Through Georgia." If it would have been all the same to General Sherman, I wish he had gone around by the way of the Gulf of Mexico, instead of marching through Georgia.

MARK TWAIN

8❀

HONOLULU (S. I.), APRIL, 1866.

OFF

Mounted on my noble steed Hawaii (pronounced Hah-wy-ye—stress on second syllable), a beast that cost thirteen dollars and is able to go his mile in three—with a bit of margin to it—I departed last Saturday week for—for any place that might turn up.

SATURDAY IN HONOLULU

Passing through the market place we saw that feature of Honolulu under its most favorable auspices—that is, in the full glory of Saturday afternoon, which is a festive day with the natives. The native girls by twos and threes and parties of a dozen, and sometimes in whole platoons and companies, went cantering up and down the neighboring streets astride of fleet but homely horses, and with their gaudy riding habits streaming like banners behind them. Such a troop of free and easy riders, in their natural home, which is the saddle, makes a gay and graceful and exhilarating spectacle. The riding habit I speak of is simply a long, broad scarf, like a tavern tablecloth brilliantly colored, wrapped around the loins once, then apparently passed up between the limbs and each end thrown back-

ward over the same, and floating and flapping behind on
both sides beyond the horse's tail like a couple of fancy
flags; and then, with a girl that throws her chest forward
and sits up like a major general and goes sweeping by like
the wind. "Gay?" says Brown, with a fine irony; "oh, you
can't mean it!"

The girls put on all the finery they can scare up on
Saturday afternoon—fine black silk robes; flowing red
ones that nearly put your eyes out; others as white as
snow; still others that discount the rainbow; and they
wear their hair in nets, and trim their jaunty hats with
fresh flowers, and encircle their dusky throats with home-
made necklaces of the brilliant vermilion-tinted blossom
of the ohia; and they fill the markets and the adjacent
streets with their bright presences, and smell like thunder
with their villainous coconut oil.

Occasionally you see a heathen from the sunny isles
away down in the South Seas, with his face and neck tattooed till he looks like the customary unfortunate from
Reese River who has been blown up in a mine. Some are
tattooed a dead blue color down to the upper lip—masked,
as it were—leaving the natural light yellow skin of Mi-
cronesia unstained from thence down; some with broad
marks drawn down from hair to neck, on both sides of
the face, and a strip of the original yellow skin, two inches
wide, down the center—a gridiron with a spoke broken
out; and some with the entire face discolored with the
popular mortification tint, relieved only by one or two
thin, wavy threads of natural yellow running across the
face from ear to ear, and eyes twinkling out of this darkness, from under shadowing hat brims, like stars in the
dark of the moon.

native staple food

tourists

POI FOR SALE

Moving among the stirring crowds, you come to the poi merchants, squatting in the shade on their hams, in true native fashion, and surrounded by purchasers. (The Sandwich Islanders always squat on their hams, and who knows but they may be the old original "ham sandwiches"? The thought is pregnant with interest.) The poi looks like common flour paste, and is kept in large bowls formed of a species of gourd, and capable of holding from one to three or four gallons. Poi is the chief article of food among the natives, and is prepared from the kalo or taro plant (*k* and *t* are the same in the Kanaka alphabet, and so are *l* and *r*). The taro root looks like a thick, or, if you please, a corpulent sweet potato, in shape, but is of a light purple color when boiled. When boiled it answers as a passable substitute for bread. The buck Kanakas bake it under ground, then mash it up well with a heavy lava pestle, mix water with it until it becomes a paste, set it aside and let it ferment, and then it is poi—and a villainous mixture it is, almost tasteless before it ferments and too sour for a luxury afterward. But nothing in the world is more nutritious. When solely used, however, it produces acrid humors, a fact which sufficiently accounts for the blithe and humorous character of the Kanakas. I think there must be as much of a knack in handling poi as there is in eating with chopsticks. The forefinger is thrust into the mess and stirred quickly round several times and drawn as quickly out, thickly coated, just as if it were poulticed; the head is thrown back, the finger inserted in the mouth and the poultice stripped off and swallowed—the eye closing gently, meanwhile, in a languid sort of ecstasy. Many a different finger goes into the same bowl and many a different kind of dirt and shade and quality of flavor is added to the virtues of its contents. One tall gentleman, with nothing in the world on but a soiled and greasy shirt, thrust in his finger and tested the poi, shook his head, scratched it with the useful finger, made another test, prospected among his hair, caught something and ate it; tested the poi again, wiped the grimy perspiration from his brow with the universal hand, tested again, blew his nose—"Let's move on, Brown," said I, and we moved.

AWA FOR SALE—DITTO FISH

Around a small shanty was collected a crowd of natives buying the awa root. It is said that but for the use of this root the destruction of the people in former times by venereal diseases would have been far greater than it was, and by others it is said that this is merely a fancy. All agree that poi will rejuvenate a man who is used up and his vitality almost annihilated by hard drinking, and that in some kinds of diseases it will restore health after all medicines have failed; but all are not willing to allow to the awa the virtues claimed for it. The natives manufacture an intoxicating drink from it which is fearful in its effects when persistently indulged in. It covers the body with dry, white scales, inflames the eyes, and causes premature decrepitude. Although the man before whose establishment we stopped has to pay a government license of eight hundred dollars a year for an exclusive right to sell awa root, it is said that he makes a small fortune every twelvemonth; while saloonkeepers, who pay a thousand dollars a year for the privilege of retailing whiskey, etc., only make a bare living.

We found the fish market crowded; for the native is very fond of fish, and eats the article raw. Let us change the subject.

OLD-TIME SATURDAYS

In old times here Saturday was a grand gala day indeed. All the native population of the town forsook their labors, and those of the surrounding country journeyed to the city. Then the white folks had to stay indoors, for every street was so packed with charging cavaliers and cavalier-esses that it was next to impossible to thread one's way through the cavalcades without getting crippled. In the afternoon the natives were wont to repair to the plain, outside the town, and indulge in their ancient sports and pastimes and bet away their week's earnings on horse races. One might see two or three thousand, some say five thousand, of these wild riders, skurrying over the plain in a mass in those days. And it must have been a fine sight.

At night they feasted and the girls danced the lascivious hula-hula—a dance that is said to exhibit the very perfec-tion of educated motion of limb and arm, hand, head, and body, and the exactest uniformity of movement and ac-curacy of "time." It was performed by a circle of girls with no raiment on them to speak of, who went through with an infinite variety of motions and figures without prompting, and yet so true was their "time," and in such perfect concert did they move that when they were placed in a straight line, hands, arms, bodies, limbs, and heads waved, swayed, gesticulated, bowed, stooped, whirled, squirmed, twisted, and undulated as if they were part and parcel of a single individual; and it was difficult to believe they were not moved in a body by some exquisite piece of mechanism.

Of late years, however, Saturday has lost most of its quondam gala features. This weekly stampede of the natives interfered too much with labor and the interests of the white folks, and by sticking in a law here, and preaching a sermon there, and by various other means, they gradually broke it up. The demoralizing hula-hula was forbidden to be performed, save at night, with closed doors, in presence of few spectators, and only by permission duly procured from the authorities and the payment of ten dollars for the same. There are few girls nowadays able to dance this ancient national dance in the highest perfection of the art.

making Puritan lang.

THE GOVERNMENT PRISON

Cantering across the bridge and down the firm, level, gleaming white coral turnpike that leads toward the south, or the east, or the west, or the north (the points of the compass being all the same to me, inasmuch as, for good reasons, I have not had an opportunity thus far of discovering whereabouts the sun rises in this country—I know where it sets, but I don't know how it gets there nor which direction it comes from), we presently arrived at a massive coral edifice which I took for a fortress at first, but found out directly that it was the government prison. A soldier at the great gate admitted us without further authority than my countenance, and I suppose he thought he was paying me a handsome compliment when he did so; and so did I until I reflected that the place was a penitentiary. However, as far as appearances went, it might have been the King's palace, so neat and clean and white, and so full of the fragrance of flowers was the establishment, and I was satisfied.

We passed through a commodious office, whose walls were ornamented with linked strands of polished handcuffs and fetters, through a hall, and among the cells above and below. The cells for the men were eight or ten feet high, and roomy enough to accommodate the two prisoners and their hammocks, usually put in each, and have space left for several more. The floors were scrubbed clean, and were guiltless of spot or stain of any kind, and the painfully white walls were unmarred by a single mark or blemish. Through ample gratings, one could see the blue sky and get his hair blown off by the cool breeze. They call this a prison—the pleasantest quarters in Honolulu.

There are four wards, and one hundred and thirty-two prisoners can be housed in rare and roomy comfort within them.

There were a number of native women in the female department. Poor devils, they hung their heads under the prying eyes of our party as if they were really ashamed of being there.

In the condemned cell and squatting on the floor, all swathed in blankets, as if it were cold weather, was a brown-faced, gray-bearded old scalawag, who, in a frolicsome mood, had massacred three women and a batch of children—his own property, I believe—and reflects upon that exploit with genuine satisfaction to this hour, and will go to the gallows as tranquilly indifferent as a white man would go to dinner.

OUT AT THE BACK DOOR

The prison yard—that sad enclosure which, in the prisons of my native America, is a cheerless barren and yieldeth no vegetation save the gallows tree, with its sorrowful human fruit—is a very garden! The beds, bordered by rows of inverted bottles (the usual style here), were filled with all manner of dainty flowers and shrubs: Chinese mulberry and orange trees stood here and there, well stocked with fruit; a beautiful little pine tree—rare, and imported from the far South Seas—occupied the center, with sprays of gracefully arching green spears springing outward like parasol tops, at marked and regular intervals, up its slender stem, and diminishing in diameter with mathematical strictness of graduation, till the sprouting plume at the top stood over a perfect pyramid. Vines clambered everywhere and hid from view and clothed with beauty everything that might otherwise have been suggestive of chains and captivity. There was nothing here to remind one of the prison save a brace of dovecotes, containing several pretty birds brought hither from "strange, strange lands beyond the sea." These, sometimes, may pine for liberty and their old free life among the clouds or in the shade of the orange groves, or abroad on the breezy ocean—but if they do, it is likely they take it out in pining, as a general thing.

CAPTAIN TAIT, SCRIPTURAL STUDENT

Against one wall of the prison house stands an airy little building which does duty as a hospital. A harmless old lunatic, named Captain Tait, has his quarters here. He has a wife and children in the town, but he prefers the prison

hospital, and has demanded and enjoyed its hospitality
(slip of the pen—no joke intended) for years. He visits his
family at long intervals—being free to go and come as he
pleases—but he always drifts back to the prison again after
a few days. His is a religious mania, and he professes to
read sixty chapters of the Bible every day, and write them
down in a book. He was about down to chapter thirty-
five when I was introduced to him, I should judge, as it
was nearly two in the afternoon.

I said, "What book are you reading, Captain?"

"The precious of the precious—the book of books—the
Sacred Scriptures, sir."

"Do you read a good deal in it?"

"Sixty chapters every day (with a perceptible show of
vanity, but a weary look in the eye withal)—sixty chapters every day, and write them all down in a plain, legible
hand."

"It is a good deal. At that rate, you must ultimately get
through, and run short of material."

"Ah, but the Lord looks out for his own. I am in His
hands—He does with me as He wills. I often read some
of the same chapters over again, for the Lord tells me what
to read, and it is not for me to choose. Providence always
shows me the place."

"No hanging fire?—I mean, can you always depend
on—on this information coming to time every day, so
to speak?"

"Always—always, sir. I take the sacred volume in my
hand, in this manner, every morning, in a devout and
prayerful spirit, and immediately, and without any voli-
tion on my part, my fingers insert themselves between the
leaves—so directed from above (with a sanctified glance

aloft)—and I know that the Lord desires me to open at that place and begin. I never have to select the chapter myself—the Lord always does it for me."

I heard Brown mutter, "The old man appears to have a good thing, anyway—and his poi don't cost him anything, either; Providence looks out for his regular sixty, the prison looks out for his hash, and his family looks out for itself. I've never seen any sounder maniac than him, and I've been around considerable."

GENERAL GEORGE WASHINGTON

We were next introduced to General George Washington, or, at least, to an aged, limping Negro man, who called himself by that honored name. He was supposed to be seventy years old, and he looked it. He was as crazy as a loon, and sometimes, they say, he grows very violent. He was a Samson in a small way; his arms were corded with muscle, and his legs felt as hard as if they were made of wood. He was in a peaceable mood at present, and strongly manacled. They have a hard time with him occasionally, and some time or other he will get in a lively way and eat up the garrison of that prison, no doubt. The native soldiers who guard the place are afraid of him, and he knows it.

His history is a sealed book—or at least all that part of it which transpired previously to the entry of his name as a pensioner upon the Hawaiian Government fifteen years ago. He was found carrying on at a high rate at one of the other islands, and it is supposed he was put ashore there from a vessel called the *Olive Branch*. He has evidently been an old sailor, and it is thought he was one of a party of Negroes who fitted out a ship and sailed from a New

England port some twenty years ago. He is fond of talking in his dreamy, incoherent way, about the Blue Ridge in Virginia, and seems familiar with Richmond and Lynchburg. I do not think he is the old original General W.

ALOFT

Upstairs in the prison are the handsome apartments used by the officers of the establishment; also a museum of quaint and curious weapons of offense and defense, of all nations and all ages of the world. The prison is to a great extent a self-supporting institution, through the labor of the convicts farmed out to load and unload ships and work on the highways, and I am not sure but that it supports itself and pays a surplus into the public treasury besides, but I have no note of this, and I seldom place implicit confidence in my memory in matters where figures and finance are concerned and have not been thought of for a fortnight. This government prison is in the hands of W. C. Parke, Marshal of the Kingdom, and he has small need to be ashamed of his management of it. Without wishing to betray too much knowledge of such matters, I should say that this is the model prison of the western half of the world, at any rate.

MARK TWAIN

9

HONOLULU, APRIL, 1866.

SAD ACCIDENT

I have just met an estimable lady—Mrs. Captain Jollop-
son, whose husband (with her assistance) commands the
whaling bark *Lucretia Wilkerson*—and she said:

"Oh, I've never *had* such a time of it! I'm clean out of
luck, I do believe. The wind's been dead ahead with me all
this day. It appears to me that I can't do no way but that
it comes out wrong. First, I turned out this morning and
says I, 'Here's a go—eight bells and no duff yet! I just
know it's going to blow great guns for *me* today.' And so
it's come out. Start fair, sail fair; otherwise, just the re-
verse. Well, I hove on my dress and cleared for the market,
and took the big basket, which I don't do when I'm alone,
because I'm on the short lay when it comes to eating; but
when the old man's in port, it's different, you know, and I
go fixed when I recruit for him—never come back in ballast then, because he's on the long lay, and it's expensive
too; you can depend on it, his leakage and shrinkage shows
up on his home bills when he goes out of port, and it's all
on account of recruiting, too—though he says it's on account of toggery for me, which is a likely yarn, when I
can't even buy a set of new halliards for my bonnet but he
growls, and what few slops I do have I've got to smuggle

'em; and yet, bless you, if we were to ship 'em the freight
on mine wouldn't pay primage on his—but where was I?
Oh, yes—I hove on my dress and hove down toward the
market, and while I was laying off and on before the post
office, here comes a shipkeeper round the corner three
sheets in the wind and his deadlights stove in, and I see
by the way he was bulling that if he didn't sheer off and
shorten sail he'd foul my larboard stuns'l-boom, which I
had my basket on—because, you see, he'd been among his
friends having a bit of a gam, and had got about one fid
too much aboard, and his judgment had fetched away in
the meantime, and so he steered bad, and was making
latitude all the time when he ought to have been making
longitude, and here he was to wind'ard of me, but making
so much leeway that—well, you see how it was. I backed off
fast as I could, and sung out to him to port his helm, but it
warn't no use; he'd everything drawing and I had considerable sternway, and he just struck me a little abaft the beam,
and down I went, head on, and skunned my elbow!"

I said, "Bless my life!"

And she said, "Well you may say it! My! such a jolt! It
started everything. It's worse'n being pulled! I shouldn't
wonder if I'd have to be hove down—" and then she
spread her hand alongside of her mouth and sung out,
"Susy, ahoy!" to another woman, who rounded to to wait
for her, and the two fell off before the wind and sailed
away together.

TRANSLATION

"Eight bells" stands for the closing of a watch—two to
an hour, four hours to a watch, six watches in a day—on
board ship.

"Duff" is Jack Tar's dessert—a sort of dough, with dried apples or something of the kind in it on extra occasions.

"Cleared" for the market—a ship "clears" for her voyage when she takes out her papers at the customhouse.

"Short lay" and "long lay"—these phrases are confined to the whaling interest. Neither the officers nor men get any wages on a whaleship, but receive, instead, a proportion of all the bone and oil taken; Jack usually gets about the one-hundred-and-twentieth part of all the "catch" (or profits of the voyage), for his share, and this is called a "long lay"; the captain generally gets a tenth, twelfth, or fourteenth, which is a "short lay," and the other officers in proportion. Some captains also have perquisites besides their "lay"—a dollar or more on every barrel of the "catch," over a certain number. The luckiest captain of the lot made fifty thousand dollars last season. Very good for a few months work. When a ship is ready to sail and must suddenly supply the place of some seaman who has fallen sick, candidates will take advantage of the circumstances and demand as short a "lay" as a second mate's to ship as the last man and complete the crew. I am informed (but I do not believe it), that this is termed the "Lay of the Last Minstrel."

"Recruit"—the whaling voyage to the North Seas occupies about seven months; then the vessel returns to Honolulu, transships her oil to the States, refits, and goes over to the coast of California about November or December, to put in her idle time catching humpback whales or devilfish, returning here along in March and April to "recruit"—that is, procure vegetables, and especially potatoes, which are a protective against scurvy, and give the men a few days run on shore, and then off for the north

again as early in the spring as possible. Those vessels which
do not consider the coast fishing profitable, because of the
"stoving" of boats by the savage humpbacks and the con-
sequent loss of men and material, go to "west'ard," as they
term going down to the line after sperm whales; and when
they have finished this "between season," they go over and
"recruit" at Japan, and from thence proceed directly north.

"Leakage and Shrinkage"—when a whaler returns here
with her cargo, the United States consul estimates its
probable value in the East, and buys the interests of the
officers and men on behalf of the owners of the ship, and
pays for the same in gold. To secure the shipowner against
loss, a bill of contingencies is brought against poor Jack by
the consul (leakage and shrinkage being among the items),
which reduces the profits of his long voyage about one half
or two thirds. For instance, take the case of the whaling
bark ——— last year. The consul considered oil to be worth
between one dollar and seventy-five cents and two dollars
a gallon (in greenbacks) in the States; he put it down at
one dollar and seventy-five cents to be on the safe side,
and then reduced as follows:

First—premium to be paid for money, and difference
between gold and paper—so much. (Jack must be paid
in gold.)

Second—an allowance of eight percent, for probable
leakage and shrinkage of the oil on its homeward voyage.

Third—freight on the homeward voyage—paid by Jack.

Fourth—interest and insurance on the cargo hence to
the States—paid by Jack.

Fifth—commission of the owner at home (2½ percent)
for selling the cargo—paid by Jack.

And after all these reductions, what do you suppose the

consul paid Jack for his one-hundred-and-twentieth "lay" in a cargo of oil worth over $1.75 a gallon at home? He paid him seventy-four cents a gallon. As a general thing, the shipowner at home makes a princely profit out of this "gouging" of the sailorman; but instances have occurred —rarely, however—where the price set by the consul here was so much above the real value of the oil at home, that all the gouging was not sufficient to save the shipowner from loss.

"Home Bills"—it makes no difference how much money a sailor brings into port, he is soon head over heels in debt. In order to secure his services on a voyage, the ship is obliged to assume this indebtedness. The item is entered against Jack on the ship's books at the home port in the East as his "home bill." If the voyage proves lucky, the ship gets even on Jack's home bill by subtracting it from his "lay"; but if she takes no oil she must pay the bill anyhow, and is "out and injured," of course. These "home bills" are first assumed by one of the professional "sharks" in New Bedford and New London who furnish crews to ships; say Jack owes fifty dollars; the shark enters his name for a voyage, assumes his debt, advances him a dollar or so for a farewell spree, and takes his note for $150; and the shipowner agrees to cash it at the end of six months. Ships have left port responsible for five thousand dollar home bills, lost four or five men by desertion, been to great trouble and expense to supply other men, and then had no luck and failed to catch a single whale.

"Slops"—improvident Jack is apt to leave port short of jackets, trousers, shirts, tobacco, pipes, letter paper, and so forth and so on. The ship takes a large quantity of these things along, and supplies them to him at extremely healthy prices, so that sometimes, after a long, unlucky voyage, no wages and heavy home bills and bills for "slops," Jack will return to port very considerably in debt to the ship, and the ship must stand the loss, for an unprofitable voyage squares all such accounts. In squaring up a voyage before the consul, the ship captain piles up the slop bills as high as he can get them, though it does not put a single cent in his own pocket; he forgets, in his enthusiasm for his owner's interest, that while he is gouging Jack for the benefit of "the firm," the firm are gouging himself, and Jack too, by the system of consular assessment I have mentioned above. The captain says to the consul:

"Put down three pair of boots on this man's slop bill."

Jack: "But I didn't have but one pair, sir."

Captain: "Belay! Don't talk back; you might have had 'em if you'd a' wanted 'em. And put him down for eleven pair of socks."

Jack: "But I only had two pair, sir."

Captain: "Well, ——— it, is that any o' my fault? Warn't they there for anybody that wanted 'em? And set him down for two ream of letter paper."

Jack: "Why, I never writ a letter whilst I was gone, sir."

Captain: "Hold your yop! Do you cal'late for me to be responsible for all your dam foolishness? You might have had four ream, if you'd wanted it. And set on ten percent for other truck, which I don't recollect what it was."

And so Jack is gouged by the captain, for the owner's exclusive benefit, and both are fleeced by that same owner with strict impartiality. Perhaps the captain's "lay" will go East to be sold, and "the firm" will sell at a dollar and a half and then report to him that the market had fallen and they only got a dollar for it. Thus ungrateful are they to the captain who gouged the seaman on his "slops" for their sole benefit.

"Primage"—this term obtains in most seaports. No man can tell now what gave it birth, for it is very ancient, and its origin is long ago forgotten. It is a tax of five percent on a ship's freight bills, and in old times went to her captain. In our day, however, it goes to the shipowner with the other freight money (although it forms a separate item in the freight bill), or is turned over to the agent who procured a cargo for a vessel, as his commission. When you engage for the shipment of a lot of freight, you make no mention of this five percent primage, but you perfectly understand that it will be added, and you must pay it; therefore, when you are ostensibly shipping at twenty cents, you are really shipping at twenty-one.

"Laying off and on"—a sailor phrase, sufficiently well understood by landsmen to need no explanation.

"Shipkeeper"—a man who stands guard on a whaler and takes care of the ship when the boats and the crew are off after whales.

"Bulling"—a term usually applied to the chafing of vessels together when riding at anchor in harbors subject to chopping swells. Some whalers say that one reason why they avoid San Francisco is that this "bulling" process in our bay is more damaging to their vessels, frequently, than a long voyage.

"Gam"—the whaleman's phrase for gossip—very common here.

"Fid"—the whaleman's term for our "smile"—drink. A fid is an instrument which the sailor uses when he splices the main brace on board ship.

"Fetched away"—a nautical phrase signifying to break

loose from fastenings in a storm—such as the fetching away of furniture, rigging, etc.

"Skunned"—after examining various authors I have discovered that this is a provincial distortion of our word "skinned."

"Pulled"—a term signifying the arraigning of a ship's officers before the courts by the crew to answer for alleged cruelties practiced upon them on the high seas—such as the "pulling" of captains and mates by the crews of the *Mercury*, the *White Swallow*, the *Great Republic*, etc., in the San Francisco courts. Here is another reason why, out of the eighty-seven American whale ships that will fish in the north seas this summer, only about sixteen will venture to touch at San Francisco either going or coming: they find it safer and cheaper to rendezvous and procure supplies here, and save 4,200 miles extra sailing, than to start from, and return to, San Francisco and run the chance of getting "pulled." Honolulu would not amount to anything at all without her whaling trade, and so Jack cannot "pull" his captain here—no matter what his grievance was, he could not easilly get it before these courts; the lawyer who ventured to take his case would stand a fair chance of being run out of town by the enraged community. But the whaler man says, 'You drop into 'Frisco and great Neptune! your men'll pull you before you get your anchor down—and there you are for three months, on expenses, waiting on them courts; and they'll go in and swear to the infernalest pack of lies, and the jury'll believe every word of it, and the judge'll read you a sermon that'll take the hair off your head, and then he'll take and jam you into a jail. Oh, no; it don't pay a whale ship to stop at San Francisco."

"Hove down"—in ports where there are [no] docks, damaged vessels are hauled out and "hove down" on their sides when repairs to their bottoms are required.

By this time, if you will go back and read the first paragraphs of this letter you may be able to understand them.

Every section of our Western Hemisphere seems supplied with a system of technicalities, etiquette, and slang, peculiar to itself. The above chapter is intended to give you a somewhat exaggerated idea of the technicalities of conversation in Honolulu—bred from the great whaling interest which centers here, and naturally infused into the vocabulary of the place. Your favorite California similes were bred from the technicalities of surface mining; those of Washoe come from the profound depths of the "main lead," and those of the Honoluluian were born of whalebone, blubber, and the traffic of the seas. Perhaps no single individual would use more than two or three of the nautical and whaling phrases I have quoted, in any one conversation, but you might hear all of them in the course of a week, if you talked with a good many people.

And etiquette varies according to one's surroundings. In the mining camps of California, when a friend tenders you a "smile" or invites you to take a "blister," it is etiquette to say, "Here's hoping your dirt'll pan out gay." In Washoe, when you are requested to "put in a blast," or invited to take "your regular pison," etiquette admonishes you to touch glasses and say, "Here's hoping you'll strike it rich in the lower level." And in Honolulu, when your friend the whaler asks you to take a "fid" with him, it is simple etiquette to say, "Here's eighteen hundred barrels, old salt!" But, "Drink hearty!" is universal. That is the orthodox reply, the world over.

In San Francisco sometimes, if you offend a man, he proposes to take his coat off, and inquires, "Are you on it?" If you are, you can take your coat off, too. In Virginia City, in former times, the insulted party, if he were a true man, would lay his hand gently on his six-shooter and say, "Are you heeled?" But in Honolulu, if Smith offends Jones, Jones asks (with a rising inflection on the last word, which is excessively aggravating), "How much do you weigh?" Smith replies, "Sixteen hundred and forty pound—and you?" "Two ton to a dot, at a quarter past eleven this forenoon—peel yourself; you're my blubber!"

APOLOGETIC AND EXPLANATORY

When I began this letter I meant to furnish some facts and figures concerning the great Pacific whaling traffic, to the end that San Francisco might take into consideration the expediency of making an effort to divert the patronage of the fleet to herself, if it seemed well to do so; and chiefly I meant to try and explain why that patronage does not gravitate to that center naturally and of its own accord. True, many know the reason already, and need no explanation, but many more do not understand it so well or know so much about it. But not being in a sufficiently serious mood today, I have wisely left for my next letter the discussion of a subject of such overwhelming gravity.

MARK TWAIN

10🏵

HONOLULU, APRIL, 1866.

THE WHALING TRADE

The whaling trade of the north seas—which is by no means insignificant—centers in Honolulu. Shorn of it this town would die—its business men would leave and its real estate would become valueless, at least as city property, though Honolulu might flourish afterwards as a fine sugar plantation, the soil being rich and scarcely needing irrigation.

The San Francisco Chamber of Commerce might do worse than make an effort to divert the whaling trade to her city. Honolulu fits out and provisions a majority out of ninety-six whalers this year, and receives a very respectable amount of money for it. Last year she performed this service for only fifty-one vessels—so you can see how the trade is increasing. Sailors always spend all their money before they leave port. Last year they spent $150,000 here, and will doubtless spend double as much when this year's fleet returns. It is said that in the palmy days of whaling, fifteen or twenty years ago, they have squandered as high as a million and a half in this port at the end of a successful voyage. There have been vast fleets of whale ships fitted out here and provisioned and recruited in a single year, in those days, and everything promises that the whaling interest will now move steadily forward, under the impetus of the long-continued high rates of oil and bone, until it eclipses in importance any degree it has ever attained in former times. In chartering vessels to carry home the "catch" of whalers; in equipping them, and supplying and recruiting them; and in relieving their crews of their money at the end of the season, San Francisco might manage to get several hundred thousands a year out of the whaling trade if she could get it into her hands, or a million or so, should whaling again reach its former high prosperity.

It costs from one thousand dollars all the way up to twenty thousand to provision and fit a whaler here for her voyage to the north seas, including paying off crew, and taking them "by and large," the average is about six thousand dollars to each vessel. Of the ninety-six ships which go north from here this season, only forty-nine will fit here—the other forty-seven, being the increase in tonnage and on their first voyage, were equipped at home. The home equipment is generally for two full seasons— so Honolulu will not get the job of supplying these new ships for a couple of years yet; but after that she will have their whole custom, unless, perhaps, San Francisco can make a satisfactory bid for the whaling trade in the meantime.

There have been over four hundred whalers in the north seas at one time in the palmy days of the trade, two thirds of which were supplied in this market, and paid Honolulu over a million for doing it, even at the moderate prices of those days.

CONCERNING OIL AND BONE

Oil is valuable, but whalebone is more so.

Sperm whales are chiefly caught at the "line," or "west-'ard," as they term it. They do not yield any bone, but the oil is worth from 75 to 100 percent more than any other at the present time.

Humpbacks and devilfish are caught on the coast of California, "between seasons." The yield is called "coast oil." They yield no bone.

Ochotsk whales yield about twenty percent less bone than the Arctic whale, and it is worth four to five cents a pound less than Arctic.

The "catch" is a term which signifies the fruits of a voyage. The average catch for three years past of ships sailing out of this port, was about 650 barrels of oil a year to each vessel, and eight thousand pounds of bone.

CONSULAR PRICES

The consular prices at which crews of whalers were paid off here in the fall of 1865 were as follows: whale oil, 64¢ a gallon; coast oil, 60¢; sperm oil, 92¢. Ochotsk bone, 74¢ a pound; Arctic, 78¢—in gold. These prices were not one half what the articles were worth in the Eastern markets—in currency.

PAST AND PRESENT

The "palmy days of whaling"—the phrase which one hears here as often as he hears in California of matters which transpired "in an early day" there, or in Washoe of "the flush times of '63"—refers to a period some fifteen years gone by. But the "palmy days," in a modified form, lasted clear up to 1853. Let me give a few figures: The fleet brought to this port in 1853: oil, 4,000,-000 gallons; bone, 2,020,264 pounds. Then for several years the yield gradually fell away, till in 1858 the figures were: oil, considerable under 3,000,000 gallons; bone, 1,614,710 pounds. Five years after, in 1863, in the midst of the war, the catch had fallen away down to: oil, 732,-031 gallons; bone, 337,043 pounds. Still lower in 1864: oil, 642,362 gallons; bone, 339,331 pounds. But in 1865, in spite of the pirate *Shenandoah*, the trade almost held its own; it had "struck bottom," as we say in Washoe, and was ready to start up again. The yield was: oil, 621,434 gallons; bone, 337,394 pounds.

These last figures were for sixty-seven ships, all told—fifty-one of which went from here. We may look for better results this season, with ninety-six vessels in the fleet; and next year the "palmy days" may come again, for everything that can be turned into a whale ship by any process known to art is being bought up or chartered in the East now for this trade, and in due time the icy solitudes of the north seas will once more become populous with the winged servants of commerce.

WHAT COMMANDS THE WHALER PATRONAGE

I have talked whaler talk and read whaling statistics and asked questions about the whaling interest every now and then for two or three weeks, and have discovered that it was easy to get plausible information concerning every point connected with this commerce save one, and that was: Why is it that this remote port, in a foreign country, is made the rendezvous of the whaling fleet, instead of the seemingly more eligible one of San Francisco, on our own soil? This was a "stunner." Most people would venture a chance shot at one portion of the mystery, but nobody was willing to attempt its entire solution. The truth seems to be that there is no main, central, prominent reason for it, but it is made up of a considerable bundle of reasons, neither of which is especially important when taken by itself.

SAN FRANCISCO VS. HONOLULU

1. See how the case stands: In Honolulu it is not a holiday job to ship a crew; natives comprise it chiefly, and the Government frowns upon their employment as sailors, because it causes the agricultural interests to suffer for want of labor, and you see the plantations build up the whole kingdom, while the whaling trade only builds up Honolulu and one or two smaller seaports. So the Government first made the whalers enter into bonds of one hundred dollars for each man; that is, to insure the return of that man to the kingdom; the bond was increased, until now it is three hundred dollars, and shipping taxes of various kinds have been instituted, which amount altogether to about six hundred dollars for each man, which must be paid in gold to the Government when the man ships. Ships usually go out under bonds of three thousand to ten thousand dollars for the return of their crews. The bond system, which was intended to keep the Kanakas all at home, don't work; the whalers still are obliged to take natives or go without crews. So, urged by the agricultural interest, an attempt will be made in the legislature, which convenes two weeks hence, to pass a bill entirely forbidding the shipping of natives. If this is accomplished, it will give San Francisco one good chance to get the whaling

patronage; and it is a better and more permanent and safer thing to have than rich but ephemeral mines. In favor of San Francisco, it is acknowledged that as soon as it became the established whaling rendezvous, whaling crews would repair to it, and men could be shipped at small expense and without bonds.

2. It is twenty-one hundred miles from San Francisco to Honolulu—so that these whalers, by coming here, do forty-two hundred miles more sailing than they need to do, and waste about a month and a half of time in doing it.

3. They cannot insure directly, here. The policies must go all the way to the East, and then maybe the insurance office may approve them and maybe it may reject them, and perchance the ship may be lost in the meantime.

In San Francisco insurance could be directly effected.

4. Here the whole whaling fleet, nearly, is paid off at once, and in gold, and of course exchange goes up to a high figure; started at five or six, last fall, and went up to ten percent premium. It stands at two and a half even now, when there is no especial call for money.

In San Francisco it need never go to two and a half at any time. Whalemen's bills are the best paper in the country, being always sure and prompt; scarcely a single failure to pay them is recorded.

5. Facilities for transshipment of oil eastward would be much greater in San Francisco than here.

6. Facilities for chartering, equipping, provisioning, and recruiting whalers would be much greater and cheaper in San Francisco than here.

7. Here it takes a mild eternity for a whaler or his agent to communicate with the shipowner at home.

In San Francisco, your steamers, overland stages, and telegraphs bring them face to face.

I think I have stated the case fairly. In facilities for shipping crews, in economy of time and distance of travel of a voyage, in facilities for insuring, in cheapness of money, in facilities for transshipping cargoes, ditto ditto for chartering and equipping vessels, and ditto ditto for communicating with owners, Honolulu cannot begin to compete with San Francisco.

Then why does the whaling fleet rendezvous in a remote port in a foreign land, instead of a convenient one at home?

AN ATTEMPT AT A SOLUTION

I have got the question answered by piecemeal by many different persons, and I will jot down the several items here. They say it is hard to get crews in San Francisco, but they confess that this would not be the case if that city became the established rendezvous. They say men can "run away" so easily there, and put the ship in for their "home bills," etc., but that here they can't get off the Islands. They say the ship is preyed upon by everybody, and fleeced for everything from spun yarn up to salt beef. They say their ships are worn out by "bulling" in the harbor there, but the harbor is smooth and roomy here. And they say, finally (and then the old sea dogs gnash their teeth and swear till the air turns blue around them), that "there's more land sharks (lawyers) in 'Frisco than there's fiddlers in hell, I tell you; and you'll get 'pulled' before your anchor's down!" If there is a main, central count in the indictment against San Francisco that is it. A whaler can be snatched up ("pulled") by his men and

the land sharks, and hauled into court in San Francisco
with the utmost facility, but they cannot touch him here.
The lawyer who took charge of a sailor's complaint against
his captain might as well emigrate—he could practice no
more in Honolulu. True, when a case is so flagrant that it
cannot possibly be overlooked, a sort of trial is sometimes
had, but it never amounts to much.

The above are the whaling captain's arguments—or
were, in the first place, but from their mouths they have
gone into everybody's else, and belong to nobody in particular now. Then there are other arguments which you
hear oftener from other people than from the whalers
themselves. For instance, several persons have explained
about in this wise: In San Francisco the agent transacts the
captain's business exactly as it is done here, and then brings
in a bill, item by item, for commissions—a bill that any
man can understand in a minute, and it looks expensive;
but here the agent, with fine sagacity, charges no commissions—at least they do not appear on the surface—they
are faithfully wrung into the general bill in a sort of
"debtor to sundries" fashion, though, and nobody notices
it, and consequently nobody grumbles!

Another powerful argument may be stated thus: A
whaleman don't amount to much in San Francisco, but
here he is the biggest frog in the pond. Up there the agent
lets him dance attendance until more important business is
attended to, and then goes out with him and assists him in
just such of his concerns as absolutely require assistance,
and then leaves him to paddle his own canoe with the remainder; but here the agent welcomes the old salt like a
long-lost brother, and makes him feel that he is a man of
consequence—and so he is, and should be so treated in

San Francisco; and the agent attends closely to all the whaler's shore business, of every kind whatever, if it is desired, and thus the captain's stay in port is a complete holiday.

A SUGGESTION

If I were going to advise San Franciscans as to the best strategy to employ in order to secure the whaling trade, I would say, cripple your facilities for "pulling" sea captains on every pretense that sailors can trump up, and show the whaler a little more consideration when he is in port. All other objections will die of themselves.

A STEP MADE

A nucleus is already formed up there. Swift & Allen have opened a branch of their New Bedford house in San Francisco, and their ships (they have eight at sea now) will rendezvous there hereafter. They are going to add several vessels to their fleet this season. Sixteen whalers, and possibly many more, will rendezvous at San Francisco this year. Those captains who have tried that port during the past two years are satisfied with it—all but one or two, who have been "pulled."

MARK TWAIN

11🌸

HONOLULU, APRIL, 1866.

PARADISE AND THE PARI (JOKE)

I have ridden up the handsome Nuuanu Valley; noted the mausoleum of the departed kings of Hawaii by the wayside; admired the neat residences, surrounded by beautiful gardens that border the turnpike; stood, at last, after six miles of travel, on the famous *Pari*—the "divide," we would call it—and looked down the precipice of six or eight hundred feet, over which old Kamehameha I drove the army of the king of Oahu three quarters of a century ago; and gazed upward at the sharp peak close at my left, springing several hundred feet above my head like a colossal church spire—stood there and saw the sun go down and the little plain below and the sea that bordered it become shrouded in thick darkness; and then saw the full moon rise up and touch the tops of the billows, skip over the gloomy valley and paint the upper third of the high peak as white as silver; and heard the ladies say: "Oh, beautiful!—and *such* a strong contrast!" and heard the gentlemen remark: "By George! talk about scenery! how's that?"

It was all very well, but the same place in daylight does not make so fine a picture as the Kalihi Valley (pro-

96

nounced Kah-lee-he, stress on the second syllable). All citizens talk about the *Pari;* all strangers visit it the first thing; all scribblers write about it—but nobody talks or writes about or visits the *Pari's* charming neighbor, the Kalihi Valley. I think it was a fortunate accident that led me to stumble into this enchanted ground.

ANOTHER PARADISE

For a mile or two we followed a trail that branched off from the terminus of the turnpike that leads past the government prison, and bending close around the rocky point of a foothill, we found ourselves fairly in the valley, and the panorama began to move. After a while the trail took the course of a brook that came down the center of the narrowing canyon, and followed it faithfully throughout its eccentric windings. On either side the ground rose gradually for a short distance, and then came the mountain barriers—densely wooded precipices on the right and left, that towered hundreds of feet above us, and up which one might climb about as easily as he could climb up the side of a house.

It was a novel sort of scenery, those mountain walls. Face around and look straight across at one of them, and sometimes it presented a bold, square front, with small inclination out of the perpendicular; move on a little and look back, and it was full of sharp ridges, bright with sunlight, and with deep, shady clefts between; and what had before seemed a smooth boulder, set in among the thick shrubbery on the face of the wall, was now a bare rampart of stone that projected far out from the mass of green foliage, and was as sharply defined against the sky as if it had been built of solid masonry by the hand of man. Ahead

the mountains looked portly—swollen, if you please—
and were marked all over, up and down, diagonally and
crosswise, by sharp ribs that reminded one of the fan-
tastic ridges which the wind builds of the drifting snow on
a plain. Sometimes these ridges were drawn all about the
upper quarter of a mountain, checking it off in velvety
green squares and diamonds and triangles, some beaming
with sunlight and others softly shaded—the whole upper
part of the mountain looking something like a vast green
veil thrown over some object that had a good many edges
and corners to it—then a sort of irregular "eaves" all
around, and from this the main body of the mountain
swept down, with a slight outward curve, to the valley
below. All over these highlands the forest trees grew so
thickly that, even close at hand, they seemed like solid
banks of foliage. These trees were principally of two kinds
—the koa and the kukui—the one with a very light green
leaf and the other with a dark green. Occasionally there
were broad alternate belts of each extending diagonally
from the mountain's bases to their summits, and here and
there, in the midst of the dark green, were great patches
of the bright light-colored leaves, so that, to look far down
the valley, along the undulating front of the barrier of
peaks, the effect was as if the sun were streaming down
upon it through breaks and rifts in the clouds, lighting up
belts at intervals all along, and leaving those intervening
darkened by the shadows of the clouds; and yet there was
not a shred of a cloud in the whole firmament! It was
very soft, and dreamy, and beautiful. And following
down the two tall ridges that walled the valley in, we
saw them terminate at last in two bold, black headlands
that came together like a V, and across this gate ran a

narrow zone of the most brilliant light green tint (the shoal water of the distant sea, between reef and shore), and beyond this the somber blue of the deeper water stretched away to the horizon. The varied picture of the lights and shadows on the wooded mountains, the strong, dark outlines of the gate, and the bright green water and the belt of blue beyond, was one replete with charming contrasts and beautiful effects—a revelation of fairyland itself.

The mountain stream beside us, brawling over its rocky bed, leaped over a miniature precipice occasionally, and then reposed for a season in a limpid pool at her base, reflecting the dank and dripping vines and ferns that clung to the wall and protruded in bunches and festoons through breaks in the sparkling cascade. On the gentle rising ground about us were shady groves of forest trees—the kou, the koa, the breadfruit, the lau hala, the orange, lime, kukui, and many others; and, handsomest of all, the ohia, with its feathery tufts of splendid vermilion-tinted blossoms, a coloring so vivid as to be almost painful to the eye. Large tracts were covered with large hau (how) bushes, whose sheltering foliage is so thick as to be almost impervious to rain. It is spotted all over with a rich yellow flower, shaped something like a teacup, and sometimes it is further embellished by innumerable white bell-shaped blossoms, that grow upon a running vine with a name unknown to me. Here and there were wide crops of bushes completely overgrown and hidden beneath the glossy green leaves of another species of vine, and so dense was this covering that it would hardly be possible for a bird to fly through it. Then there were open spaces well carpeted with grass, and sylvan avenues that wound hither and thither till they lost themselves among the trees. In one open spot a vine of the species I last mentioned had taken possession of two tall dead stumps and wound around and about them, and swung out from their tops and twined their meeting tendrils together into a faultless arch. Man, with all his art, could not have improved its symmetry.

Verily, with its rank luxuriance of vines and blossoms, its groves of forest trees, its shady nooks and grassy lawns, its crystal brook and its wild and beautiful mountain scenery, with that charming far-off glimpse of the sea, Kalihi is the Valley of Enchantment come again!

SAM BRANNAN'S PALACE

While I am on the subject of scenery, I might as well speak of Sam Brannan's palace, or "the Bungalow," as it is popularly called. Years ago it was built and handsomely furnished by Shillaber, now of San Francisco, at a cost of between thirty and forty thousand dollars, and in the day of its glory must have considerably outshone its regal neighbor, the palace of the king. It was a large mansion, with compact walls of coral; dimensions, say, sixty or seventy feet front and eighty feet depth, perhaps, including the ample veranda or portico in front; this portico was supported by six or eight tall fluted Corinthian columns, some three feet in diameter; a dozen coral steps led up to the portico from the ground, and these extended the whole length of the front; there were four rooms on the main floor, some twenty-four feet square, each, and about twenty feet high, besides a room or so of smaller dimensions. When its white paint was new, this must have been a very stately edifice. But finally it passed into Brannan's hands—for the sum of thirty thousand dollars (never mind the particulars of the transaction)—and it has been going to decay for the past ten years. It has arrived there now, and it is the completest ruin I ever saw. One or two of the pillars have fallen, and lie like grand Theban ruins, diagonally across the wide portico; part of the roof of the portico has caved down, and a huge gridiron of plasterless lathing droops from above and threatens the head of the apostrophizing stranger; the windows are dirty, and some of them broken; the shutters are unhinged; the elegant doors are marred and splintered; within, the floors are strewn with debris from the shattered ceilings, weeds grow in damp mold in obscure corners; lizards peep curiously out from unsuspected hiding places and then skurry along the walls and disappear in gaping crevices; the summer breeze sighs fitfully through the desolate chambers, and the unforbidden sun looks down through many a liberal vent in roof and ceiling. The spacious grounds without are rank with weeds, and the fences are crazy with age and chronic debility. No more complete and picturesque ruin than the Bungalow exists today in the Old World or the New. It is the most discouraged-looking pile the sun visits on its daily round, perhaps. In the sorrowful expression of its deserted halls, its fallen columns, and its decayed magnificence, it seems to proclaim, in the homely phrase of California, that it has "got enough pie."

Thomas Jefferson John Quincy Adams, of San Francisco, agent for the State Agricultural Society of California, and agent of pretty much all the other institutions of the kind in the world, including the Paris Exhibition, who has traveled all over these islands during the past eight months, and gathered more information, and collected more silk worms and flowers and seeds, and done more work, and stayed longer in people's houses an uninvited guest, and got more terrific hints and had a rougher time generally, on an imperceptible income, than any other man the century has produced, is Sam Brannan's trusted agent to put the Bungalow in elegant repair and draw on him for five thousand dollars for the purpose. It is not possible for me to say when the work will be commenced or who will take the daring contract—but I *can* say that so small a sum as five thousand dollars expended on the Bungalow would only spoil it as an attractive ruin, without making it amount to much as a human habitation. Let it alone, Brannan, and give your widely known and much discussed agent another job.

THE KING'S PALACE

The King's palace stands not far from the melancholy Bungalow, in the center of grounds extensive enough to accommodate a village. The place is surrounded by neat and substantial coral walks, but the gates pertaining to them are out of repair, and so was the soldier who admitted us—or at any rate his uniform was. He was an exception, however, for the native soldiers usually keep their uniforms in good order.

The palace is a large, roomy frame building, and was very well furnished once, though now some of the appurtenances have lost some of their elegance. But the King don't care, I suppose, as he spends nearly all his time at his modest country residence at Waikiki. A large apartment in the center of the building serves as the royal council chamber; the walls are hung with life-size portraits of various European monarchs, sent hither as tokens of that cousinly regard which exists between all kings, at least on paper. To the right is the reception room or hall of audience, and to the left are the library and a sort of anteroom or private audience chamber. In one of these are life-size portraits of old Kamehameha the Great and one or two queens and princes. The old war-horse had a dark brown, broad and beardless face, with native intelligence apparent in it, and something of a crafty expression about the eye; hair white with age and cropped short; in the picture he is clad in a white shirt, long red vest and with the famous feather war cloak over all. We were permitted to examine the original cloak. It is very ample in its dimensions, and is made entirely of the small, silky, bright yellow feathers of the man-of-war or tropic bird, closely woven into a strong, coarse netting of grass by a process which promises shortly to become a lost art, inasmuch as only one native, and he an old man, is left who understands it in its highest elegance. These feathers are rare and costly, because each bird has but two of them—one under each wing—and the birds are not plenty. It required several generations to collect the materials and manufacture this cloak, and had the work been performed in the United States, under our fine army contract system, it would have cost the Government more millions of dollars than I can estimate without a large arithmetic and a blackboard. In old times, when a king put on his gorgeous feather war cloak, it meant trouble; some other king and his subjects were going to catch it. We were shown other war cloaks, made of yellow feathers, striped and barred with broad bands of red ones—fine specimens of barbaric splendor. The broken spear of a terrible chief who flourished seven hundred years ago, according to the tradition, was also brought out from among the sacred relics of a former age and displayed. It is said that this chieftain stood seven feet high without his boots (he was permanently without them), and was able to snake an enemy out of the ranks with this spear at a distance of forty to sixty and even a hundred feet; and the spear, of hard, heavy, native wood, was once thirty feet long. The name of this pagan hero is sounded no more from the trumpet of fame, his bones lie none knows where, and the record of his gallant deeds is lost. But he was a "brick," we may all depend upon that. How the wood of the weapon has managed to survive seven centuries of decay, though, is a question calculated to worry the antiquaries.

But it is sunrise, now, and time for honest people to begin to "turn in."

MARK TWAIN

12✿

HAWAIIAN LEGISLATURE

I have been reporting the Hawaiian Legislature all day. This is my first visit to the Capitol. I expected to be present on the 25th of April and see the King open his parliament in state and hear his speech, but I was in Maui then and Legislatures had no charms for me.

The Government of the Hawaiian Kingdom is composed of three estates, viz.: The King, the Nobles, and the Commons or Representatives. The Nobles are members of the Legislature by right of their nobility—by blood, if you please—and hold the position for life. They hold the right to sit, at any rate, though that right is not complete until they are formally commissioned as Legislators by the King. Prince William, who is thirty-one years of age, was only so commissioned two years ago, and is now occupying a seat in the parliament for the first time. The King's Ministers belong to the Legislature by virtue of their office. Formerly the Legislative Assembly consisted of a House of Nobles and a House of Representatives, and worked separately, but now both estates sit and vote together. The object of the change was to strengthen the hands of the Nobles by giving them a chance to overawe the Commons (the latter

being able to outvote the former by about three to one),
and it works well. The handful of Nobles and Ministers,
being backed by the King and acting as his mouthpieces,
outweigh the common multitude on the other side of the
House, and carry things pretty much their own way. It is
well enough, for even if the Representatives were to assert
their strength and override the Nobles and pass a law
which did not suit the King, his Majesty would veto the
measure and that would be the end of it, for there is no
passing a bill over *his* veto.

Once, when the legislative bodies were separate and the
Representatives did not act to suit the late King (Kamehameha IV), he took Cromwell's course—prorogued the
parliament instanter and sent the members about their
business. When the present King called a convention, a
year or two ago, to frame a new constitution, he wanted
a property qualification to vote incorporated (universal
suffrage was the rule before) and desired other amend-
ments, which the convention refused to sanction. He dis-
missed them at once, and fixed the constitution up to suit
himself, ratified it, and it is now the fundamental law of
the land, although it has never been formally ratified and
accepted by the people or the Legislature. He took back a
good deal of power which his predecessors had surrendered
to the people, abolished the universal suffrage clause, and
denied the privilege of voting to all save such as were possessed of a hundred dollars worth of real estate or had an
income of seventy-five dollars a year. And, if my opinion
were asked, I would say he did a wise thing in this last-
named matter.

The King is invested with very great power. But he is
a man of good sense and excellent education, and has

an extended knowledge of business, which he acquired through long and arduous training as Minister of the Interior under the late King, and therefore he uses his vast authority wisely and well.

THE CAPITOL—AN AMERICAN
SOVEREIGN SNUBBED

The Legislature meets in the Supreme Court room, an apartment which is larger, lighter, and better fitted and furnished than any courtroom in San Francisco. A railing across the center separates the Legislators from the visitors.

When I got to the main entrance of the building, and was about to march boldly in, I found myself confronted by a large placard, upon which was printed:

NO ADMITTANCE BY THIS ENTRANCE EXCEPT TO
MEMBERS OF THE LEGISLATURE AND FOREIGN
OFFICIALS.

It shocked my republican notions somewhat, but I pocketed the insinuation that I was not high-toned enough to go in at the front door, and went around and entered meekly at the back one. If ever I come to these islands again I will come as the Duke of San Jose, and put on as many frills as the best of them.

THE KING'S FATHER

I found the Legislature to consist of half a dozen white men and some thirty or forty natives. It was a dark assemblage. The Nobles and Ministers (about a dozen of them altogether) occupied the extreme left of the hall, with David Kalakaua (the King's Chamberlain) and Prince

William at the head. The President of the Assembly, His Royal Highness M. Kekuanaoa, and the Vice President (Rhodes) sat in the pulpit, if I may so term it.

The President is the King's father. He is an erect, strongly built, massive featured, white-haired, swarthy old gentleman of eighty years of age or thereabouts. He was simply but well dressed, in a blue cloth coat and white vest, and white pantaloons, without spot, dust, or blemish upon them. He bears himself with a calm, stately dignity, and is a man of noble presence. He was a young man and a distinguished warrior under that terrific old fighter, Kamehameha I, more than half a century ago, and I could not help saying to myself, "This man, naked as the day he was born, and war club and spear in hand, has charged at the head of a horde of savages against other hordes of savages far back in the past, and reveled in slaughter and carnage; has worshiped wooden images on his bended knees; has seen hundreds of his race offered up in heathen temples as sacrifices to hideous idols, at a time when no missionary's foot had ever pressed this soil, and he had never heard of the white man's God; has believed his enemy could secretly pray him to death; has seen the day, in his childhood, when it was a crime punishable by death for a man to eat with his wife, or for a plebeian to let his shadow fall upon the King—and now look at him: an educated Christian; neatly and handsomely dressed; a high-minded, elegant gentleman; a traveler, in some degree, and one who has been the honored guest of royalty in Europe; a man practiced in holding the reins of an enlightened government, and well versed in the politics of his country and, in general, practical information. Look at him, sitting there presiding over the deliberations of a legislative body, among whom are white men—a grave, dignified, statesmanlike personage, and as seemingly natural and fitted to the place as if he had been born in it and had never been out of it in his lifetime. Lord! how the experiences of this old man's strange, eventful life must shame the cheap inventions of romance!"

Kekuanaoa is not of the blood royal. He derives his princely rank from his wife, who was a daughter of Kamehameha the Great. Under other monarchies the male line takes precedence of the female in tracing genealogies, but here the opposite is the case—the female line takes precedence. Their reason for this is exceedingly sensible, and I recommend it to the aristocracy of Europe: They say it is easy to know who a man's mother was, but, etc., etc.

A COMPREHENSIVE SLUR

The mental caliber of the Legislative Assembly is up to the average of such bodies the world over—and I wish it were a compliment to say it, but it is hardly so. I have seen a number of legislatures, and there was a comfortable majority in each of them that knew just about enough to come in when it rained, and that was all. Few men of first-class ability can afford to let their affairs go to ruin while they fool away their time in legislatures for months on a stretch. Few such men care a straw for the small-beer distinction one is able to achieve in such a place. But your chattering, one-horse village lawyer likes it, and your solemn ass from the cow counties, who don't know the Constitution from the Lord's Prayer, enjoys it, and these you will always find in the assembly; the one gabble-gabble-gabbling threadbare platitudes and "give-me-liberty-or-give-me-death" buncombe from morning till night, and the other asleep, with his slab-soled brogans set up like a couple of gravestones on the top of his desk.

Among the Commons in this Legislature are a number of Kanakas with shrewd, intelligent faces, and a "gift of gab" that is appalling. The Nobles are able, educated, fine-looking men, who do not talk often, but when they do, they generally say something—a remark which will not apply to all their white associates in the same house. If I were not ashamed to digress so often I would like to expatiate a little upon the noticeable fact that the nobility of this land, as a general thing, are distinguishable from the common herd by their large stature and commanding presence, and also set forth the theories in vogue for accounting for it, but for the present I will pass the subject by.

IN SESSION—BILL RAGSDALE

At 11 A.M. His Royal Highness the President called the house to order. The roll call was dispensed with for some reason or other, and the chaplain, a venerable looking white man, offered up a prayer in the native tongue; and I must say that this curious language, with its numerous vowels and its entire absence of hissing sounds, fell very softly and musically from his lips. A white chief clerk read the journal of the preceding day's proceedings in English, and then handed the document to Bill Ragsdale, a "half white" (half white and half Kanaka), who translated and clattered it off in Kanaka with a volubility that was calculated to make a slow-spoken man like me distressingly nervous.

Bill Ragsdale stands up in front of the Speaker's pulpit, with his back against it, and fastens his quick black eye upon any member who rises, lets him say half a dozen sentences, and then interrupts him, and repeats his speech in a loud, rapid voice, turning every Kanaka speech into English and every English speech into Kanaka, with a readiness and felicity of language that are remarkable— waits for another installment of talk from the member's lips and goes on with his translation as before. His tongue is in constant motion from eleven in the forenoon till four in the afternoon, and why it does not wear out is the affair of Providence, not mine. There is a spice of deviltry in the fellow's nature, and it crops out every now and then when he is translating the speeches of slow old Kanakas who do not understand English. Without departing from the spirit of a member's remarks, he will, with apparent unconsciousness, drop in a little voluntary contribution occasionally in the way of a word or two that will make the gravest speech utterly ridiculous. He is careful not to venture upon such experiments, though, with the remarks of persons able to detect him. I noticed when he trans-lated for His Excellency David Kalakaua, who is an ac-complished English scholar, he asked, "Did I translate you correctly, Your Excellency?" or something to that effect. The rascal.

FAMILIAR CHARACTERISTICS

This Legislature is like all other legislatures. A wooden-head gets up and proposes an utterly absurd something or other, and he and half a dozen other woodenheads discuss it with windy vehemence for an hour, the remainder of the house sitting in silent patience the while, and then a sensible man—a man of weight—a big gun—gets up and shows the foolishness of the matter in five sentences; a vote is taken and the thing is tabled. Now, on one occasion, a Kanaka member, who paddled over here from some barren rock or other out yonder in the ocean—some scalawag who wears nothing but a pair of socks and a plug hat when he is at home, or possibly is even more scantily arrayed in the popular malo—got up and gravely gave notice of a bill to authorize the construction of a suspension bridge from Oahu to Hawaii, a matter of a hundred and fifty miles! He said that natives would prefer it to the inter-island schooners, and they wouldn't suffer from seasickness on it. Up came Honorables Ku and Kulaui, and Kowkow and Kiwawhoo and a lot of other clacking geese, and harried and worried this notable internal improvement until some sensible person rose and choked them off by moving the previous question. Do not do an unjust thing now, and imagine Kanaka legislatures do stupider things than other similar bodies. Rather blush to remember that once, when a Wisconsin legislature had the affixing of a penalty for the crime of arson under consideration, a member got up and seriously suggested that when a man committed the damning crime of arson they ought either to hang him or make him marry the girl! To my mind the suspension-bridge man was a Solomon compared to this idiot.

(I shall have to stop at this point and finish this subject tomorrow. There is a villain over the way, yonder, who has been playing "Get Out of the Wilderness" on a flute ever since I sat down here tonight—sometimes fast, sometimes slow, and always skipping the first note in the second bar—skipping it so uniformly that I have got to waiting and painfully looking out for it latterly. Human nature cannot stand this sort of torture. I wish his funeral was to come off at half past eleven o'clock tomorrow and I had nothing to do. I would attend it.)

EXPLANATORY

It has been six weeks since I touched a pen. In explanation and excuse I offer the fact that I spent that time (with the exception of one week) on the island of Maui. I only got back yesterday. I never spent so pleasant a month before, or bade any place good-bye so regretfully. I doubt if there is a mean person there, from the homeliest man on the island (Lewers) down to the oldest (Tallant). I went to Maui to stay a week and remained five. I had a jolly time. I would not have fooled away any of it writing letters under any consideration whatever. It will be five or six weeks before I write again. I sail for the island of Hawaii tomorrow, and my Maui notes will not be written up until I come back.

MARK TWAIN

13🏵

LEGISLATURE CONTINUED—

THE SOLONS AT WORK

The first business that was transacted today was the introduction of a bill to prohibit the intermarrying of old persons with young ones, because of the nonfruitfulness of such unions. The measure was discussed, laughed over, and finally tabled. I will remark here that I noticed that there seemed to be no regular order of business observed. Motions, resolutions, notices, introduction and third reading of bills, etc., were jumbled together. This may be convenient enough for the members, but it must necessarily be troublesome to the clerks and reporters.

Then a special committee reported back favorably a bill to prohibit Chinamen from removing their male children from the Islands, and the report was adopted—which I thought was rather hard on the Chinamen.

WAR

Next "the gentleman from Kohala" offered a resolution requesting the Minister of the Interior to bring his books into the House and separate the "Bishop of England's" printing account from his omnibus of "sundries," and show just how my lord's account with the government printing office stood. [Sensation.]

A member jumped up and moved to amend by requesting a general inquisition into printing affairs, and to strike out the offensive clause particularizing the bishop's bill.

The Minister of the Interior (an Englishman—Dr. Hutchinson) opposed the motion, angrily—said it "showed the animus of the thing the way it stood." He said he was ready to produce the books, and went at once and brought them in.

Another member moved to table the original motion.

Harris, Minister of Finance, wanted the motion to stand unamended; he said it showed the animus of the thing, too; said it was the old insinuation, emanating from outside the walls of this House—that the Minister of the Interior was diverting the public funds to the support of the Anglican Church; the ancient insinuation that he was recreant to his duty, etc.; said the animus was prominent enough in the language of the resolution, which denied to the Lord Bishop of Honolulu the title which all the world recognized as his, and called him the "Bishop of England"; said the bishop always paid his bills; he (Harris) always paid his bills, and gave money frequently to the Anglican Church; was a member of it; would like to know of a single solitary instance where the Congregationalist member from Kohala had ever contributed one dollar, one shilling, one infinitesimal fraction of a farthing to the support of the Reformed Catholic Church of the Lord Bishop; but a King's Minister couldn't be honest, oh, no! and a Minister couldn't be a gentleman—certainly not! impossible!—oh, utterly!

And so forth and so on, wandering further and further

from the question before the House, and quacking about stuff that had no more to do with the subject under discussion than the Decalogue has got to do with the Declaration of Independence. This man was on his feet every five minutes for an hour. One timid Commoner feebly moved the previous question once, with a vague hope of shutting up the Minister, but he never got a second, and was snubbed in a moment, and "went in his hole," as they say in California.

The original motion was finally tabled, but it made a fearful stir among the Ministers during its brief existence. It created a bitter discussion, and showed how malignant are the jealousies that rankle in the breasts of the rival religious denominations here.

The Vice President said he was sorry the motion had been offered; that it was an insult to the Government, to the Bishop of Honolulu, to the House, and to all parties concerned, and it grieved him to have to put it to a vote.

In the debate, His Excellency Minister Harris was the champion of the Reformed Catholic Church (though, to save my soul, I could not see what *any* church had to do— that is, openly and aboveboard—with the question before the House). He was the champion; and without any ill feeling toward him I will yet express the conviction that about two more such champions would bring ruin and destruction upon any cause under the sun.

MINISTER HARRIS

Mr. Harris is six feet high, bony and rather slender, middle-aged; has long, ungainly arms; stands so straight that he leans back a little; has small side whiskers; from my distance his eyes seemed blue, and his teeth looked too regular and too white for an honest man; he has a long head the wrong way—that is, up and down; and a bogus Roman nose and a great, long, cadaverous undertaker's countenance, displayed upon which his ghastly attempts at humorous expressions were as shocking as a facetious leer on the face of a corpse. He is a native of New Hampshire, but is unworthy of the name of American. I think, from his manner and language today, that he belongs, body and soul and boots, to the King of the Sandwich Islands and the "Lord Bishop of Honolulu."

He has no command of language—or ideas. His oratory is all show and pretense; he makes considerable noise and a great to-do, and impresses his profoundest incoherencies with an oppressive solemnity and ponderous windmill gesticulations with his flails. He raises his hand aloft and looks piercingly at the interpreter and launches out into a sort of prodigious declamation, thunders upward higher and higher toward his climax—words, words, awful four-syllable words, given with a convincing emphasis that almost inspires them with meaning, and just as you take a sustaining breath and "stand by" for the crash, his poor little rocket fizzes faintly in the zenith and goes out ignominiously. The sensation one experiences is the same a miner feels when he puts in a blast which he thinks will send the whole top of a mountain to the moon, and after running a quarter of a mile in ten seconds to get out of the way, is disgusted to hear it make a trifling, dull report, discharge a pipeful of smoke, and barely jolt half a bushel of dirt. After one of these incomprehensible ravings, Mr. Harris bends down and smiles a horrid smile of self-complacency in the face of the Minister of the Interior; bends to the other side and continues it in the face of the

Minister of Foreign Affairs; beams it serenely upon the admiring lobby, and finally confers the remnants of it upon the unhappy interpreter—all of which pantomime says as plainly as words could say it: "Eh?—but wasn't it an awful shot?" Harris says the weakest and most insipid things, and then tries by the expression of his countenance to swindle you into the conviction that they are the most blighting sarcasms. And in seven years I have never lost my cheerfulness and wanted to lay me down in some secluded spot and die, and be at rest, until I heard him try to be funny today. If I had had a double-barreled shotgun, I would have blown him into a million fragments. Harris deals in long paragraphs of personalities, that would not be permitted in any other legislature. This man has the reputation of being an "able" man; yet he was talking pretty much all the time today, and all the good sound sense or point there was in his vaporings could have been boiled down into half a page of foolscap. Harris is *not* a man of first-class abilities—but that is only my opinion, you know—not Harris'. He knows some things, though. He knows that his salary of four thousand dollars is little enough, in all conscience (especially as he gets nothing as Acting Attorney General, and is not allowed to engage in outside business), and he knew enough on one occasion to vote against reducing his pay to three thousand dollars when his single vote was necessary to kill the proposed economy. He is an inveterate official barnacle, and is generally well supplied with offices—some people say the Hawaiian Government is a wheelbarrow, and that Harris is the wheel.

The Legislature voted an appropriation yesterday to have the photographs of its members taken and hung up in the Capitol. If they had known I was going to paint Harris, they might have saved about three dollars. Harris, you won't do.

If I had time now I would write you a little something about Harris. Under the circumstances, though, I feel it my duty to pass on to something else.

MINISTER HUTCHINSON

Next to His Excellency Mr. Harris, His Majesty's Minister of Finance, sits His Excellency Mr. Hutchinson, His Majesty's Minister of the Interior—an Englishman. He has sandy hair, sandy mustache, sandy complexion—is altogether one of the sandiest men I ever saw, so to speak: is a tall, stoop-shouldered, middle-aged, lowering-browed, intense-eyed, irascible man, and looks like he might have his little prejudices and partialities. He has got one good point, however—he don't talk.

THE OTHER MINISTERS

Near Dr. Hutchinson sit His Excellency the Governor of Oahu (born in this country of Italian and American parentage, and considered an American) and His Excellency M. De Varigny, Acting Minister of Foreign Affairs —a Frenchman. These are merely sensible, unpretentious men—nothing particularly remarkable about their manner or appearance. If Varigny were as hopelessly bad as his English pronunciation, nothing but a special intervention of Providence could save him from perdition hereafter.

THE MILLENNIUM AT HAND

I have found at least one startling peculiarity about this Hawaiian Legislature. They do not accuse its members of being stained with bribery and corruption. It is a new and pleasant sensation to me. Some people ascribe this singular purity to innate virtue, while others less charitable say the members are not offered bribes because they are such leaky vessels that they would be sure to let it out. Doubtless, in some cases one theory is correct, and the other correct in other cases. I hope it is somehow that way; at any rate, I haven't time to discuss it.

LEGISLATIVE ETIQUETTE

Legislative etiquette is of a low grade everywhere, I believe. I find no exception to the rule here. All hands smoke during the session, from the highest down to the pock-marked messenger. Cow-county members—or perhaps I should say taro-patch members—lay the sides of their faces on the desks, encircle them with their arms, and go to sleep for a few moments at a time. I know they must put their feet on the desks sometimes, but I could not catch them at it. I saw them eating crackers and cheese, though, and freely excused them for it, because they hold long, fatiguing sessions—from eleven till four o'clock, without intermission. I am grieved to say that their etiquette is a shade superior to that of the early Washoe legislature. "Horse Williams" was a member of one of them, and he used to always prop his vast feet upon his desk and get behind them and eat a raw turnip during prayer by the chaplain.

MORE CHARACTERISTICS

So much for the Legislature. I came away and left them at the favorite occupation of such bodies—crowding the finance officer's estimates to the utmost limit. The last thing they did was to provide a clerk for the sheriff of Maui, with a salary of one thousand dollars, which was well enough, considering that for two thousand a year and some trifling perquisites, that officer acts as sheriff of the island of Maui, postmaster of Lahaina, customhouse officer, tax collector of the island of Lanai, and probably does a little in a general way in the missionary line, though he is better at entertaining a temporary guest, as I am aware; but you know the inevitable result—every sheriff of every little dab of rock in this group will have to have a thousand-dollar clerk now.

MR. BROWN DISAPPOINTED

Brown has been keeping a sharp lookout for the King for nearly three months, now. When we came out of the Capitol, we heard His Majesty had been at the door a few minutes before. Said the impetuous child of nature:

"Blame that King, ain't I ever—"

"Peace, son!" said I; "respect the sacred name of royalty."

A CORRECTION

Speaking of the King reminds me of something which ought to be said and might as well be said in this paragraph. Some people in California have an idea that the King of the Sandwich Islands is a man who spends his time idling about the town of Honolulu with individuals of questionable respectability, and drinking habitually and to excess. This impression is wrong. Before he ascended the throne he was "faster" than was well for him or for his good name, but, like the hero of Agincourt, he renounced his bad habits and discarded his Falstaffs when he became

King, and since that time has conducted himself as becomes his high position. He attends closely to his business, makes no display, does not go about much, and in manners and habits is a thorough gentleman. He only appears in the streets when his affairs require it, and then he goes well mounted or in his carriage, and decently and properly attended.

And while upon this subject I will remark that His Majesty's income is amply sufficient for the modest state he indulges in. The Legislature appropriates sixteen thousand dollars a year to his use, and his estates (called the "Royal Domain") yield him twenty thousand a year besides. The present palace is to be pulled down and a new one erected. The Legislature has just made an appropriation of forty thousand dollars to begin the work and carry it on for the next two years. There was nothing said about what it is ultimately to cost—wherefore I surmise that it is the design of the Government to build a palace well worthy of the name.

MARK TWAIN

14🌸

"HOME AGAIN"

I have just got back from a three weeks' cruise on the island of Hawaii and an eventful sojourn of several days at the great volcano. But of that trip I will speak hereafter. I am too badly used up to do it now. I only want to write a few lines at present by the *Live Yankee*, merely to keep my communications open, as the soldiers say.

THE LATE PRINCESS

I find Hawaiian politics in a state of unusual stir on account of the death of the King's sister, Her Royal Highness the Princess Victoria Kamamalu Kaahumanu, heir presumptive to the crown. She was something over twenty-seven years old, and had never been married, although she was formally betrothed to Prince William and the marriage day appointed more than once, but circumstances interfered and the nuptials were never consummated.

The Princess was a granddaughter of old Kamehameha the Conqueror, and like all of that stock, was talented. She was the last female descendant of the old warrior.

The care of her infancy was confided to Dr. A. F. [correctly G. P.] Judd (afterward so honorably distinguished in Hawaiian history). Subsequently Hon. John Ii was appointed her guardian by the King. She was carefully educated in the Royal Chiefs' School, which was at that time presided over by the earliest friends of the Hawaiians, the American missionaries. (It is now in the hands of the gentlemen of the Royal Hawaiian Church, otherwise the "Reformed Catholic Church," a sort of nondescript wildcat religion imported here from England.) She became an accomplished pianist and vocalist, and for many years sat at the melodeon and led the choir in the great stone church here. From her infancy it was expected that she would one day fill the throne, and therefore great importance was attached to her acts, and they were duly observed and noted as straws calculated to show how the wind would be likely to set in her ultimate official life. Consequently the strong friendship she manifested for the missionaries was regarded with jealous eye in certain quarters, and frequent attempts were made to diminish her partiality for them. The late Mr. Wyllie, Minister of Foreign Affairs (a native of Scotland), once sent for Hon. Mr. Ii, and endeavored to get him to use his influence in dissuading the Princess and Mrs. Bishop (a high chiefess) who visited California in the *Ajax* lately, from further attendance upon the church choirs. He said it was very improper and out of character for princesses to sing in a choir, and that such personages in England would not do such a thing. The effort was fruitless, however; Victoria continued her former course, and remained faithful to her early friends. She was urged to desert them and go over to the Reformed Catholic Church, but she steadfastly refused.

The Princess was distinguished as the founder and Perpetual President of a benevolent association called "Aha Hui Kaahumanu"—an organization partaking of the benevolent character of Freemasonry, but without its secrecy. It was composed of her countrywomen, and supported by their subscriptions; its membership was exceedingly numerous, and its ramifications extended all over the several islands of the group. Its objects were to secure careful nursing of its members when sick, and their decent burial after death. The society always formed in procession and followed deceased members to the grave, arrayed in a uniform composed of a white robe and a scarf, which indicated the official rank of the wearer by its color.

The Princess was possessed of immense landed estates, and formerly kept up considerable state. She rode in a fine carriage, and had her guards and sentries about her several residences, in European fashion.

The natives have always been remarkable for the extravagant love and devotion they show toward their chiefs; it almost amounts to worship. When Victoria was a girl of fifteen, she made an excursion through the island of Hawaii (the realm of the ancient founders of her race), with her guardian and a retinue of servants, and was everywhere received with a wild enthusiasm by her people. In Hilo, they came in multitudes to the house of the reverend missionary, where she was stopping, and brought with them all manner of offerings—poi, taro, bananas, pigs, fowls—anything they [could] get hold of which was valuable in their eyes—and many of them stinted and starved themselves for the time being, no doubt, to do this honor to a princess who could not use or carry away the hundredth part of what they lavished upon her. And for hours and even days together the people thronged around the place and wept and chanted their distressing songs, and wailed their agonizing wails; for joy at the return of a loved one and sorrow at his death are expressed in precisely the same way with this curious people.

MOURNING FOR THE DEAD

The Princess died on Tuesday, May 29th, and on Wednesday the body was conveyed to the King's palace, there to lie in state about four weeks, which is royal custom here. The chamber is still darkened, and its walls and ceilings draped and festooned with solemn black. The corpse is attired in white satin, trimmed with lace and ruche, and reposes upon the famous yellow-feather war cloak of the kings of Hawaii; a simple coronet of orange blossoms, interwoven with white feathers, adorns the head that was promised a regal diadem; six kahili bearers stand upon each side, and these are surrounded by a guard of honor in command of one of the high chiefs; a party of chief women are in constant attendance, and officers of the household troops and of the volunteer forces are on duty about the palace; the old Queen Dowager sleeps in the chamber every night. Candelabras burn day and night at the head and feet of the corpse, and shed a funereal twilight over it, and over the silent attendants and the dark and dismal symbols of woe. Every evening a new chant, composed by some chief woman several days before and carefully rehearsed, is sung. All this in the death chamber.

Outside, on the broad verandas and in the ample palace yard, a multitude of common natives howl and wail, and weep and chant the dreary funeral songs of ancient Hawaii, and dance the strange dance for the dead. Numbers of these people remain there day after day and night after night, sleeping in the open air in the intervals of their mourning ceremonies.

I am told these things. I have not seen them. The King has ordered that no foreigner shall be permitted to enter the palace gates before the last night previous to the funeral. The reason why this order was issued is, I am told, that the performances at the palace at the time the corpse of the late King lay there in state were criticized and commented upon too freely. These performances were considerably toned down while the missionaries were in power, but under the more liberal regime of the new Reformed Catholic dispensation, they fell back toward their old-time barbarous character. The gates were thrown open and everybody went in and saw and heard what may be termed the funeral orgies of the dead King. The term is coarse, but perhaps it is a better one than a milder one would be. And then scribblers like myself wrote column after column about the matter in the public prints, and the subject was discussed and criticized in private circles and inveighed against in the pulpits. All this was harassing and disagreeable to the parties nearest concerned, and hence the present order forbidding any but Hawaiian citizens and lenient friends from witnessing the ceremonies. So strong is some people's curiosity, however, that the law has already been violated several times within the past week by strangers, who entered the tabooed grounds in disguise. They were discovered, however, and quietly turned out.

The deceased Princess has lain in state now for more than three weeks—yet still the nightly wailing goes on in the palace yard, and the crowds of natives who conduct it increases steadily by influx from the other islands, and the lamentations grow more extravagant all the time. The missionary efforts to discourage and break up this weird custom, inherited from the old pagan days, are quietly rebuked in a little advertisement which appears over the signature of the King's Chamberlain in the public papers today, wherein he invites all natives to come to the palace grounds and stay there night and day and take part in the wailing for the departed. That looks like a disposition on the part of the authorities not only to check the progress of civilization, but to go backward a little.

THE COFFIN

The Legislature have appropriated six thousand dollars to defray the funeral expenses of the Princess. The obsequies will take place the latter part of next week. I have seen the coffin (it is not quite finished yet), and certainly it is the most elegant piece of burial furniture I ever saw. It is made of those two superb species of native wood, kou and koa. The former is nearly as dark as ebony; the latter is like fine California laurel, richly grained and clouded with mahogany. Both woods have an ironlike hardness, and are exceedingly close in grain, and when highly polished and varnished, nothing in the shape of wood can be more brilliant, more lustrous, more beautiful. It produces a sort of ecstasy in me to look at it, and holds me like a mesmeric fascination. There is nothing extraordinary about the fashioning—the planning and construction—of this coffin, but still it is beautiful. The wood is so splendidly burnished, and so gracefully grained and clouded.

The silver tablet upon the coffin, upon which is to be inscribed the name and title of the deceased, is to cost five hundred dollars. I go into these minor details to show you that royal state in the Sandwich Islands approaches as near to its European models as the circumstances of the case will admit.

HOW FUNERALS OF DEAD CHIEFS WERE CELEBRATED IN OLD TIMES

If a Sandwich Islands missionary comes across a stranger, I think he weighs him and measures him and judges him (in defiance of the injunction to "judge not, etc.") by an ideal which he has created in his own mind—and if that stranger falls short of that ideal in any particular, the good missionary thinks he falls just that much short of what he ought to be in order to stand a chance for salvation; and with a tranquil simplicity of self-conceit, which is marvelous to a modest man, he honestly believes that the Almighty, of a necessity, thinks exactly as he does. I violate the injunction to judge not, also. I judge the missionary, but, with a modesty which is entitled to some credit, I freely confess that my judgment may err. Now, therefore, when I say that the Sandwich Islands missionaries are pious; hard-working; hard-praying; self-sacrificing; hospitable; devoted to the well-being of this people and the interests of Protestantism; bigoted; puritanical; slow; ignorant of all white human nature and natural ways of men, except the remnant of these things that are left in their own class or profession; old fogy—fifty years behind the age; uncharitable toward the weaknesses of the flesh; considering all shortcomings, faults, and failings in the light of crimes, and having no mercy and no forgiveness for such—when I say this about the missionaries, I do it with the explicit understanding that it is only *my* estimate of them—not that of a Higher Intelligence—not that of even other sinners like myself. It is only *my* estimate, and it may fall far short of being a just one.

Now, after the above free confession of my creed, I think I ought to be allowed to print a word of defense of these missionaries without having that eternal charge of "partiality and prejudice" launched at me that is generally sure to be discharged at any man here who ventures—in certain quarters—to give them any credit or offer to defend them from ill-natured aspersions.

Mr. Staley, my Lord Bishop of Honolulu—who was built into a lord by the English Bishop of Oxford and shipped over here with a fully equipped "Established Church" in his pocket—has frequently said that the natives of these islands are morally and religiously in a worse condition today than they were before the American missionaries ever came here. Now that is not true—and in that respect the statement bears a very strong family likeness to many other of the bishop's remarks about our missionaries. Our missionaries are our missionaries—and even if they were our devils, I would not want any English prelate to slander them. I will not go into an argument to prove that the natives have been improved by missionary labor—because facts are stronger than argument. Above I have stated how the natives are now singing and wailing every night—queerly enough, but innocently and harmlessly—out yonder in the palace yard, for the dead Princess. Following is some account of the style of conducting this sort of thing shortly before the traduced missionaries came. I quote from Jarves' *History of the Sandwich Islands:*

The ceremonies observed on the death of any important personage were exceedingly barbarous. The hair was shaved or cut close, teeth knocked out and sometimes the ears were mangled. Some tattooed their tongues in a corresponding manner to the other parts of their bodies. Frequently the flesh was cut or burnt, eyes scooped out, and other even more painful personal outrages inflicted. But these usages, however shocking they may appear, were innocent compared with the horrid saturnalia which immediately followed the death of a chief of the highest rank. Then the most unbounded license prevailed; law and restraint were cast aside, and the whole people appeared more like demons than human beings. Every vice and crime was allowed. Property was destroyed, houses fired, and old feuds revived and avenged. Gambling, theft, and murder were as open as the day; clothing was cast aside as a useless incumbrance; drunkenness and promiscuous prostitution prevailed throughout the land, no women, excepting the widows of the deceased, being exempt from the grossest violation. There was no passion however lewd, or desire however wicked, but could be gratified with impunity during the continuance of this period which happily, from its own violence, soon spent itself. No other nation was ever witness to a custom which so entirely threw off all moral and legal restraints and incited the evil passions to unresisted riot and wanton debauchery.

It is easy to see, now, that the missionaries have made a better people of this race than they formerly were; and

I am satisfied that if that old-time national spree were still a custom of the country, my Lord Bishop would not be in this town today saying hard things about the missionaries. No; his excellent judgment would have impelled him to take to the woods when the Princess died.

WHO SHALL INHERIT THE THRONE?

The great bulk of the wealth, the commerce, the enterprise, and the spirit of progress in the Sandwich Islands centers in the Americans. Americans own the whaling fleet; they own the great sugar plantations; they own the cattle ranches; they own their share of the mercantile depots and the lines of packet ships. Whatever of commercial and agricultural greatness the country can boast of it owes to them. Consequently the question of who is likely to succeed to the crown in case of the death of the present King, is an interesting one to American residents, and therefore to their countrymen at home. The incumbent of the throne has it in his power to help or hinder them a good deal. The King is not married; and if he dies without leaving an heir of his own body or appointing a successor, the crown will be likely to fall upon either His Highness Prince William C. Lunalilo, or David Kalakaua. The former is of the highest blood in the kingdom— higher than the King himself, it is said—and Kalakaua is descended from the ancient kings of the island of Hawaii. King Keoua (father of Kamehameha the Great), great-great-grandfather of the present King, was also the great-great-grandfather of Prince William; but from Kamehameha the lines diverge, and if there is any kinship between William and Kamehameha V, it is distant. They both had a common ancestor in King Umi, however, a gentleman who flourished several hundred years ago. Prince William is called eleventh in descent from Umi, and the present King only fourteenth, which confers seniority of birth and rank upon the former. But this subject is tanglesome.

PRINCE WILLIAM

Prince William is a man of fine, large build; is thirty-one years of age; is affable, gentlemanly, open, frank, manly; is as independent as a lord and has a spirit and a will like the old Conqueror himself. He is intelligent, shrewd, sensible—is a man of first-rate abilities, in fact. He has a right handsome face, and the best nose in the Hawaiian Kingdom, white or otherwise; it is a splendid beak, and worth being proud of. He has one most unfortunate fault—he drinks constantly; and it is a great pity, for if he would moderate this appetite, or break it off altogether, he could become a credit to himself and his nation. I like this man, and I like his bold independence, and his friendship for and appreciation of the American residents; and I take no pleasure in mentioning this failing of his. If I could print a sermon that would reform him, I would cheerfully do it.

DAVID KALAKAUA

Hon. David Kalakaua, who at present holds the office of King's Chamberlain, is a man of fine presence, is an educated gentleman and a man of good abilities. He is approaching forty, I should judge—is thirty-five, at any rate. He is conservative, politic, and calculating, makes little display, and does not talk much in the Legislature. He is a quiet, dignified, sensible man, and would do no discredit to the kingly office.

The King has power to appoint his successor. If he does such a thing, his choice will probably fall on Kalakaua. In case the King should die without making provision for a successor, it would be the duty of the Legislature to select a king from among the dozen high chiefs, male and female, who are eligible under the Hawaiian Constitution. Under these circumstances, if Prince William were thoroughly redeemed from his besetting sin, his chances would be about even with Kalakaua's.

FUNERAL MUSIC

It is two o'clock in the morning, and I have just been up toward the palace to hear some of the singing of the numerous well-born watchers (of both sexes) who are standing guard in the chamber of death. The voices were very pure and rich, and blended together without harshness or discord, and the music was exceedingly plaintive and beautiful. I would have been glad enough to get closer. When the plebeians outside the building resumed their distressing noise I came away. In the distance I hear them at it yet, poor, simple, loving, faithful, Christian savages.

POSTSCRIPT

The *Swallow* arrived here on Monday morning, with Anson Burlingame, United States Minister to China, and General Van Valkenburgh, United States Minister to Japan. Their stay is limited to fourteen days, but a strong effort will be made to persuade them to break that limit and pass the Fourth of July here. They are paying and receiving visits constantly, of course, and are cordially welcomed. Burlingame is a man who would be esteemed, respected, and popular anywhere, no matter whether he were among Christians or cannibals.

The people are expecting McCook, our new Minister to these islands, every day.

Whartenby and Mackie, of Nevada (Cal.), arrived here in the last vessel, and will start back in a week or two. They came merely for recreation.

Several San Franciscans have come to Honolulu to locate permanently. Among them Dr. A. C. Buffum; he has a fair and growing practice. Judge Jones is another; he has already more law practice on his hands than he can well attend to. And lastly, J. J. Ayers, late one of the proprietors of the *Morning Call,* has arrived, with material for starting a newspaper and job office. He has not made up his mind yet, however, to try the experiment of a newspaper here. Sanford, last chief engineer of the *Ajax,* came in the last vessel, and proposes to settle in the islands— perhaps in the sugar line. He has gone to Maui to see what the chances are in that deservedly famous sugar-producing region.

A letter arrived here yesterday morning giving a meager account of the arrival on the island of Hawaii of nineteen poor starving wretches, who had been buffeting a stormy sea in an open boat for forty-three days! Their ship, the *Hornet,* from New York, with a quantity of kerosene on board, had taken fire and burned in latitude 2 degrees north and longitude 135 degrees west. Think of their sufferings for forty-three days and nights, exposed to the scorching heat of the center of the torrid zone, and at the mercy of a ceaseless storm! When they had been entirely out of provisions for a day or two and the cravings of hunger became insupportable, they yielded to the ship-

wrecked mariner's final and fearful alternative, and solemnly drew lots to determine who of their number should
die to furnish food for his comrades—and then the morning mists lifted and they saw land. They are being cared
for at Sanpohoihoi [Laupahoehoe], a little seaside station
I spent a night at two weeks ago. This boatload was in
charge of the captain of the *Hornet*. He reports that the
remainder of the persons in his ship (twenty in number)
left her in two boats, under command of the first and
second mates, and the three boats kept company until the
night of the nineteenth day, when they got separated. No
further particulars have arrived here yet, and no confirma-
tion of the above sad story.

DINNER TO THE ENVOYS

The American citizens of Honolulu, anxious to show
to their distinguished visitors the honor and respect due
them, have invited them to partake of a dinner upon some
occasion before their departure. Burlingame and General
Van Valkenburgh have accepted the invitation and will
inform the committee this evening what day will best suit
their convenience.

MARK TWAIN

15❀

BURNING OF THE CLIPPER
SHIP *HORNET* AT SEA

Detailed Account of the Sufferings of Officers and Crew, As Given by the Third Officer and Members of the Crew.

In the postscript to a letter which I wrote two or three days ago, and sent by the ship *Live Yankee*, I gave you the substance of a letter received here from Hilo by Walker, Allen & Co., informing them that a boat containing fifteen men, in a helpless and starving condition, had drifted ashore at Laupahoehoe, Island of Hawaii, and that they had belonged to the clipper ship *Hornet*, Mitchell master, and had been afloat on the ocean since the burning of that vessel, about one hundred miles north of the equator, on the 3d of May—forty-three days.

The third mate and ten of the seamen have arrived here and are now in the hospital. Captain Mitchell, one seaman named Antonio Passene, and two passengers (Samuel and Henry Ferguson, of New York City, young gentlemen, aged respectively eighteen and twenty-eight) are still at Hilo, but are expected here within the week.

In the captain's modest epitome of this terrible romance,

which you have probably published, you detect the fine old hero through it. It reads like Grant.

THE THIRD MATE

I have talked with the seamen and with John S. Thomas, third mate, but their accounts are so nearly alike in all substantial points, that I will merely give the officer's statement and weave into it such matters as the men mentioned in the way of incidents, experiences, emotions, etc. Thomas is very intelligent and a very cool and self-possessed young man, and seems to have kept a pretty accurate log of his remarkable voyage in his head. He told his story, of three hours' length, in a plain, straightforward way, and with no attempt at display and no straining after effect. Wherever any incident may be noted in this paper where any individual has betrayed any emotion, or enthusiasm, or has departed from strict, stoical self-possession, or had a solitary thought that was not an utterly unpoetical and essentially practical one, remember that Thomas, the third mate, was not that person. He has been eleven days on shore, and already looks sufficiently sound and healthy to pass almost anywhere without being taken for an invalid. He has the marks of a hard experience about him though, when one looks closely. He is very much sunburned and weatherbeaten, and looks thirty-two years old. He is only twenty-four, however, and has been a sailor fifteen years. He was born in Richmond, Maine, and still considers that place his home.

SAILING OF THE "HORNET"—PACIFIC RAILROAD IRON

The following is the substance of what Thomas said:

The *Hornet* left New York on the 15th of January last, unusually well manned, fitted, and provisioned—as fast and as handsome a clipper ship as ever sailed out of that port. She had a general cargo—a little of everything; a large quantity of kerosene oil in barrels; several hundred cases of candles; also four hundred tons Pacific Railroad iron and three engines. The third mate thinks they were dock engines, and one of the seamen thought they were locomotives. Had no gales and no bad weather; nothing but fine sailing weather, and she went along steadily and well—fast, very fast, in fact. Had uncommonly good weather off Cape Horn; he had been around that Cape seven times—each way—and had never seen such fine weather there before. On the 12th of April, in latitude, say, 35 south and longitude 95 west, signaled a Prussian bark; she set Prussian ensign, and the *Hornet* responded with her name, expressed by means of Merritt's system of signals. She was sailing west—probably bound for Australia. This was the last vessel ever seen by the *Hornet's* people until they floated ashore at Hawaii in the longboat —a space of sixty-four days.

THE SHIP ON FIRE

At seven o'clock on the morning of the 3d of May, the chief mate and two men started down into the hold to draw some "bright varnish" from a cask. The captain told him to bring the cask on deck—that it was dangerous to have it where it was, in the hold. The mate, instead of obeying the order, proceeded to draw a can full of the varnish first. He had an "open light" in his hand, and the liquid took fire; the can was dropped, the officer in his consternation neglected to close the bung, and in a few seconds the fiery torrent had run in every direction, under bales of rope, cases of candles, barrels of kerosene, and all sorts of freight, and tongues of flame were shooting upward through every aperture and crevice toward the deck.

The ship was moving along under easy sail, the watch on duty were idling here and there in such shade as they could find, and the listlessness and repose of morning in the tropics was upon the vessel and her belongings. But as six bells chimed, the cry of "Fire!" rang through the ship, and woke every man to life and action. And following the fearful warning, and almost as fleetly, came the fire itself. It sprang through hatchways, seized upon chairs, table, cordage, anything, everything—and almost before the bewildered men could realize what the trouble was and what was to be done the cabin was a hell of angry flames. The mainmast was on fire—its rigging was burnt asunder! One man said all this had happened within eighteen or twenty minutes after the first alarm—two others say in ten minutes. All say that one hour after the alarm, the main- and mizzenmasts were burned in two and fell overboard.

Captain Mitchell ordered the three boats to be launched instantly, which was done—and so hurriedly that the longboat (the one he left the vessel in himself) had a hole as large as a man's head stove in her bottom. A blanket was stuffed into the opening and fastened to its place. Not a single thing was saved, except such food and other articles as lay about the cabin and could be quickly seized and thrown on deck. Thomas was sent into the longboat to receive its proportion of these things, and, being barefooted at the time, and bareheaded, and having no clothing on save an undershirt and pantaloons, of course he never got a chance afterward to add to his dress. He lost everything he had, including his logbook, which he had faithfully kept from the first. Forty minutes after the fire alarm, the provisions and passengers were on board the three boats, and they rowed away from the ship—and to some distance, too, for the heat was very great. Twenty minutes afterward the two masts I have mentioned, with their rigging and their broad sheets of canvas wreathed in flames, crashed into the sea.

All night long the thirty-one unfortunates sat in their frail boats and watched the gallant ship burn; and felt as men feel when they see a tried friend perishing and are powerless to help him. The sea was illuminated for miles around, and the clouds above were tinged with a ruddy hue; the faces of the men glowed in the strong light as they shaded their eyes with their hands and peered out anxiously upon the wild picture, and the gunwales of the boats and the idle oars shone like polished gold.

At five o'clock on the morning after the disaster, in latitude 2 degrees 20 minutes north, longitude 112 degrees 8 minutes west, the ship went down, and the crew of the *Hornet* were alone on the great deep, or, as one of the seamen expressed it, "We felt as if sombody or something had gone away—as if we hadn't any home any more."

Captain Mitchell divided his boat's crew into two watches and gave the third mate charge of one and took the other himself. He had saved a studding sail from the ship, and out of this the men fashioned a rude sail with their knives; they hoisted it, and taking the first and second mates' boats in tow, they bore away upon the ship's course (northwest) and kept in the track of vessels bound to or from San Francisco, in the hope of being picked up.

THEIR WATER, PROVISIONS, ETC.

I have said that in the few minutes' time allowed him, Captain Mitchell was only able to seize upon the few articles of food and other necessaries that happened to lie about the cabin. Here is the list: Four hams, seven pieces of salt pork (each piece weighed about four pounds), one box of raisins, one hundred pounds of bread (about one barrel), twelve two-pound cans of oysters, clams, and assorted meats; six buckets of raw potatoes (which rotted so fast they got but little benefit from them), a keg with four pounds of butter in it, twelve gallons of water in a forty-gallon tierce or "scuttle butt," four one-gallon demijohns full of water, three bottles of brandy, the property of passengers; some pipes, matches, and a hundred pounds of tobacco; had no medicines. That was all these poor fellows had to live on for forty-three days—the whole thirty-one of them!

Each boat had a compass, a quadrant, a copy of Bowditch's *Navigator* and a nautical almanac, and the captain's and chief mate's boat had chronometers.

RATIONS

Of course, all hands were put on short allowance at once. The day they set sail from the ship each man was allowed a small morsel of salt pork—or a little piece of potato, if he preferred it—and half a sea biscuit three times a day. To understand how very light this ration of bread was, it is only necessary to know that it takes seven of these sea biscuits to weigh a pound. The first two days they only allowed one gill of water a day to each man; but for nearly a fortnight after that the weather was lowering and stormy, and frequent rain squalls occurred. The rain was caught in canvas, and whenever there was a shower the forty-gallon cask and every other vessel that would hold water was filled—even all the boots that were watertight were pressed into this service, except such as the matches and tobacco were deposited in to keep dry. So for fourteen days. There were luxurious occasions when there was plenty of water to drink. But after that how they suffered the agonies of thirst for four long weeks!

HOPING AGAINST HOPE

For seven days the boats sailed on, and the starving men ate their fragment of biscuit and their morsel of raw pork in the morning, and hungrily counted the tedious hours until noon and night should bring their repetitions of it. And in the long intervals they looked mutely into each other's faces, or turned their wistful eyes across the wild sea in search of the succoring sail that was never to come.

"Didn't you talk?" I asked one of the men.

"No; we were too downhearted—that is, the first week or more. We didn't talk—we only looked at each other and over the ocean."

And thought, I suppose. Thought of home—of shelter from storms—of food and drink and rest.

The hope of being picked up hung to them constantly —was ever present to them, and in their thoughts, like hunger. And in the captain's mind was the hope of making the Clarion Islands, and he clung to it many a day.

The nights were very dark. They had no lantern and could not see the compass, and there were no stars to steer by. Thomas said, of the boat, "She handled easy, and we steered by the feel of the wind in our faces and the heave of the sea." Dark and dismal and lonesome work was that! Sometimes they got a fleeting glimpse of the sailor's friend, the North Star, and then they lighted a match and hastened anxiously to see if their compass was faithful to them—for it had to be placed close to an iron ringbolt in the stern, and they were afraid, during those first nights, that this might cause it to vary. It proved true to them, however.

SUMPTUOUS FARE

On the fifth day a notable incident occurred. They caught a dolphin! And while their enthusiasm was still at its highest over this stroke of good fortune, they captured another. They made a trifling fire in a tin plate and warmed the prizes—to cook them was not possible—and divided them equitably among all hands and ate them.

On the sixth day two more dolphins were caught.

Two more were caught on the seventh day, and also a small bonita, and they began to believe they were always going to live in this extravagant way; but it was not to be; these were their last dolphins, and they never could get another bonita, though they saw them and longed for them often afterward.

RATIONS REDUCED

On the eighth day the rations were reduced about one half. Thus—breakfast, one fourth of a biscuit, an ounce of ham, and a gill of water to each man; dinner, same quantity of bread and water, and four oysters or clams; supper, water and bread the same, and twelve large raisins or fourteen small ones, to a man. Also, during the first twelve or fifteen days, each man had one spoonful of brandy a day, then it gave out.

This day, as one of the men was gazing across the dull waste of waters as usual, he saw a small, dark object rising and falling upon the waves. He called attention to it, and in a moment every eye was bent upon it in intensest interest. When the boat had approached a little nearer, it was discovered that it was a small green turtle, fast asleep. Every noise was hushed as they crept upon the unconscious slumberer. Directions were given and hopes and fears expressed in guarded whispers. At the fateful moment—a moment of tremendous consequence to these famishing men—the expert selected for the high and responsible office stretched forth his hand, while his excited comrades bated their breath and trembled for the success of the enterprise, and seized the turtle by the hind leg and handed him aboard! His delicate flesh was carefully divided among the party and eagerly devoured—after being "warmed" like the dolphins which went before him.

THE BOATS SEPARATE

After the eighth day I have ten days unaccounted for— no notes of them save that the men say they had their two or three ounces of food and their gill of water three times a day—and then the same weary watching for a saving sail by day and by night, and the same sad "hope deferred that maketh the heart sick," was their monotonous experience. They talked more, however, and the captain labored without ceasing to keep them cheerful. (They have always a word of praise for the "old man.")

The eighteenth day was a memorable one to the wanderers on the lonely sea. On that day the boats parted company. The captain said that separate from each other there were three chances for the saving of some of the party where there could be but one chance if they kept together.

The magnanimity and utter unselfishness of Captain Mitchell (and through his example, the same conduct in his men) throughout this distressing voyage, are among its most amazing features. No disposition was ever shown by the strong to impose upon the weak, and no greediness, no desire on the part of any to get more than his just share of food, was ever evinced. On the contrary, they were thoughtful of each other and always ready to care for and assist each other to the utmost of their ability. When the time came to part company, Captain Mitchell and his crew, although theirs was much the more numerous party (fifteen men to nine and seven respectively in the other boats), took only one third of the meager amount of provisions still left, and passed over the other two thirds to be divided up between the other crews; these men could starve, if need be, but they seem not to have known how to be mean.

After the division the captain had left for his boat's share two thirds of the ham, one fourth of a box of raisins, half a bucket of biscuit crumbs, fourteen gallons of water, three cans of "soup-and-bully." (That last expression of the third mate's occurred frequently during his narrative, and bothered me so painfully with its mysterious incomprehensibility, that at length I begged him to explain to me what this dark and dreadful "soup-and-bully" might be. With the consul's assistance he finally made me understand the French dish known as "soup bouillon" is put up in cans like preserved meats, and the American sailor is under the impression that its name is a sort of general title which describes any description of edible whatever which is hermetically sealed in a tin vessel, and with that high contempt for trifling conventionalities which distinguishes his class, he has seen fit to modify the pronunciation into "soup-and-bully.")

The captain told the mates he was still going to try to make the Clarion Isles, and that they could imitate his example if they thought best, but he wished them to freely follow the dictates of their own judgment in the matter. At eleven o'clock in the forenoon the boats were all cast loose from each other, and then, as friends part from friends whom they expect to meet no more in life, all hands hailed with a fervent "God bless you, boys; good-bye!" and the two cherished sails drifted away and disappeared from the longing gaze that followed them so sorrowfully.

ANOTHER CAPTURE

On the afternoon of this eventful eighteenth day two "boobies" were caught—a bird about as large as a duck, but all bone and feathers—not as much meat as there is on a pigeon—not nearly so much, the men say. They ate them raw—bones, entrails, and everything—no single morsel was wasted; they were carefully apportioned among the fifteen men. No fire could be built for cooking purposes —the wind was so strong and the sea ran so high that it was all a man could do to light his pipe.

A GOOD FRIEND GONE

At eventide the wanderers missed a cheerful spirit—a plucky, strong-hearted fellow, who never drooped his head or lost his grip—a staunch and true good friend, who was always at his post in storm or calm, in rain or shine—who scorned to say die, and yet was never afraid to die—a little trim and taut old rooster, he was, who starved with the rest, but came on watch in the stern sheets promptly every day at four in the morning and six in the evening for eighteen days and crowed like a maniac! Right well they named him Richard of the Lion Heart! One of the men said with honest feeling: "As true as I'm a man, Mr. Mark Twain, if that rooster was here today and any man dared to abuse the bird, I'd break his neck!" Richard was esteemed by all and by all his rights were respected. He received his little ration of bread crumbs every time the men were fed, and, like them, he bore up bravely and never grumbled and never gave way to despair. As long as he was strong enough, he stood in the stern sheets or mounted the gunwale as regularly as his watch came round, and crowed his two-hour talk, and when at last he grew feeble in the legs and had to stay below, his heart was still stout and he slapped about in the water on the bottom of the boat and crowed as bravely as ever! He felt that under circumstances like these America expects every rooster to do his duty, and he did it. But is it not to the high honor of that boat's crew of starving men that, tortured day and night by the pangs of hunger as they were, they refused to appease them with the blood of their humble comrade? Richard was transferred to the chief mate's boat and sailed away on the eighteenth day.

RELIGIOUS SERVICES

The third mate does not remember distinctly, but thinks morning and evening prayers were begun on the nineteenth day. They were conducted by one of the young Fergusons, because the captain could not read the prayer book without his spectacles, and they had been burned with the ship. And ever after this date, at the rising and the setting of the sun, the storm-tossed mariners reverently bowed their heads while prayers went up for "they that are helpless and far at sea."

AN INCIDENT

On the morning of the twenty-first day, while some of the crew were dozing on the thwarts and others were buried in reflection, one of the men suddenly sprang to his feet and cried, "A sail! a sail!" Of course, sluggish blood bounded then and eager eyes were turned to seek the welcome vision. But disappointment was their portion, as usual. It was only the chief mate's boat drifting across their path after three days' absence. In a short time the two parties were abreast each other and in hailing distance. They talked twenty minutes; the mate reported "all well" and then sailed away, and they never saw him afterward.

FURTHER REDUCTION OF RATIONS

On the twenty-fourth day Captain Mitchell took an observation and found that he was in latitude 16 degrees north and longitude 117 degrees west—about a thousand miles from where his vessel was burned. The hope he had cherished so long that he would be able to make the Clarion Isles deserted him at last; he could only go before the wind, and he was now obliged to attempt the best thing the southeast trades could do for him—blow him to the "American group" or to the Sandwich Islands—and therefore he reluctantly and with many misgivings turned his prow towards those distant archipelagoes. Not many mouthfuls of food were left, and these must be economized. The third mate said that under this new program of proceedings "we could see that we were living too high; we had got to let up on them raisins, or the soup-and-

bullies, one, because it stood to reason that we warn't going to make land soon, and so they wouldn't last." It was
a matter which had few humorous features about it to
them, and yet a smile is almost pardonable at this idea, so
gravely expressed, of "living high" on fourteen raisins at
a meal.

The rations remained the same as fixed on the eighth
day, except that only two meals a day were allowed, and
occasionally the raisins and oysters were left out.

What these men suffered during the next three weeks
no mortal man may hope to describe. Their stomachs and
intestines felt to the grasp like a couple of small tough
balls, and the gnawing hunger pains and the dreadful
thirst that was consuming them in those burning latitudes
became almost insupportable. And yet, as the men say,
the captain said funny things and talked cheerful talk until he got them to conversing freely, and then they used
to spend hours together describing delicious dinners they
had eaten at home, and earnestly planning interminable
and preposterous bills of fare for dinners they were going
to eat on shore, if they ever lived through their troubles
to do it, poor fellows. The captain said plain bread and
butter would be good enough for him all the days of his
life, if he could only get it.

But the saddest things were the dreams they had. An
unusually intelligent young sailor named Cox said: "In
those long days and nights we dreamed all the time—not
that we ever slept. I don't mean—no, we only sort of
dozed—three fourths of the faculties awake and the other
fourth benumbed into the counterfeit of a slumber; oh,
no—some of us never slept for twenty-three days, and no
man ever saw the captain asleep for upward of thirty. But

we barely dozed that way and dreamed—and always of such feasts! bread, and fowls, and meat—everything a man could think of, piled upon long tables, and smoking hot! And we sat down and seized upon the first dish in our reach, like ravenous wolves, and carried it to our lips, and —and then we woke up and found the same starving comrades about us, and the vacant sky and the desolate sea!"

These things are terrible even to think of.

RATIONS STILL FURTHER REDUCED

It even startles me to come across that significant heading so often in my notebook, notwithstanding I have grown so familiar with its sound by talking so much with these unfortunate men.

On the twenty-eighth day the rations were: One teaspoonful of bread crumbs and about an ounce of ham for the morning meal; a spoonful of bread crumbs alone for the evening meal, and one gill of water three times a day! A kitten would perish eventually under such sustenance.

At this point the third mate's mind reverted painfully to an incident of the early stages of their sufferings. He said there were two between-decks, on board the *Hornet*, who had been lying there sick and helpless for he didn't know how long; but when the ship took fire, they turned out as lively as anyone under the spur of the excitement. One was a "Portyghee," he said, and always of a hungry disposition; when all the provisions that could be got had been brought aft and deposited near the wheel to be lowered into the boats, "that sick Portyghee watched his chance, and when nobody was looking, he harnessed the provisions and ate up nearly a quarter of a bar'l of bread before the old man caught him, and he had more than two notions to put his lights out." The third mate dwelt upon this circumstance as upon a wrong he could not fully forgive, and intimated that the Portyghee stole bread enough, if economized in twenty-eighth-day rations, to have run the longboat party three months.

THEY CAPTURE A PRIZE

Four little flying fish, the size of the sardines of these latter days, flew into the boat on the night of the twenty-eighth day. They were divided among all hands and devoured raw. On the twenty-ninth day they caught another, and divided it into fifteen pieces, less than a teaspoonful apiece.

On the thirtieth day they caught a third flying fish and gave it to the revered old captain—a fish of the same poor little proportions as the others—four inches long—a present a king might be proud of under such circumstances— a present whose value, in the eyes of the men who offered it, was not to be found in the Bank of England—yea, whose vaults were not able to contain it! The old captain refused to take it; the men insisted; the captain said no— he would take his fifteenth—they must take the remainder. They said in substance, though not in words, that they would see him in Jericho first! So the captain had to eat the fish.

I believe I have done the third mate some little wrong in the beginning of this letter. I have said he was as self-possessed as a statue—that he never betrayed emotion or enthusiasm. He never did except when he spoke of "the old man." It always thawed through his ice then. The men were the same way; the captain is their hero—their true and faithful friend, whom they delight to honor.

I said to one of these infatuated skeletons, "But you wouldn't go quite so far as to die for him?" A snap of the finger—"As quick as that!—I wouldn't be alive now if it hadn't been for him." We pursued the subject no further.

RATIONS STILL FURTHER REDUCED

I still claim the public's indulgence and belief. At least Thomas and his men do through me. About the thirty-second day the bread gave entirely out. There was nothing left, now, but mere odds and ends of their stock of provisions. Five days afterward, on the thirty-seventh day—latitude 16 degrees 30 minutes north, and longitude 170 degrees west—kept off for the "American group"—"which don't exist and never will, I suppose," said the third mate. Ran directly over the ground said to be occupied by these islands—that is, between latitude 16 degrees and 17 degrees north, and longitude 133 degrees to 136 degrees west. Ran over the imaginary islands and got into 136 degrees west, and then the captain made a dash for Hawaii, resolving that he would go till he fetched land, or at any rate as long as he and his men survived.

THE LAST RATION!

On Monday, the thirty-eighth day after the disaster, "We had nothing left," said the third mate, "but a pound and a half of ham—the bone was a good deal the heaviest part of it—and one soup-and-bully tin." These things were divided among the fifteen men, and they ate it all —two ounces of food to each man. I do not count the ham bone, as that was saved for the next day. For some time now the poor wretches had been cutting their old boots into small pieces and eating them. They would also pound wet rags to a sort of pulp and eat them.

STARVATION FARE

On the thirty-ninth day the ham bone was divided up into rations, and scraped with knives and eaten. I said: "You say the two sick men remained sick all through, and after awhile two or three had to be relieved from standing watch; how did you get along without medicines?"

The reply was: "Oh, we couldn't have kept them if we'd had them; if we'd had boxes of pills, or anything like that, we'd have eaten them. It was just as well—we couldn't have kept them, and we couldn't have given them to the sick men alone—we'd have shared them around all alike, I guess." It was said rather in jest, but it was a pretty true jest, no doubt.

After apportioning the ham bone, the captain cut the canvas cover that had been around the ham into fifteen equal pieces, and each man took his portion. This was the last division of food that the captain made. The men broke up the small oaken butter tub and divided the staves among themselves, and gnawed them up. The shell of the little green turtle, heretofore mentioned, was scraped with knives and eaten to the last shaving. The third mate chewed pieces of boots and spit them out, but ate nothing except the soft straps of two pairs of boots—ate three on the thirty-ninth day and saved one for the fortieth.

THE AWFUL ALTERNATIVE

The men seem to have thought in their own minds of the shipwrecked mariner's last dreadful resort—cannibalism; but they do not appear to have conversed about it. They only thought of the casting lots and killing one of their number as a possibility; but even when they were eating rags and bone and boots and shell and hard oak wood, they seem to have still had a notion that it was remote. They felt that some one of the company must die soon—which one they well knew; and during the last there or four days of their terrible voyage they were patiently but hungrily waiting for him. I wonder if the subject of these anticipations knew what they were thinking of? He must have known it—he must have felt it. They had even calculated how long he would last; they said to themselves, but not to each other, I think they said, "He will die Saturday—and then!"

There was one exception to the spirit of delicacy I have mentioned—a Frenchman, who kept an eye of strong personal interest upon the sinking man and noted his failing strength with untiring care and some degree of cheerfulness. He frequently said to Thomas: "I think he will go off pretty soon, now, sir. And then we'll eat him!" This is very sad.

Thomas and also several of the men state that the sick "Portyghee," during the five days that they were entirely out of provisions, actually ate two silk handkerchiefs and a couple of cotton shirts, besides his share of the boots and bones and lumber.

THE CAPTAIN'S BIRTHDAY

Captain Mitchell was fifty-six years old on the 12th of June—the fortieth day after the burning of the ship and the third day before the boat's crew reached land. He said it looked somewhat as if it might be the last one he was going to enjoy. He had no birthday feast except some bits of ham canvas—no luxury but this, and no substantials save the leather and oaken bucket staves.

Speaking of the leather diet, one of the men told me he was obliged to eat a pair of boots which were so old and rotten that they were full of holes; and then he smiled gently and said he didn't know, though, but what the holes tasted about as good as the balance of the boot. This man was still very feeble, and after saying this he went to bed.

LAND HO!

At eleven o'clock on the 15th of June, after suffering all that men may suffer and live for forty-three days, in an open boat, on a scorching tropical sea, one of the men feebly shouted the glad tidings, "Land ho!" The "watch below" were lying in the bottom of the boat. What do you suppose they did? They said they had been cruelly disappointed over and over again, and they dreaded to risk another experience of the kind—they could not bear it—they lay still where they were. They said they would not trust to an appearance that might not be land after all. They would wait.

Shortly it was proven beyond question that they were almost to land. Then there was joy in the party. One man is said to have swooned away. Another said the sight of the green hills was better to him than a day's rations, a strange figure for a man to use who had been fasting for forty days and forty nights.

The land was the island of Hawaii, and they were off Laupahoehoe and could see nothing inshore but breakers. I was there a week or two ago and it is a very dangerous place. When they got pretty close to shore, they saw cabins, but no human beings. They thought they would lower the sail and try to work in with the oars. They cut the ropes and the sail came down, and then they found they were not strong enough to ship the oars. They drifted help-lessly toward the breakers, but looked listlessly on and cared not a straw for the violent death which seemed about to overtake them after all their manful struggles, their privations, and their terrible sufferings. They said, "It was good to see the green fields again." It was all they cared for. The "green fields" were a haven of rest for the weary wayfarers; it was sufficient; they were satisfied; it was nothing to them that death stood in their pathway; they had long been familiar to him; he had no terrors for them.

Two of Captain Spencer's natives saw the boat, knew by the appearance of things that it was in trouble, and dashed through the surf and swam out to it. When they climbed aboard, there were only five yards of space be-tween the poor sufferers and a sudden and violent death. Fifteen minutes afterward the boat was beached upon the shore, and a crowd of natives (who are the very incar-nation of generosity, unselfishness, and hospitality) were around the strangers dumping bananas, melons, taro, poi—anything and everything they could scrape together that could be eaten—on the ground by the cartload; and if Mr. Jones, of the station, had not hurried down with his stew-ard, they would soon have killed the starving men with kindness. As it was, the sick "Portyghee" really ate six bananas before Jones could get hold of him and stop him. This is a fact. And so are the stories of his previous ex-ploits. Jones and the Kanaka girls and men took the mar-iners in their arms like so many children and carried them up to the house, where they received kind and judicious attention until Sunday evening, when two whaleboats came from Hilo, Jones furnished a third, and they were taken in these to the town just named, arriving there at two o'clock Monday morning.

REMARKS

Each of the young Fergusons kept a journal from the day the ship sailed from New York until they got on land once more at Hawaii. The captain also kept a log every day he was adrift. These logs, by the captain's direction, were to be kept up faithfully as long as any of the crew were alive, and the last survivor was to put them in a bottle, when he succumbed, and lash the bottle to the inside of the boat. The captain gave a bottle to each officer of the other boats, with orders to follow his example. The old gentleman was always thoughtful.

The hardest berth in that boat, I think, must have been that of provision keeper. This office was performed by the captain and the third mate; of course they were always hungry. They always had access to the food, and yet must not gratify their craving appetites.

The young Fergusons are very highly spoken of by all the boat's crew, as patient, enduring, manly, and kindhearted gentlemen. The captain gave them a watch to themselves—it was the duty of each to bail the water out of the boat three hours a day. Their home is in Stamford, Connecticut, but their father's place of business is New York.

In the chief mate's boat was a passenger—a gentlemanly young fellow of twenty years, named William Lang, son of a stockbroker in New York.

The chief mate, Samuel Hardy, lived at Chatham, Massachusetts; second mate belonged in Shields, England; the cook, George Washington (Negro), was in the chief mate's boat, and also the steward (Negro); the carpenter was in the second mate's boat.

CAPTAIN MITCHELL

To this man's good sense, cool judgment, perfect discipline, close attention to the smallest particulars which could conduce to the welfare of his crew or render their ultimate rescue more probable, that boat's crew owe their lives. He has shown brain and ability that make him worthy to command the finest frigate in the United States, and a genuine unassuming heroism that [should] entitle him to a Congressional Medal. I suppose some of the citizens of San Francisco who know how to appreciate this kind of a man will not let him go on hungry forever after he gets there. In the above remarks I am only echoing the expressed opinions of numbers of persons here who have never seen Captain Mitchell, but who judge him by his works—among others Hon. Anson Burlingame and our Minister to Japan, both of whom have called at the hospital several times and held long conversations with the men. Burlingame speaks in terms of the most unqualified praise of Captain Mitchell's high and distinguished abilities as evinced at every point throughout his wonderful voyage.

THE SICK

Captain Mitchell, one sailor, and the two Fergusons are still at Hilo. The two first mentioned are pretty feeble, from what I can learn. The captain's sense of responsibility kept him strong and awake all through the voyage; but as soon as he landed, and that fearful strain upon his faculties was removed, he was prostrated—became the feeblest of the boat's company.

The seamen here are doing remarkably well, considering all things. They already walk about the hospital a little; and very stiff-legged, because of the long inaction their muscles have experienced.

When they came ashore at Hawaii, no man in the party had had any movement of his bowels for eighteen days, several not for twenty-five or thirty, one not for thirty-seven, and one not for forty-four days. As soon as any of the men can travel, they will be sent to San Francisco.

I have written this lengthy letter in a great hurry in order to get it off by the bark *Milton Badger*, if the thing be possible, and I may have made a good many mistakes, but I hardly think so. All the statistical information in it comes from Thomas, and he may have made mistakes, because he tells his story entirely from memory, and although he has naturally a most excellent one, it might well be pardoned for inaccuracies concerning events which transpired during a series of weeks that never saw his mind strongly fixed upon any thought save the weary longing for food and water. But the logbooks of the captain and the two passengers will tell the terrible romance from the first day to the last in faithful detail, and these I shall forward by the next mail if I am permitted to copy them.

MARK TWAIN

16❀

A MONTH OF MOURNING

For a little more than a month, the late Princess—Her Royal Highness Victoria Kamamalu Kaahumanu, heir presumptive to the crown and sister to the King—lay in state at Iolani Palace, the royal residence. For a little over a month, troops of natives of both sexes, drawn here from the several islands by the great event, have thronged past my door every evening on their way to the palace. Every night, and all night long, for more than thirty days, multitudes of these strange mourners have burned their candlenut torches in the royal inclosure, and sung their funeral dirges, and danced their hula-hulas, and wailed their harrowing wail for the dead. All this time we strangers have been consumed with curiosity to look within those walls and see the pagan deviltry that was going on there. But the thing was tabu (forbidden—we get our word "taboo" from the Hawaiian language) to foreigners—haoles. The grounds were thrown open to everybody the first night, but several rowdy white people acted so unbecomingly—so shamefully, in fact—that the King placed a strict tabu upon their future admittance. I was absent—on the island of Hawaii [Maui]—at that time, and so I lost that one single opportunity to gratify my curiosity in this matter.

Last night was to behold the grand finale, inasmuch as the obsequies were to transpire today, and therefore I was a good deal gratified to learn that a few foreigners would be allowed to enter a side gate and view the performances in the palace yard from the veranda of Dr. Hutchinson's house (Minister of the Interior). I got there at a little after 8 P.M.

NIGHT SCENE IN THE PALACE GROUNDS

The veranda we occupied overlooked the royal grounds, and afforded an excellent view of the two thousand or twenty-five hundred natives sitting, densely packed together, in the glare of the torches, between our position and the palace, a hundred feet in front of us. It was a wild scene—those long rows of eager, dusky faces, with the light upon them; the band of hula girls in the center, showily attired in white bodices and pink skirts, and with wreaths of pink and white flowers and garlands of green leaves about their heads; and the strongly illuminated torchbearers scattered far and near at intervals through the large assemblage and standing up conspicuously above the masses of sitting forms. Light enough found its way to the broad verandas of the palace to enable us to see whatever transpired upon them with considerable distinctness. We could see nothing there, however, except two or three native sentries in red uniforms, with gleaming muskets in their hands.

Presently some one said: "Oh, there's the King!"

"Where?"

"There—on the veranda—now, he's just passing that—
No; it's that blasted Harris."

That isn't really his Christian name, but he is usually
called by that or a stronger one. I state this by way of
explanation. Harris is the Minister of Finance and Attorney General, and I don't know how many other things.
He has three marked points: He is not a second Solomon;
he is as vain as a peacock; he is as "cheeky" as—however, there is no simile for *his* "cheek." In the Legislature,
the other day, the Speaker was trying to seat a refrac-
tory member; the member knew he was strictly in order,
though, and that his only crime was his opposition to the
Ministry, and so he refused to sit down. Harris whispered
to the interpreter: "Tell the Speaker to let *me* have the
chair a moment." The speaker vacated his place; Harris
stepped into it, rapped fiercely with the gavel, scowled
imperiously upon the intrepid commoner, and ordered him
to sit down. The man declined to do it. Harris commanded
the Sergeant-at-Arms to seat him. After a trial, that officer said the bold representative of the people refused to
permit him to seat him. Harris ordered the Sergeant to
take the man out of the house—remove him by force!
[Sensation—tempest, I should rather say.] The poor hum-
bled and browbeaten country members threw off their
fears for the moment and became men; and from every
part of the house they shouted: "Come out of that chair!
leave that place! put him out! put out the ———!" (I
have forgotten the Hawaiian phrase, but it is equivalent to
"miserable dog.") And this terrible man, who was going
to perform such wonders, vacated the Speaker's chair, and
went meekly back to his own place, leaving the stout opponent of the Ministry master of the field. The Legislature

adjourned at once, and the excited and triumphant Kanakas burst forth into a stirring battle hymn of the old
days of Kamehameha the Great. Harris was an American
once (he was born in Portsmouth, N. H.), but he is no
longer one. He is *hoopilimeaai* to the King. How do you
like that, Mr. H.? How do you like being attacked in your
own native tongue?

(NOTE TO THE READER: That long native word means
—well, it means Uriah Heep boiled down—it means the
soul and spirit of obsequiousness. No genuine American
can be other than obedient and respectful toward the Government he lives under and the flag that protects him,
but no such American can ever be hoopilimeaai to anybody.)

I hope the gentle reader will pardon this digression; but
if the gentle reader don't want to do it, he can let it alone.

A GLIMPSE OF THE HEATHEN AGES

About half past eight o'clock a dozen native women
rose up and began the sad mourning rites. They locked
arms and swayed violently backward and forward; faced
around and went through a number of quick gestures with
hands, heads, and bodies; turned and twisted and mingled
together—heads and hands going all the time, and their
motions timed to a weird howling which it would be rather
complimentary to call singing; and finished up spreading
their arms abroad and throwing their heads and bodies
far backward simultaneously, and all uttering a deafening
squall at the same moment.

"Well, if there's anything between the Farallones and
Fiddler's Green as devilish as that, I wish I may—"

"Brown," I said, "these solemn and impressive funeral

rites of the ancient times have been rescued from the oblivion to which the ignorant missionaries consigned them forty years ago, by the good and wise Lord Bishop Staley, and it ill beseems such as you to speak irreverently of them. I cannot permit you to say more in this vein in my presence."

When the women had finished, the multitude clapped their hands boisterously in token of applause.

A number of native boys next stood up and went through a performance a good deal like that which I have just described, singing at the same time a strange, unmusical chant. The audience applauded again. (Harris came out once more on that part of the veranda which could be seen best by the great assemblage, and assumed an attitude and expression so suggestive of his being burdened with the cares of state of sixty or seventy kingdoms, that, if I had been a stranger, I must have said to myself: "The trifles Richelieu had to contend with were foolishness to what this man has got on his hands.")

CHRISTIANITY AND CIVILIZATION
IN WARM QUARTERS

Next, about twenty native women dressed in black rose up and sang some hymns like ours, but in the Kanaka tongue, and made good music of them. Some of the voices were very rich and sweet, the harmony was excellent and the time perfect. Every now and then, while this choir sang (and, in fact, all the evening), old-time natives scattered through the crowd would suddenly break out into a wild heartbroken wail that would almost startle one's pulse into stillness. And there was one old fellow near the center who would get up often, no matter what was going on, and branch forth into a sort of singsong recitation, which he would eventually change into a stump speech; he seemed to make a good many hits judging by the cordial applause he got from a coterie of admirers in his immediate vicinity.

MORE HEATHEN DEVILTRY

A dozen men performed next—howled and distorted their bodies and flung their arms fiercely about, like very maniacs.

"God bless my soul, just listen at that racket! Your opinion is your opinion, and I don't quarrel with it; and my opinion is my opinion; and I say, once for all, that if I was Mayor of this town I would just get up here and read the Riot Act once, if I died for it the next—"

"Brown, I cannot allow this language. These touching expressions of mourning were instituted by the good bishop, who has come from his English home to teach this poor benighted race to follow the example and imitate the sinless ways of the Redeemer, and did not he mourn for the dead Lazarus? Do not the sacred scriptures say 'Jesus wept'?"

I overheard this person Brown muttering something about the imitation being rather overdone or improved on, or something of that kind, but I paid no attention to it. The man means well; his ignorance is his misfortune— not his crime.

Twenty Kanakas in striped knit shirts now filed through the dense crowd and sat down in a double row on the ground; each bore an immense gourd, more than two feet long, with a neck near one end and a head to it; the outer, or largest end, was a foot in diameter; these things were dry and hollow, and are the native tom-toms or drums. Each man set his gourd on end, and supported it with a hand on each side; at a given signal every drummer launched out into a dismal chant and slapped his drum twice in quick succession with his open hands; then three times; then twice again; then—well, I cannot describe it; they slapped the drums in every conceivable way, and the sound produced was as dull and dry as if the drums had been solid stone; then they held them above their heads a few moments, or over their shoulders, or in front of their faces, or behind their necks, and then brought them simultaneously to the gound with a dead, hollow thump; and then they went on slapping them as before. They kept up this most dreary and unexciting performance for twenty minutes or more, and the great concourse of natives watched every motion with rapt and eager admiration, and loudly applauded the musicians.

Brown muttered (under the vile pretense of not intending to be overheard): "Jesus wept."

"Brown," I said, "your conduct is shameful. It has always been conceded that in following the example set us by the Savior we may be allowed some latitude. But I will not argue with a man who is so bigoted, faultfinding, and uncharitable. I will have nothing further to say to you upon this subject."

"He—he wept."

I thought I heard those words, but Brown's head was out of the window, and I was not certain. I was already irritated to that degree that to speak would be to lose my temper, and therefore I allowed the suspected mutinous language to pass unnoticed.

THE CELEBRATED NATIONAL DANCE ("HULA-HULA")

After the drumming came the famous hula-hula we had heard so much about and so longed to see—the lascivious dance that was wont to set the passions of men ablaze in the old heathen days, a century ago. About thirty buxom young Kanaka women, gaily attired as I have before remarked, in pink and white, and with heads wreathed with flowers and evergreens, formed themselves into half a dozen rows of five or six in a row, shook the reefs out of their skirts, tightened their girdles and began the most unearthly caterwauling that was ever heard, perhaps; the noise had a marked and regular time to it, however, and they kept strict time to it with writhing bodies; with heads and hands thrust out to the left; then to the right; then a step to the front and the left hands all projected simultaneously forward, and the right hands placed on the hips; then the same repeated with a change of hands; then a mingling together of the performers—quicker time, faster and more violently excited motions—more and more complicated gestures—(the words of their fierce chant meantime treating in broadest terms, and in detail, of things which may be vaguely hinted at in a respectable newspaper, but not distinctly mentioned)—then a convulsive writhing of the person, continued for a few moments and ending in a sudden stop and a grand caterwaul in chorus (great applause).

"Jesus wept."

I barely heard the words, and that was all. They sounded like blasphemy. I offered no rebuke to the utterer, because I could not disguise from myself that the gentle grief of the Savior was but poorly imitated here—that the heathen orgies resurrected by the Lord Bishop of Honolulu were not warranted by the teachings of the Master whom he professes to serve.

Minister Harris emerging from the Palace veranda at this moment with the weight of his sixty kingdoms bearing down on him heavier than ever, and it being past midnight, I judged it time to go home, and I did so.

WHOSE CIRCUS IT WAS

It is reported that the King has said: "The foreigners like their religion—let them enjoy it, and freely. But the religion of my fathers is good enough for me." Now that is all right. At least I think so. And I have no fault to find with the natives for the lingering love they feel for their ancient customs. But I do find fault with Bishop Staley for reviving those customs of a barbarous age at a time when they had long been abandoned and were being forgotten—when one more generation of faithful adherence to the teachings of the American missionaries would have buried them forever and made them memories of the past —things to be talked of and wondered at, like the old laws that made it death for a plebeian to stand erect in the presence of his king, or for a man to speak to his wife on a tabu day—but never imitated.

For forty years before the bishop brought his Royal Hawaiian Established Reformed Catholic Church here, the kings and chiefs of this land had been buried with the quiet, simple, Christian rites that are observed in England and America, and no man thought of anything more being necessary. But one of the first things Bishop Staley did when he arrived here a few years ago was to write home that the missionaries had deprived the natives of their innocent sports and pastimes (such as the lascivious hula-hula, and the promiscuous bathing in the surf of nude natives of opposite sexes), and one of the next things he did was to attend a hula-hula at Waikiki with his holy head tricked out in the flower and evergreen trumpery worn by the hula girls. When the late king died, the bishop revived the half-forgotten howling and hula dancing and other barbarisms in the palace yard, and officiated there as a sort of master of ceremonies. For many a year before he came, that wretchedest of all wretched musical abortions, the tom-tom, had not been heard near the heart of Honolulu; but he has reinstated it and brought it into its ancient esteem and popularity. The old superstitions of this people were passing away far faster than is the case with the inhabitants of the unfrequented and sparsely populated country districts of America, France, and Wales, but Bishop Staley is putting a stop to progress in this direction.

We owe the strange and unpleasant scenes of last night to him—there are not ten white men in the kingdom who have ever seen their like before in public—and I am told that he is appalled at the work of his own hands—that he is ashamed—that he dreads to think of the comments it will provoke in Christian lands—in a word, that he finds, too late, that he has made a most melancholy blunder.

BISHOP STALEY

If I may speak freely, I think this all comes of elevating a weak, trivial-minded man to a position of rank and power—of making a bishop out of very inferior material —of trying to construct greatness out of constitutional insignificance. My estimate of Bishop Staley is not carelessly formed; there is evidence to back it. He gossips habitually; he lacks the common wisdom to keep still that deadly enemy of a man, his own tongue; he says ill-advised things in public speeches, and then in other public speeches denies that he ever said them; he shows spite, a trait which is not allied to greatness; he is fond of rushing into print, like mediocrity the world over, and is vainer of being my Lord Bishop over a diocese of fifteen thousand men and women (albeit they belong to other people's churches) than some other men would be of wielding the worldwide power of the Pope; and finally, every single important act of his administration has evinced a lack of sagacity and an unripeness of judgment which might be forgiven a youth, but not a full-grown man—or, if that seems too severe, which might be forgiven a restless, visionary nobody, but not a bishop. My estimate of Bishop Staley may be a wrong one, but it is at least an honest one.

Persons who are intimate with Bishop Staley say he is a good man, and a well educated and cultivated one, and that in social life he is companionable, pleasant, and liberal spirited when church matters are not the topic of conversation. This is no doubt true; but it is my province to speak of him in his official, not in his private capacity. He has shown the temerity of an incautious, inexperienced, and immature judgment in rushing in here fresh from the heart and home of a high English civilization and throwing down the gauntlet of defiance before a band of stern, tenacious, unyielding, tireless, industrious, devoted old Puritan knights who have seen forty years of missionary service; whose time was never fooled away in theorizing, but whose lightest acts always meant business; who landed here two score years ago, full of that fervent zeal and resistless determination inherited from their Pilgrim fore-fathers, and marched forth and seized upon this people with a grip of iron, and infused into their being, wrought into their very natures, the spirit of democracy and the religious enthusiasm that animated themselves; whose grip is still upon the race and can never be loosened till they, of their own free will and accord, shall relax it. He showed a marvelous temerity—one weak, inexperienced man against a host of drilled and hardy veterans; and among them great men—men who would be great in wider and broader spheres than that they have chosen here. He miscalculated the force, the confidence, the determination of that Puritan spirit which subdued America and under-lies her whole religious fabric today—which has subdued these islanders, and whose influence over them can never be unseated.

THE REFORMED CATHOLIC CHURCH— THE "COURT RELIGION"

His church was another miscalculation. It was a mistake to appeal by imposing ceremonies and showy display to a people imbued with a thorough Puritan distaste for such things, and who had never been much accustomed to any-thing of the kind at any period of their history. There is little in common between the simple evergreen decora-tions and the tom-toms and the hula-hulas of the natives, and the cheap magnificence of the bishop's cathedral altar, his gaudily painted organ pipes and the monotonous and unattractive ceremonials of his church service.

He is fighting with good nerve, but his side is weak. The moneyed strength of these islands—their agriculture, their commerce, their mercantile affairs—is in the hands of

Americans—republicans; the religious power of the country is wielded by Americans—republicans; the whole people are saturated with the spirit of democratic Puritanism, and they are—republicans. This is a *republic*, to the very marrow, and over it sit a King, a dozen Nobles and half a dozen Ministers. The field of the Royal Hawaiian Established Church is thus so circumscribed that the little cathedral in Nuuanu Street, with its thirty pews of ten-individual capacity each, is large enough to accommodate it in its entirety, and have room to spare.

And this is the bugbear that has kept the American missionaries in hot water for three or four years! The Bishop of Honolulu ought to feel flattered that a chance so slim as his, and a power so feeble as his, has been able to accomplish it. But at the same time he ought to feel grateful, because, if let alone, he and his church must infallibly have been and remained insignificant. I do not say this ill-naturedly, for I bear the Bishop no malice, and I respect his sacred office; I simply state a palpable fact.

I will say a word or two about the Reformed Catholic Church, to the end that strangers may understand its character. Briefly, then, it is a miraculous invention. One might worship this strange production itself without breaking the first commandment, for there is nothing like it in the heavens above or in the earth beneath, or in the water under the earth. The Catholics refuse to accept it as Catholic, the Episcopalians deny that it is the church they are accustomed to, and of course the Puritans claim no kindred with it. It is called a child of the Established Church of England, but it resembles its parent in few particulars. It has got an altar which is gay with fiery velvet, showy white trimmings, vases of flowers, and other mantel ornaments. (It was once flanked by imposing, seven-branched candlesticks, but these were obnoxious and have been removed.) Over it is a thing like a gilt signboard, on which is rudely painted two processions—four personages in each—marching solemnly and in single file toward the crucified Savior in the center, and bringing their baggage with them. The design of it is a secret known only to the artist and his Maker. Near the pulpit is a red canopied shower bath—I mean it looks like one—upon which is inscribed, "Separated unto the Gospel of God." The bishop sits under it at a small desk, when he has got nothing particular to do. The organ pipes are colored with a groundwork of blue, which is covered all over with a flower work wrought in other colors. Judging by its striking homeliness, I should say that the artist of the altar piece had labored here also. Near the door of the church, but inside, of course, stands a small pillar, surmounted by a large shell. It may be for holy water or it may be a contribution box. If the latter be the case, I must protest that this ghastly pun—this mute suggestion to shell out—is ill suited to the sacred character of the place, and it is only with the profoundest pain that I force myself to even think for a moment upon so distressing a circumstance. Against the wall is a picture of the future cathedral of Honolulu—a more imposing structure than the present one; that many a year may elapse before it is built is no wish of mine. A dozen acolytes—Chinese, Kanaka, and half-white boys, arrayed in white robes, hold positions near the altar, and during the early part of the service they sing and go through some performances suggestive of the regular Catholic services; after that, the majority of the boys go off on furlough. The bishop reads a chapter from the Bible; then the organist leaves his instrument and sings a litany peculiar to this church, and not to be heard elsewhere; there is nothing stirring or incendiary about his mild, nasal music; the congregation join the chorus; after this a third clergyman preaches the sermon; these three ecclesiastics all wear white surplices. I have described the evening services. When the bishop first came here, he indulged in a good deal of showy display and ceremony in his church, but these proved so distasteful, even to Episcopalians, that he shortly modified them very much.

I have spoken rather irreverently once or twice in the above paragraph, and am ashamed of it. But why write it over? I would not be likely to get it any better. I might make the matter worse.

"And say that—"

"Brown, have you, in defiance of all my reproofs, been looking over my shoulder again?"

"Yes, but that's all right, you know—that's all right. Just say—just say that the bishop works as hard as any man, and makes the best fight he can—and that's a credit to him, anyway."

"Brown, that is the first charitable sentiment I have ever heard you utter. At a proper moment I will confer upon you a fitting reward for it. But for the present, good night, son. Go, now. Go to your innocent slumbers. And wash your feet, Brown—or perhaps it is your teeth—at any rate you are unusually offensive this evening. Remedy the matter. Never mind explaining—good night."

THE ROMAN CATHOLIC MISSION

The French Roman Catholic Mission here, under the Right Reverend Lord Bishop Maigret, goes along quietly

and unostentatiously; and its affairs are conducted with a
wisdom which betrays the presence of a leader of distinguished ability. The Catholic clergy are honest, straightforward, frank, and open; they are industrious and devoted to their religion and their work; they never meddle;
whatever they do can be relied on as being prompted by a
good and worthy motive. These things disarm resentment
—prejudice cannot exist in their presence. Consequently,
Americans are never heard to speak ill or slightingly of the
French Catholic Mission. Their religion is not nondescript
—it is plain, out-and-out, undisguised, and unmistakable
Catholicism. You know right where to find them when
you want them. The American missionaries have no quarrel with these men; they honor and respect and esteem
them—and bid them Godspeed. There is an anomaly for
you—Puritan and Roman Catholic striding along, hand
in hand, under the banner of the Cross!

MARK TWAIN

17 ❀

HONOLULU, JULY 1, 1866.

FUNERAL OF THE PRINCESS

At ten o'clock yesterday morning, the court, members of the Legislature and various diplomatic bodies assembled at the Iolani Palace, to be present at the funeral of the late Princess. The sermon was preached by the Rev. Mr. Parker, pastor of the great stone church—of which the Princess was a member, I believe, and whose choir she used to lead in the days of her early womanhood. To the day of her death she was a staunch, unwavering friend and ally of the missionaries, and it is a matter of no surprise that Parker, always eloquent, spoke upon this occasion with a feeling and pathos which visibly moved the hearts of men accustomed to conceal their emotions.

The Bishop of Honolulu, ever zealous, had sought permission to officiate in Parker's stead, but after duly considering the fact that the Princess had always regarded the bishop with an unfriendly eye and had persistently refused to have anything to do with his church, his request was denied. However, he demanded and was granted the place of honor in the procession, although it belonged properly to the officiating clergyman. The bishop also claimed that inasmuch as the Royal Mausoleum was consecrated ground, it would be sacrilegious to allow a Calvinistic minister to officiate there when the body was consigned to the tomb, and so he was allowed to conduct that portion of the obsequies himself. However, he explained that it was not the custom of his church to read a burial service or offer up a prayer over such as had never belonged to that church, and therefore the departed Princess was consigned to her last resting place with no warmer or kindlier a recommendation than a meager, noncommittal benediction—a sort of chilly funereal politeness—nothing more. But then we should not blame the bishop in this matter, because he has both authority and example to sustain his position, as I find by reference to a "Review" by W. D. Alexander of one of his "Pastoral Addresses." I quote from Alexander:

"Only last December, Thomas Powell, near Peterborough in England, wished to have his son buried in the parish churchyard, and a Dissenting minister to officiate. When the friends had gathered around the grave, a messenger arrived from the clergyman of the Established Church, one Ellaby, stating that he was ready to perform the Episcopal service. This was courteously declined, upon which the rector issued from the church and forbade the burial. Even the right of silent interment was denied them, and when the afflicted father would himself perform the last sad offices at the grave of his child the spade was wrenched from his hand by the sexton."

In offering this defense of the Bishop of Honolulu, I do so simply with an unselfish wish to do him justice and save him from hasty and injurious criticism, and *not* through a mean desire to curry favor with him.

THE GRAND FUNEREAL PAGEANT

As the hour of eleven approached, large bodies of white and native residents, chiefly on horseback, moved toward the palace through the quiet streets, to see the procession form. All business houses were closed, of course, and many a flag, half-mast high, swung lazily in the summer air.

The procession began to move at eleven, amid the solemn tolling of bells and the dull booming of minute guns from the heights overlooking the city. A glance of the eye down the procession revealed a striking and picturesque spectacle—large bodies of women, in melancholy black, and roofed over with a far-reaching double line of black umbrellas; troops of men and children, in black; carriages, with horses clad from head to foot in sable velvet; and in strong contrast with all this were the bright colors flashing here and there along the pageant—swarthy Zouaves in crimson raiment; soldiers, in blue and white and other lively hues; mounted lancers, with red and white pennants fluttering from their weapons; nobles and great officers in splendid uniforms; and—conspicuous amid its gloomy surroundings—the catafalque, flanked on either side with gorgeously tinted kahilis. The slow and measured tread of the marching squadrons; the mournful music of the bands; the chanting of the virtues of the dead and the warrior deeds of her ancestors, by a gray and venerable woman here and there; the wild wail that rang out at times from some bereaved one to whom the occasion brought back the spirit of the buried past—these completed the effect.

THE KAHILIS

The kahilis are symbols of mourning which are sacred to the aristocracy. They are immense plumes, mounted upon tall poles, and are made of feathers of all bright and beautiful colors; some are a rich purple; some crimson; others brown, blue, white, and black, etc. These are all dyed, but the costly kahilis formed of the yellow feather of royalty (tabu to the common herd) were tinted by the hand of nature, and come from the tropic bird, which, as I have said in a previous letter, has but two of them—one under each wing. One or two kahilis, also, made of red feathers from a bird called by sailors the marlinspike bird, had no artificial coloring about them. These feathers are very long and slender (hence the fowl's name), and each bird's tail is furnished with two, and only two, of them. The birds of the Sandwich Islands seem uncommonly indigent in the matter of strictly ornamental feathers. A dozen or more of these gaudy kahilis were upheld by pallbearers of high blood and fenced in the stately catafalque with a varicolored wall as brilliant as a rainbow. Through the arches of the catafalque could be seen the coffin, draped with that badge and symbol of royalty, the famous yellow-feather war cloak, whose construction occupied the toiling hands of its manufacturers during nine generations of Hawaiian kings.

"STYLE"

We have here, in this little land of fifty thousand inhabitants, the complete machinery, in its minutest details, of a vast and imposing empire, done in miniature. We have all the sounding titles, all the grades and castes, all the pomp and circumstance, of a great monarchy. To the curious, the following published program of the procession will not be uninteresting. After reading the long list of dignitaries, etc., and remembering the sparseness of the population, one is almost inclined to wonder where the material for that portion of the procession devoted to "Hawaiian Population Generally" is going to be procured.

UNDERTAKER

ROYAL SCHOOL   KAWAIAHAO SCHOOL   ROMAN CATHOLIC
SCHOOL   MAEMAE SCHOOL

HONOLULU FIRE DEPARTMENT

MECHANICS' BENEFIT UNION

ATTENDING PHYSICIANS

KONOHIKIS (SUPERINTENDENTS) OF THE CROWN LANDS, KONOHIKIS
OF THE PRIVATE LANDS OF HIS MAJESTY

KONOHIKIS OF PRIVATE LANDS OF HER
LATE ROYAL HIGHNESS

GOVERNOR OF OAHU AND STAFF

HULUMANU (MILITARY COMPANY)

THE PRINCE OF HAWAII'S OWN (MILITARY COMPANY)

HOUSEHOLD TROOPS

THE KING'S HOUSEHOLD SERVANTS

SERVANTS OF HER LATE ROYAL HIGHNESS

PROTESTANT CLERGY   THE CLERGY OF THE ROMAN CATHOLIC
CHURCH

HIS LORDSHIP LOUIS MAIGRET, THE RIGHT REV. BISHOP OF
ARATHEA, VICAR-APOSTOLIC OF THE HAWAIIAN ISLANDS

THE CLERGY OF THE HAWAIIAN REFORMED CATHOLIC CHURCH

HIS LORDSHIP THE RIGHT REV. BISHOP OF HONOLULU

ESCORT HAWAIIAN CAVALRY
LARGE KAHILIS
SMALL KAHILIS
PALLBEARERS

HEARSE

ESCORT HAWAIIAN CAVALRY
LARGE KAHILIS
SMALL KAHILIS
PALLBEARERS

HER MAJESTY QUEEN EMMA'S CARRIAGE

HIS MAJESTY'S STAFF

CARRIAGE OF HER LATE ROYAL HIGHNESS

CARRIAGE OF HER MAJESTY THE QUEEN DOWAGER

THE KING'S CHANCELLOR

CABINET MINISTERS

HIS EXCELLENCY THE MINISTER RESIDENT OF THE UNITED
STATES, JAMES MCBRIDE

H. I. M.'S COMMISSIONER, MONS. DESNOYERS

H. B. M.'S ACTING COMMISSIONER, W. L. GREEN
JUDGES OF SUPREME COURT
PRIVY COUNCILLORS
MEMBERS OF LEGISLATIVE ASSEMBLY
CONSULAR CORPS
CIRCUIT JUDGES
CLERKS OF GOVERNMENT DEPARTMENTS
MEMBERS OF THE BAR
COLLECTOR GENERAL, CUSTOMHOUSE OFFICERS AND OFFICERS
OF THE CUSTOMS
MARSHAL AND SHERIFFS OF THE DIFFERENT ISLANDS
KING'S YEOMANRY
FOREIGN RESIDENTS
AHA HUI KAAHUMANU
HAWAIIAN POPULATION GENERALLY
HAWAIIAN CAVALRY
POLICE FORCE

DETAILS

The Aha Hui Kaahumanu—a benevolent society instituted (and presided over) by the late Princess for the nursing of the sick and the burial of the dead—was numerously
represented. It is composed solely of native women. They
were dressed in black, and wore sashes of different colors.

His Majesty the King, attended by a guard of nobles
and princes, whose uniforms were splendid, with bright
colors and loops and braids of gold, rode with his venerable
father in the first carriage in the rear of the catafalque.
The Bishop of Honolulu occupied the place of honor
in that portion of the procession which preceded the
catafalque.

The servants of the King and the late Princess would
have made quite a respectable procession by themselves.
They numbered two hundred and fifty, perhaps.

Four or five poodle dogs, which had been the property
of the deceased, were carried in the arms of individuals
among these servants of peculiar and distinguished trust-
worthiness. It is likely that all the Christianity the Ha-

waiians could absorb would never be sufficient to wean them from their almost idolatrous affection for dogs. And these dogs, as a general thing, are the smallest, meanest, and most spiritless, homely, and contemptible of their species.

As the procession passed along the broad and beautiful Nuuanu Street, an innocent native would step out occasionally from the ranks, procure a slice of watermelon or a pineapple or a lighted pipe from some dusky spectator, and return to his place and enjoy the refreshing luxury as he kept step with the melancholy music.

When we had thoroughly examined the pageant, we retired to a back street and galloped ahead to the mausoleum, two miles from the center of the town, and sat down to wait. This mausoleum is a neat edifice, built of dressed blocks of coral; has a high, sharp, slated roof, and its form is that of a Greek cross. The remains of the later kings repose in it, but those of ancient times were hidden or burned, in compliance with a custom of the dark ages; some say, to prevent evil-disposed persons from getting hold of them and thus being enabled to pray a descendant to death; others say, to prevent the natives from making fishhooks out of them, it being held that there were superior fishhook virtues in the bones of a high chief. There are other theories for accounting for this custom, but I have forgotten what they are. It is said that it was usual to send a friend to hide the bones (after they had been stripped of the flesh and neatly tied in a bundle), and then waylay him and kill him as he came back, whereby it will be observed that to do a favor of this kind was attended with consequences which could not be otherwise than disagreeable to the party assuming the kindly office of undertaker to a dead dignitary. Of course, as you will easily divine, the man was killed to prevent the possibility of his divulging his precious secret.

The mausoleum is large enough to accommodate many dead kings and princes. It stands in the middle of a large grass-clad lawn, which is enclosed by a stone wall.

ARRIVAL OF THE PROCESSION

As the procession filed through the gate, the military deployed handsomely to the right and left and formed an avenue through which the long column of mourners passed to the tomb. The coffin was borne through the door of the mausoleum, followed by the King and his chiefs, the great officers of the kingdom, foreign consuls, ambassadors, and distinguished guests (Burlingame and General Van Valkenburgh). Several of the kahilis were then fastened to a framework in front of the tomb, there to remain until they decay and fall to pieces, or, forestalling this, until another scion of royalty dies. At this point of the proceedings the multitude set up such a dismal, heartbroken wailing as I hope never to hear again. The soldiers fired three volleys of musketry—the wailing being previously silenced to permit of the guns being heard.

His Highness Prince William, in a showy military uniform (who was formerly betrothed to the Princess but was not allowed to marry her), stood guard and paced back and forth within the door. The privileged few who followed the coffin into the mausoleum remained some time, but the King soon came out and stood in the door and near one side of it. A stranger could have guessed his rank (although he was so simply and unpretentiously dressed) by the profound deference paid him by all persons in his vicinity; by seeing his high officers receive his quiet orders and suggestions with bowed and uncovered heads; and by observing how careful those persons who came out of the mausoleum were to avoid "crowding" him (although there was room enough in the doorway for a wagon to pass, for that matter); how respectfully they edged out sideways, scraping their backs against the wall and always presenting a front view of their persons to His Majesty, and never putting their hats on until they were well out of the royal presence.

THE KING

The King is thirty-four years of age, it is said, but looks all of fifty. He has an observant, inquiring eye, a heavy, massive face, a lighter complexion than is common with his race, tolerably short, stiff hair, a moderate mustache and imperial, large stature, inclining somewhat to corpulence (I suppose he weighs fully one hundred and eighty— maybe a little over), has fleshy hands, but a small foot for his size, is about six feet high, is thoughtful and slow of movement, has a large head, firmly set upon broad shoulders, and is a better man and a better looking one than he is represented to be in the villainous popular photographs of him, for none of them are good. That last remark is surplusage, however, for no photograph ever was good, yet, of anybody—hunger and thirst and utter wretchedness overtake the outlaw who invented it! It transforms into desperadoes the meekest of men; depicts sinless innocence upon the pictured faces of ruffians; gives the wise man the stupid leer of a fool, and a fool an expression of more than earthly wisdom. If a man tries to look merely serious when he sits for his picture, the photograph makes him as solemn as an owl; if he smiles, the photograph smirks repulsively;

if he tries to look pleasant, the photograph looks silly; if he makes the fatal mistake of attempting to seem pensive, the camera will surely write him down an ass. The sun never looks through the photographic instrument that it does not print a lie. The piece of glass it prints it on is well named a "negative"—a contradiction—a misrepresentation—a falsehood. I speak feelingly of this matter, because by turns the instrument has represented me to be a lunatic, a Solomon, a missionary, a burglar, and an abject idiot, and I am neither.

The King was dressed entirely in black—dress coat and silk hat—and looked rather democratic in the midst of the showy uniforms about him. On his breast he wore a large gold star, which was half hidden by the lapel of his coat. He remained at the door a half hour, and occasionally gave an order to the men who were erecting the kahilis before the tomb. He had the good taste to make one of them substitute black crepe for the ordinary hempen rope he was about to tie one of them to the framework with. Finally he entered his carriage and drove away, and the populace shortly began to drop in his wake. While he was in view, there was but one man who attracted more attention than himself, and that was Minister Harris. This feeble personage had crepe enough around his hat to express the grief of an entire nation, and as usual he neglected no opportunity of making himself conspicuous and exciting the admiration of the simple Kanakas. Oh! noble ambition of this modern Richelieu!

A CONTRAST—HOW THEY DID IN ANCIENT TIMES

It is interesting to contrast the funeral ceremonies of the Princess Victoria with those of her great ancestor Kameha-

meha the Conqueror, who died less than fifty years ago—
in 1819, the year before the first missionaries came:

> On the 8th of May, 1819, at the age of sixty-six,
> he died, as he had lived, in the faith of his country. It
> was his misfortune not to have come in contact with
> men who could have rightly influenced his religious
> aspirations. Judged by his advantages and compared
> with the most eminent of his countrymen he may be
> justly styled not only great, but good. To this day his
> memory warms the heart and elevates the national
> feelings of Hawaiians. They are proud of their old
> warrior king; they love his name; his deeds form their
> historical age; and an enthusiasm everywhere prevails,
> shared even by foreigners who knew his worth, that
> constitutes the firmest pillar of the throne of his son.
> In lieu of human victims (the custom of that age),
> a sacrifice of three hundred dogs attended his obse-
> quies—no mean holocaust when their national value
> and the estimation in which they were held are con-
> sidered. The bones of Kamehameha, after being kept
> for a while, were so carefully concealed that all
> knowledge of their final resting place is now lost.
> There was a proverb current among the common
> people that the bones of a cruel king could not be hid;
> they made fishhooks and arrows of them, upon which,
> in using them, they vented their abhorrence of his
> memory in bitter execrations.

The account of the circumstances of his death, as written by the native historians, is full of minute detail, but
there is scarcely a line of it which does not mention or illus-

trate some bygone custom of the country. In this respect
it is the most comprehensive document I have yet met
with. I will quote it entire [from James J. Jarves, *History
of the Hawaiian or Sandwich Islands,* 2d ed., 1844, pp.
207–9]:

> When Kamehameha was dangerously sick and the
> priests were unable to cure him, they said: "Be of good
> courage and build a house for the god [his own private
> god or idol] that thou mayest recover." The chiefs
> corroborated this advice of the priests, and a place of
> worship was prepared for Kukailimoku, and conse-
> crated in the evening. They proposed also to the King,
> with a view to prolong his life, that human victims
> should be sacrificed to his deity; upon which the
> greater part of the people absconded through fear of
> death, and concealed themselves in hiding places till
> the tabu, in which destruction impended, was past. It
> is doubtful whether Kamehameha approved of the
> plan of the chiefs and priests to sacrifice men, as he
> was known to say, "The men are sacred for the King";
> meaning that they were for the service of his succes-
> sor. This information was derived from Liholiho, his
> son.
>
> After this, his sickness increased to such a degree
> that he had not strength to turn himself in his bed.
> When another season, consecrated for worship at the
> new temple (heiau), arrived, he said to his son, Liho-
> liho, "Go thou and make supplication to thy god; I
> am not able to go, and will offer my prayers at home."
> When his devotions to his feathered god, Kukaili-
> moku, were concluded, a certain religiously disposed

individual, who had a bird god, suggested to the King that through its influence his sickness might be removed. The name of this god was Pua; its body was made of a bird, now eaten by the Hawaiians, and called in their language *alae*. Kamehameha was willing that a trial should be made, and two houses were constructed to facilitate the experiment; but while dwelling in them he became so very weak as not to receive food. After lying there three days, his wives, children, and chiefs, perceiving that he was very low, returned him to his own house. In the evening he was carried to the eating house, where he took a little food in his mouth which he did not swallow; also a cup of water. The chiefs requested him to give them his counsel; but he made no reply, and was carried back to the dwelling house; but when near midnight—ten o'clock, perhaps—he was carried again to the place to eat; but, as before, he merely tasted of what was presented to him. Then Kaikioewa addressed him thus: "Here we all are, your younger brethren, your son Liholiho and your foreigner; impart to us your dying charge, that Liholiho and Kaahumanu may hear." Then Kamehameha inquired, "What do you say?" Kaikioewa repeated, "Your counsels for us." He then said, "Move on in my good way and—" He could proceed no further. The foreigner, Mr. Young, embraced and kissed him. Hoapili also embraced him, whispering something in his ear, after which he was taken back to the house. About twelve he was carried once more to the house for eating, into which his head entered, while his body was in the dwelling house immediately adjoining. It should be remarked that this frequent car-

rying of a sick chief from one house to another resulted from the tabu system, then in force. There were
at that time six houses connected with an establishment—one for worship, one for the men to eat in, an
eating house for the women, a house to sleep in, a
house in which to manufacture kapa (native cloth),
and one where, at certain intervals, the women might
dwell in seclusion.

The sick was once more taken to his house, when
he expired; this was at two o'clock, a circumstance
from which Leleiohoku derived his name. As he
breathed his last, Kalaimoku came to the eating house
to order those in it to go out. There were two aged
persons thus directed to depart; one went, the other
remained on account of love to the King, by whom
he had formerly been kindly sustained. The children
also were sent away. Then Kalaimoku came to the
house, and the chiefs had a consultation. One of them
spoke thus: "This is my thought—we will eat him
raw." Kaahumanu (one of the dead King's widows)
replied, "Perhaps his body is not at our disposal; that
is more properly with his successor. Our part in him—
his breath—has departed; his remains will be disposed
of by Liholiho."

After this conversation the body was taken into the
consecrated house for the performance of the proper
rites by the priest and the new King. The name of
this ceremony is *uko;* and when the sacred hog was
baked, the priest offered it to the dead body, and it
became a god, the King at the same time repeating the
customary prayers.

Then the priest, addressing himself to the King and chiefs, said: "I will now make known to you the rules to be observed respecting persons to be sacrificed on the burial of this body. If you obtain one man before the corpse is removed, one will be sufficient; but after it leaves this house, four will be required. If delayed until we carry the corpse to the grave, there must be ten; but after it is deposited in the grave there must be fifteen. Tomorrow morning there will be a tabu, and, if the sacrifice be delayed until that time, forty men must die."

Then the high priest, Hewahewa, inquired of the chiefs, "Where shall be the residence of King Liho-liho?" They replied, "Where indeed? You, of all men, ought to know." Then the priest observed, "There are two suitable places; one is Kau, the other is Kohala." The chiefs preferred the latter, as it was more thickly inhabited. The priest added, "These are proper places for the King's residence; but he must not remain in Kona, for it is polluted." This was agreed to. It was now break of day. As he was being carried to the place of burial the people perceived that their king was dead, and they wailed. When the corpse was removed from the house to the tomb, a distance of one chain, the procession was met by a certain man who was ardently attached to the deceased. He leaped upon the chiefs who were carrying the King's body; he desired to die with him on account of his love. The chiefs drove him away. He persisted in making numerous attempts, which were unavailing. Kalaimoku also had it in his heart to die with him, but was prevented by Hookio.

The morning following Kamehameha's death, Liholiho and his train departed for Kohala, according to
the suggestions of the priest, to avoid the defilement
occasioned by the dead. At this time if a chief died
the land was polluted, and the heirs sought a residence
in another part of the country until the corpse was
dissected and the bones tied in a bundle, which being
done, the season of defilement terminated. If the deceased were not a chief, the house only was defiled,
which became pure again on the burial of the body.
Such were the laws on this subject.

On the morning on which Liholiho sailed in his
canoe for Kohala, the chiefs and people mourned after
their manner on occasion of a chief's death, conducting themselves like madmen and like beasts. Their
conduct was such as to forbid description. The priests,
also, put into action the sorcery apparatus, that the
person who had prayed the King to death might die;
for it was not believed that Kamehameha's departure
was the effect either of sickness or old age. When the
sorcerers set up by their fireplaces sticks with a strip
of kapa flying at the top, the chief Keeaumoku, Kaahumanu's brother, came in a state of intoxication and
broke the flagstaff of the sorcerers, from which it was
inferred that Kaahumanu and her friends had been
instrumental in the King's death. On this account
they were subjected to abuse.

You have the contrast, now, and a strange one it is. This
great Queen, Kaahumanu, who was "subjected to abuse"
during the frightful orgies that followed the King's death,

in accordance with an ancient custom, afterwards became a devout Christian and a steadfast and powerful friend of the missionaries.

MARK TWAIN

POSTSCRIPT—THE MINISTERS

Burlingame and Van Valkenburgh, United States Ministers to China and Japan, are ready to sail, but are delayed by the absence of two attachés, who went to Hawaii to see the volcano, and who were not aware how slow a country this is to get around in. The journey to Hilo, which would be made anywhere else almost in eighteen or twenty hours, requires a week in the little interisland schooners.

Colonel Kalakaua, the King's Chamberlain, has invited the Ministerial party to a great *luau* (native dinner) at Waikiki.

General Van Valkenburgh has achieved a distinguished success as a curiosity finder—not hunter. Standing on the celebrated Pari, a day or two ago, and amusing himself by idly punching into the compact lava wall through which the road is cut, he crumbled away a chunk of it, and observing something white sticking to it, he instituted an examination, and found a sound, white, unmarred, and unblemished human jaw tooth firmly embedded in the lava! Now the question is, how did it get there—in the side (where a road had been cut in) of a mountain of lava —seven hundred feet above the valley? a mountain which has been there for ages, this being one of the oldest islands in the group. Burlingame was present, and saw the general unearth his prize. I have critically examined it, but, as I half expected myself, the world knows as much about how to account for the wonder now as if I had let it alone. In old times, the bones of chiefs were often thrown into the volcanoes, to make sure that no enemy could get a chance to meddle with them; and Brown has given it as his deliberate opinion that "that old snag used to belong to one of them fellows." Possibly—but the opinion comes from a source which entitles it to but little weight. However, that tooth is as notable a curiosity as any I have yet seen in the Sandwich Islands.

M. T.

18❀

HONOLULU, JULY, 1866.

AT SEA AGAIN

Bound for Hawaii, to visit the great volcano and behold the other notable things which distinguish this island above the remainder of the group, we sailed from Honolulu on a certain Saturday afternoon, in the good schooner *Boomerang*.

The *Boomerang* was about as long as two streetcars, and about as wide as one. She was so small (though she was larger than the majority of the interisland coasters) that when I stood on her deck I felt but little smaller than the Colossus of Rhodes must have felt when he had a man-of-war under him. I could reach the water when she lay over under a strong breeze. When the captain and Brown and myself and four other gentlemen and the wheelsman were all assembled on the little after portion of the deck which is sacred to the cabin passengers, it was full—there was not room for any more quality folks. Another section of the deck, twice as large as ours, was full of natives of both sexes, with their customary dogs, mats, blankets, pipes, calabashes of poi, fleas, and other luxuries and baggage of minor importance. As soon as we set sail the natives all laid down on the deck as thick as Negroes in a slave pen, and smoked and conversed and captured vermin and ate them, spit on each other, and were truly sociable.

The little low-ceiled cabin below was rather larger than a hearse, and as dark as a vault. It had two coffins on each side—I mean two bunks—though Mr. Brown, with that spirit of irreverence which is so sad a feature of his nature, preferred to call the bunk he was allotted his shelf. A small table, capable of accommodating three persons at dinner, stood against the forward bulkhead, and over it hung the dingiest whale-oil lantern that ever peopled the obscurity of a dungeon with grim and ghostly shapes. The floor room unoccupied was not extensive. One might swing a cat in it, perhaps, but then it would be fatal to the cat to do it. The hold forward of the bulkhead had but little freight in it, and from morning till night a villainous old rooster, with a voice like Balaam's ass, and the same disposition to use it, strutted up and down in that part of the vessel and crowed. He usually took dinner at six o'clock, and then, after an hour devoted to meditation, he mounted a barrel and crowed a good part of the night. He got hoarser and hoarser all the time, but he scorned to allow any personal consideration to interfere with his duty, and kept up his labors in defiance of threatened diphtheria.

Sleeping was out of the question when he was on watch. He was a source of genuine aggravation and annoyance to me. It was worse than useless to shout at him or apply offensive epithets to him—he only took these things for applause, and strained himself to make more noise. Occasionally, during the day, I threw potatoes at him through an aperture in the bulkhead, but he simply dodged them and went on crowing.

The first night, as I lay in my coffin, idly watching the

dim lamp swinging to the rolling of the ship, and snuffing the nauseous odors of bilge water, I felt something gallop over me. Lazarus did not come out of his sepulcher with a more cheerful alacrity than I did out of mine. However, I turned in again when I found it was only a rat. Presently something galloped over me once more. I knew it was not a rat this time, and I thought it might be a centipede, because the captain had killed one on deck in the afternoon. I turned out. The first glance at the pillow showed me a repulsive sentinel perched upon each end of it—cockroaches as large as peach leaves—fellows with long, quivering antennae and fiery, malignant eyes. They were grating their teeth like tobacco worms, and appeared to be dissatisfied about something. I had often heard that these reptiles were in the habit of eating off sleeping sailors' toenails down to the quick, and I would not get in the bunk anymore. I laid down on the floor. But a rat came and bothered me, and shortly afterward a procession of cockroaches arrived and camped in my hair. In a few moments the rooster was crowing with uncommon spirit and a party of fleas were throwing double somersaults about my person in the wildest disorder, and taking a bite every time they struck. I was beginning to feel really annoyed. I got up and put my clothes on and went on deck.

The above is not an attempt to be spicy; it is simply an attempt to give a truthful sketch of interisland schooner life. There is no such thing as keeping a vessel in elegant condition, I think, when she carries molasses and Kanakas.

"ROLL ON, SILVER MOON"

It was compensation for all my sufferings to come unexpectedly upon so beautiful a scene as met my eye—to

step suddenly out of the sepulchral gloom of the cabin and
stand under the strong light of the moon—in the center,
as it were, of a glittering sea of liquid silver, to see the broad
sails straining in the gale, the ship keeled over on her side,
and the angry foam hissing past her lee bulwarks, and
sparkling sheets of spray dashing high over her bows and
raining upon her decks; to brace myself and hang fast to
the first object that presented itself, with hat jammed
down and coattails whipping in the breeze, and feel that
exhilaration that thrills in one's hair and quivers down his
backbone when he knows that every inch of canvas is
drawing and the vessel cleaving through the billows at her
utmost speed. There was no darkness, no dimness, no obscurity there. All was brightness, every object was vividly
defined. Every prostrate Kanaka; every coil of rope; every
calabash of poi; every puppy; every seam in the flooring;
every bolthead; every object, however minute, showed
sharp and distinct in its every outline; and the shadow of
the broad mainsail lay black as a pall upon the deck, leaving
Brown's white upturned face glorified and his body in a
total eclipse.

I ENDEAVOR TO ENTERTAIN THE SEASICK MAN

I turned to look down upon the sparkling animalculae
of the South Seas and watch the train of jeweled fire they
made in the wake of the vessel. I—

"Oh, me!"

"What is the matter, Brown?"

"Oh, me!"

"You said that before, Brown. Such tautology—"

"Tautology be hanged! This is no time to talk to a man
about tautology when he is sick—so sick—oh, my! and

has vomited up his heart and—ah, me—oh my! hand me that soup dish, and don't stand there hanging to that bulk-head looking like a fool!"

I handed him the absurd tin shaving pot, called "berth pan," which they hang by a hook to the edge of a berth for the use of distressed landsmen with unsettled stomachs, but all the sufferer's efforts were fruitless—his tortured stomach refused to yield up its cargo.

I do not often pity this bitter enemy to sentiment—he would not thank me for it, anyhow—but now I did pity him; and I pitied him from the bottom of my heart. Any man, with any feeling, must have been touched to see him in such misery. I did not try to help him—indeed I did not even think of so unpromising a thing—but I sat down by him to talk to him and so cause the tedious hours to pass less wearily, if possible. I talked to him for some time, but strangely enough, pathetic narratives did not move his emotions, eloquent declamation did not inspirit him, and the most humorous anecdotes failed to make him even smile. He seemed as distressed and restless, at intervals—albeit the rule of his present case was to seem to look like an allegory of unconditional surrender—hopeless, helpless, and indifferent—he seemed as distressed and restless as if my conversation and my anecdotes were irksome to him. It was because of this that at last I dropped into poetry. I said I had been writing a poem—or rather, been paraphrasing a passage in Shakespeare—a passage full of wisdom, which I thought I might remember easier if I reduced it to rhyme —hoped it would be pleasant to him—said I had taken but few liberties with the original; had preserved its brevity and terseness, its language as nearly as possible, and its ideas

in their regular sequence—and proceeded to read it to him,
as follows:

POLONIUS' ADVICE TO HIS SON—
PARAPHRASED FROM HAMLET

Beware of the spoken word! Be wise;
  Bury thy thoughts in thy breast;
Nor let thoughts that are unnatural
  Be ever in acts expressed.

Be thou courteous and kindly toward all—
  Be familiar and vulgar with none;
But the friends thou hast proved in thy need,
  Hold thou fast till life's mission is done!

Shake not thy faith by confiding
  In every new-begot friend,
Beware thou of quarrels—but, in them,
  Fight them out to the bitter end.

Give thine ear unto all that would seek it,
  But to few thy voice impart;
Receive and consider all censure,
  But thy judgment seal in thy heart.

Let thy habit be ever as costly
  As thy purse is able to span;
Never gaudy, but rich—for the raiment
  Full often proclaimeth the man.

Neither borrow nor lend—oft a loan
  Both loseth itself and a friend,
And to borrow relaxeth the thrift
  Whereby husbandry gaineth its end.

But lo! above all set this law:
UNTO THYSELF BE THOU TRUE!
Then never toward any canst thou
The deed of a false heart do.

As I finished, Brown's stomach cast up its contents, and in a minute or two he felt entirely relieved and comfortable. He then said that the anecdotes and the eloquence were "no good," but if he got seasick again, he would like some more poetry.

THE ZONES OF THE EARTH CONCENTRATED

Monday morning we were close to the island of Hawaii. Two of its high mountains were in view—Mauna Loa and Hualalai. The latter is an imposing peak, but being only ten thousand feet high is seldom mentioned or heard of. Mauna Loa is fourteen thousand feet high. The rays of glittering snow and ice, that clasped its summit like a claw, looked refreshing when viewed from the blistering climate we were in. One could stand on that mountain (wrapped up in blankets and furs to keep warm), and while he nibbled a snowball or an icicle to quench his thirst he could look down the long sweep of its sides and see spots where plants are growing that grow only where the bitter cold of winter prevails; lower down he could see sections devoted to productions that thrive in the temperate zone alone; and at the bottom of the mountain he could see the home of the tufted coco palms and other species of vegetation that grow only in the sultry atmosphere of eternal summers. He could see all the climes of the world at a single glance of the eye, and that glance would only pass over a distance of eight or ten miles as the bird flies.

THE REFUGE FOR THE WEARY

We landed at Kailua (pronounced Ki-loo-ah), a little collection of native grass houses reposing under tall coconut trees—the sleepiest, quietest, Sundayest looking place you can imagine. Ye weary ones that are sick of the labor and care, and the bewildering turmoil of the great world, and sigh for a land where ye may fold your tired hands and slumber your lives peacefully away, pack up your carpet sacks and go to Kailua! A week there ought to cure the saddest of you all.

An old ruin of lava-block walls down by the sea was pointed out as a fort built by John Adams for Kamehameha I, and mounted with heavy guns—some of them 32-pounders—by the same sagacious Englishman. I was told that the fort was dismantled a few years ago, and the guns sold in San Francisco for old iron—which was very improbable. I was told that an adjacent ruin was old Kamehameha's sleeping house; another, his eating house; another, his god's house; another, his wife's eating house—for by the ancient tabu system, it was death for man and woman to eat together. Every married man's premises comprised five or six houses. This was the law of the land. It was this custom, no doubt, which has left every pleasant valley in these islands marked with the ruins of numerous house enclosures, and given strangers the impression that the population must have been vast before those houses were deserted; but the argument loses much of its force when you come to consider that the houses absolutely necessary for half a dozen married men were sufficient in themselves to form one of the deserted "villages" so frequently pointed out to the "Californian" (to the natives all whites are haoles—

how-ries—that is, strangers, or, more properly, foreigners; and to the white residents all white newcomers are "Californians"—the term is used more for convenience than anything else).

I was told, also, that Kailua was old Kamehameha's favorite place of residence, and that it was always a favorite place of resort with his successors. Very well, if Kailua suits these kings—all right. Every man to his taste; but, as Brown observed in this connection, "You'll excuse *me*."

STEWED CHICKEN—MIRACULOUS BREAD

I was told a good many other things concerning Kailua —not one of which interested me in the least. I was weary and worn with the plunging of the *Boomerang* in the always stormy passages between the islands; I was tired of hanging on by teeth and toenails; and, above all, I was tired of stewed chicken. All I wanted was an hour's rest on a foundation that would let me stand up straight without running any risk—but no information; I wanted something to eat that was not stewed chicken—I didn't care what—but no information. I took no notes, and had no inclination to take any.

Now, the foregoing is nothing but the feverish irritability of a short, rough sea voyage coming to the surface—a voyage so short that it affords no time for you to tone down and grow quiet and reconciled, and get your stomach in order, and the bad taste out of your mouth, and the unhealthy coating off your tongue. I snarled at the old rooster and the cockroaches and the national stewed chicken all the time—not because these troubles could be removed, but only because it was a sanitary necessity to snarl at something or perish. One's salt-water spleen must be growled

out of the system—there is no other relief. I pined—I
longed—I yearned to growl at the captain himself, but
there was no opening. The man had had such passengers
before, I suppose, and knew how to handle them, and so he
was polite and painstaking and accommodating—and most
exasperatingly patient and even tempered. So I said to myself, "I will take it out of your old schooner, anyhow; I
will blackguard the *Boomerang,* in the public prints, to pay
for your shameless good nature when your passengers are
peevish and actually need somebody to growl at for very
relief!"

But now that I am restored by the land breeze, I wonder
at my ingratitude; for no man ever treated me better than
Captain Kangaroo did on board his ship. As for the stewed
chicken—that last and meanest substitute for something to
eat—that soothing rubbish for toothless infants—that diet
for cholera patients in the rice-water stage—it was, of
course, about the best food we could have at sea, and so
I only abused it because I hated it as I do sardines or to-
matoes, and because it was stewed chicken, and because it
was such a relief to abuse somebody or something. But
Kangaroo—I never abused Captain Kangaroo. I hope I
have a better heart than to abuse a man who, with the
kindest and most generous and unselfish motive in the
world, went into the galley, and with his own hands baked
for me the worst piece of bread I ever ate in my life. His
motive was good, his desire to help me was sincere, but his
execution was damnable. You see, I was not sick, but nothing would taste good to me; the Kanaka cook's bread was
particularly unpalatable; he was a new hand—the regular
cook being sick and helpless below—and Captain Kangaroo, in the genuine goodness of his heart, felt for me in my

distress and went down and made that most infernal bread. I ate one of those rolls—I would have eaten it if it had killed me—and said to myself: "It is on my stomach; 'tis well; if it were on my conscience, life would be a burden to me." I carried one up to Brown and he ate a piece, but declined to experiment further. I insisted, but he said no, he didn't want any more ballast. When the good deeds of men are judged in the Great Day that is to bring bliss or eternal woe unto us all, the charity that was in Captain Kangaroo's heart will be remembered and rewarded, albeit his bread will have been forgotten for ages.

THE FAMOUS ORANGE AND COFFEE REGION

It was only about fifteen miles from Kailua to Kealakekua Bay, either by sea or land, but by the former route there was a point to be weathered where the ship would be the sport of contrary winds for hours, and she would probably occupy the entire day in making the trip, whereas we could do it on horseback in a little while and have the cheering benefit of a respite from the discomforts we had been experiencing on the vessel. We hired horses from the Kanakas, and miserable affairs they were, too. They had lived on meditation all their lives, no doubt, for Kailua is fruitful in nothing else. I will mention, in this place, that horses are plenty everywhere in the Sandwich Islands—no Kanaka is without one or more—but when you travel from one island to another, it is necessary to take your own saddle and bridle, for these articles are scarce. It is singular baggage for a sea voyage, but it will not do to go without it.

The ride through the district of Kona to Kealakekua Bay took us through the famous coffee and orange section.

I think the Kona coffee has a richer flavor than any other, be it grown where it may and call it by what name you please. At one time it was cultivated quite extensively, and promised to become one of the great staples of Hawaiian commerce; but the heaviest crop ever raised was almost entirely destroyed by a blight, and this, together with heavy American customs duties, had the effect of suddenly checking enterprise in this direction. For several years the coffee growers fought the blight with all manner of cures and preventives, but with small success, and at length some of the less persevering abandoned coffee growing altogether and turned their attention to more encouraging pursuits. The coffee interest has not yet recovered its former importance, but is improving slowly. The exportation of this article last year was over 268,000 pounds, and it is expected that the present year's yield will be much greater. Contrast the progress of the coffee interest with that of sugar, and the demoralizing effects of the blight upon the former will be more readily seen:

EXPORTATIONS

	1852	1865
Coffee, pounds	117,000	263,000
Sugar, pounds	730,000	15,318,097

Thus the sugar yield of last year was more than twenty times what it was in 1852, while the coffee yield has scarcely more than doubled.

The coffee plantations we encountered in our short journey looked well, and we were told that the crop was unusually promising.

There are no finer oranges in the world than those produced in the district of Kona; when new and fresh, they are delicious. The principal market for them is California, but of course they lose much of their excellence by so long a voyage. About 500,000 oranges were exported last year against 15,000 in 1852. The orange culture is safe and sure, and is being more and more extensively engaged in every year. We passed one orchard that contained ten thousand orange trees.

There are many species of beautiful trees in Kona—noble forests of them—and we had numberless opportunities of contrasting the orange with them. The verdict rested with the orange. Among the varied and handsome foliage of the kou, koa, kukui, breadfruit, mango, guava, peach, citron, ohia, and other fine trees, its dark, rich green cone was sure to arrest the eye and compel constant exclamations of admiration. So dark a green is its foliage, that at a distance of a quarter of a mile the orange tree looks almost black.

WOODLAND SCENERY

The ride from Kailua to Kealakekua Bay is worth taking. It passes along on high ground—say a thousand feet above sea level—and usually about a mile distant from the ocean, which is always in sight, save that occasionally you find yourself buried in the forest in the midst of a rank, tropical vegetation and a dense growth of trees, whose great boughs overarch the road and shut out sun and sea and everything, and leave you in a dim, shady tunnel, haunted with invisible singing birds and fragrant with the odor of flowers. It was pleasant to ride occasionally in the warm sun, and feast the eye upon the ever-changing panorama of the forest (beyond and below us), with its many tints, its softened lights and shadows, its billowy undulations sweeping gently down from the mountain to the sea. It was pleasant also, at intervals, to leave the sultry sun and pass into the cool, green depths of this forest and indulge in sentimental reflections under the inspiration of its brooding twilight and its whispering foliage. The jaunt through Kona will always be to me a happy memory.

MARK TWAIN

19✿

CONCERNING MATTERS AND THINGS

At one farmhouse we got some large peaches of excellent flavor while on our horseback ride through Kona. This fruit, as a general thing, does not do well in the Sandwich Islands. It takes a sort of almond shape, and is small and bitter. It needs frost, they say, and perhaps it does; if this be so, it will have a good opportunity to go on needing it, as it will not be likely to get it. The trees from which the fine fruit I have spoken of came had been planted and replanted over and over again, and to this treatment the proprietor of the orchard attributed his success.

We passed several sugar plantations—new ones and not very extensive. The crops were, in most cases, third ratoons. (NOTE: The first crop is called "plant cane"; subsequent crops which spring from the original roots, without replanting, are called "ratoons.") Almost everywhere on the island of Hawaii sugarcane matures in twelve months, both ratoons and plant, and although it ought to be taken off as soon as it tassels, no doubt, it is not absolutely necessary to do it until about four months afterward. In Kona, the average yield of an acre of ground is two tons of sugar, they say. This is only a moderate yield for these islands, but would be extraordinary for Louisiana and most other sugar-growing countries. The plantations in Kona being on pretty high ground—up among the light and frequent rains—no irrigation whatever is required.

In Central Kona there is but little idle cane land now, but there is a good deal in North and South Kona. There are thousands of acres of cane land unoccupied on the island of Hawaii, and the prices asked for it range from one dollar to a hundred and fifty an acre. It is owned by common natives, and is lying "out of doors." They make no use of it whatever, and yet, here lately, they seem disinclined to either lease or sell it. I was frequently told this. In this connection it may not be out of place to insert an extract from a book of Hawaiian travels recently published by a visiting minister of the gospel:

"Well, now, *I* wouldn't, if I was you."

"Brown, I *wish* you wouldn't look over my shoulder when I am writing; and I wish you would indulge yourself in some little respite from my affairs and interest yourself in your own business sometimes."

"Well, I don't care. I'm disgusted with these mush-and-milk preacher travels, and I wouldn't make an extract from one of them. Father Damon has got stacks of books shoemakered up by them pious bushwhackers from America, and they're the flattest reading—they are sicker than the smart things children say in the newspapers. Every preacher that gets lazy comes to the Sandwich Islands to 'recruit his health,' and then he goes back home and writes a book. And he puts in a lot of history, and some legends, and some manners and customs, and dead loads of praise of the missionaries for civilizing and Christianizing the natives, and says in considerable chapters how grateful the savage ought to be; and when there is a chapter to be filled out, and they haven't got anything to fill it out with, they shovel in a lot of Scripture—now *don't* they? You just look at Rev. Cheever's book and Anderson's—and when they come to the volcano, or any sort of heavy scenery, and it is too much bother to describe it, they shovel in another lot of Scripture, and wind up with 'Lo! what God hath wrought!' Confound their lazy melts! [*sic*] Now, *I* wouldn't make extracts out of no such bosh."

"Mr. Brown, I brought you with me on this voyage merely because a newspaper correspondent should travel in some degree of state, and so command the respect of strangers; I did not expect you to assist me in my literary labors with your crude ideas. You may desist from further straining your intellect for the present, Mr. Brown, and proceed to the nearest depot and replenish the correspondent fountain of inspiration."

"Fountain dry now, of course. Confound me if I ever chance an opinion but I've got to trot down to the soda factory and fill up that cursed jug again. It seems to me that you need more inspiration—"

"Good afternoon, Brown."

The extract I was speaking of reads as follows:

We were in North Kona. The arable uplands in both the Konas are owned chiefly by foreigners. Indeed, the best of the lands on all the Islands appear to be fast going into foreign hands; and one of the allegations made to me by a foreign resident against the missionaries was that their influence was against such a transfer. The Rev. Mr. —————— told me, however, that to prevent the lands immediately about him, once owned by the admirable Kapiolani, from going to strangers he knew not who, he had felt obliged to invest his own private funds in them.

We naturally swell with admiration when we contemplate a sacrifice like this. But while I read the generous last words of that extract, it fills me with inexpressible satisfaction to know that the Rev. Mr. ———— had his reward. He paid fifteen hundred dollars for one of those pieces of land; he did not have to keep it long; without sticking a spade into it he sold it to a foreigner for ten thousand dollars in gold. Yet there be those among us who fear to trust the precious promise, "Cast thy bread upon the waters and it shall return unto thee after many days."

I have since been told that the original fifteen hundred dollars belonged to a ward of the missionary, and that inasmuch as the latter was investing it with the main view to doing his charge the best service in his power, and doubtless would not have felt at liberty to so invest it merely to protect the poor natives, his glorification in the book was not particularly gratifying to him. The other missionaries smile at the idea of their tribe "investing their own private funds" in this free and easy, this gay and affluent way— buying fifteen hundred dollars worth of land at a dash (salary four hundred dollars a year), and merely to do a trifling favor to some savage neighbor.

NATURE'S PRINTED RECORD IN THE LAVA

At four o'clock in the afternoon we were winding down a mountain of dreary and desolate lava to the sea, and closing our pleasant land journey. This lava is the accumulation of ages; one torrent of fire after another has rolled down here in old times, and built up the island structure higher and higher. Underneath, it is honeycombed with caves; it would be of no use to dig wells in such a place; they would not hold water—you would not find any for them to hold, for that matter. Consequently, the planters depend upon cisterns.

The last lava flow occurred here so long ago that there are none now living who witnessed it. In one place it inclosed and burned down a grove of coconut trees, and the holes in the lava where the trunks stood are still visible; their sides retain the impression of the bark; the trees fell upon the burning river, and becoming partly submerged, left in it the perfect counterfeit of every knot and branch and leaf, and even nut, for curiosity seekers of a long distant day to gaze upon and wonder at.

There were doubtless plenty of Kanaka sentinels on guard hereabouts at that time, but they did not leave casts of their figures in the lava as the Roman sentinels at Herculaneum and Pompeii did. It is a pity it is so, because such things are so interesting, but so it is. They probably went away. They went away early, perhaps. It was very bad. However, they had their merits; the Romans exhibited the higher pluck, but the Kanakas showed the sounder judgment.

As usual, Brown loaded his unhappy horse with fifteen or twenty pounds of "specimens," to be cursed and worried over for a time, and then discarded for new toys of a similar nature. He is like most people who visit these islands; they are always collecting specimens, with a wild enthusiasm, but they never get home with any of them.

CAPTAIN COOK'S DEATH-PLACE

Shortly we came in sight of that spot whose history is so familiar to every schoolboy in the wide world—Kealakekua Bay—the place where Captain Cook, the great circumnavigator, was killed by the natives nearly a hundred years ago. The setting sun was flaming upon it, a summer shower was falling, and it was spanned by two magnificent rainbows. Two gentlemen who were in advance of us rode through one of these, and for a moment their garments shone with a more than regal splendor. Why did not Captain Cook have taste enough to call his great discovery the Rainbow Islands? These charming spectacles are present to you at every turn; they are as common in all the islands as fogs and wind in San Francisco; they are visible every day, and frequently at night also—not the silvery bow we see once in an age in the States, by moonlight, but barred with all bright and beautiful colors, like the children of the sun and rain. I saw one of them a few nights ago. What the sailors call "rain dogs"—little patches of rainbow—are often seen drifting about the heavens in these latitudes, like stained cathedral windows.

Kealakekua Bay is a little curve like the last kink of a snail shell, winding deep into the land, seemingly not more than a mile wide from shore to shore. It is bounded on one side—where the murder was done—by a little flat plain, on which stands a coconut grove and some ruined houses; a steep wall of lava, a thousand feet high at the upper end and three or four hundred at the lower, comes down from the mountain and bounds the inner extremity of it. From this wall the place takes its name, *Kealakekua,* which in the native tongue signifies "the pathway of the Gods." They say (and still believe, in spite of their liberal education in Christianity), that the great god Lono, who used to live upon the hillside, always traveled that causeway when urgent business connected with heavenly affairs called him down to the seashore in a hurry.

As the red sun looked across the placid ocean through the tall, clean stems of the coconut trees, like a blooming whiskey bloat through the bars of a city prison, I went and stood in the edge of the water on the flat rock pressed by Captain Cook's feet when the blow was dealt that took away his life, and tried to picture in my mind the doomed man struggling in the midst of the multitude of exasperated savages—the men in the ship crowding to the vessel's side and gazing in anxious dismay toward the shore—the—

But I discovered that I could not do it.

It was growing dark, the rain began to fall, we could see that the distant *Boomerang* was helplessly becalmed at sea, and so I adjourned to the cheerless little box of a warehouse and sat down to smoke and think, and wish the ship would make the land—for we had not eaten much for the ten hours and were viciously hungry.

THE STORY OF CAPTAIN COOK

Plain unvarnished history takes the romance out of Captain Cook's assassination, and renders a deliberate verdict of justifiable homicide. Wherever he went among the Islands, he was cordially received and welcomed by the inhabitants, and his ships lavishly supplied with all manner of food. He returned these kindnesses with insult and ill-treatment.

When he landed at Kealakekua Bay, a multitude of natives, variously estimated at from ten to fifteen thousand, flocked about him and conducted him to the principal temple with more than royal honors—with honors suited to their chiefest god, for such they took him to be. They called him Lono—a deity who had resided at that place in a former age, but who had gone away and had ever since been anxiously expected back by the people. When Cook approached the awestricken people, they prostrated themselves and hid their faces. His coming was announced in a loud voice by heralds, and those who had not time to get out of the way after prostrating themselves were trampled under foot by the following throngs. Arrived at the temple, he was taken into the most sacred part and placed before the principal idol, immediately under an altar of wood on which a putrid hog was deposited. "This was held toward him while the priest repeated a long and rapidly enunciated address, after which he was led to the top of a partially decayed scaffolding. Ten men, bearing a large hog and bundles of red cloth, then entered the temple and prostrated themselves before him. The cloth was taken from them by the priest, who encircled Cook with it in numerous folds, and afterward offered the hog to him in sacrifice. Two priests, alternately and in unison, chanted praises in honor of Lono, after which they led him to the chief idol, which, following their example, he kissed." He was anointed by the high priest—that is to say, his arms, hands, and face, were slimed over with the chewed meat of a coconut; after this nasty compliment, he was regaled with awa manufactured in the mouths of attendants and spit out into a drinking vessel; "as the last most delicate attention, he was fed with swine meat which had been masticated for him by a filthy old man" [Jarves, *op. cit.*, p. 114].

These distinguished civilities were never offered by the

Islanders to mere human beings. Cook was mistaken for their absent god; he accepted the situation and helped the natives to deceive themselves. His conduct might have been wrong, in a moral point of view, but his policy was good in conniving at the deception, and proved itself so; the belief that he was a god saved him a good while from being killed —protected him thoroughly and completely, until, in an unlucky moment, it was discovered that he was only a man. His death followed instantly. Jarves, from whose history, principally, I am condensing this narrative, thinks his destruction was a direct consequence of his dishonest personation of the god, but unhappily for the argument, the historian proves, over and over again, that the false Lono was spared time and again when simple Captain Cook of the Royal Navy would have been destroyed with small ceremony.

The idolatrous worship of Captain Cook, as above described, was repeated at every heathen temple he visited. Wherever he went, the terrified common people, not being accustomed to seeing gods marching around of their own free will and accord and without human assistance, fled at his approach or fell down and worshiped him. A priest attended him and regulated the religious ceremonies which constantly took place in his honor; offerings, chants, and addresses met him at every point. "For a brief period he moved among them an earthly god—observed, feared, and worshiped." During all this time the whole island was heavily taxed to supply the wants of the ships or contribute to the gratification of their officers and crews, and, as was customary in such cases, no return expected. "The natives rendered much assistance in fitting the ships and preparing them for their voyages."

At one time the King of the island laid a tabu upon his people, confining them to their houses for several days. This interrupted the daily supply of vegetables to the ships; several natives tried to violate the tabu, under threats made by Cook's sailors, but were prevented by a chief, who, for thus enforcing the laws of his country, had a musket fired over his head from one of the ships. This is related in "Cook's Voyages." The tabu was soon removed, and the Englishmen were favored with the boundless hospitality of the natives as before, except that the Kanaka women were interdicted from visiting the ships; formerly, with extravagant hospitality, the people had sent their wives and daughters on board themselves. The officers and sailors went freely about the island, and were everywhere laden with presents. The King visited Cook in royal state, and gave him a large number of exceeding costly and valuable presents—in return for which the resurrected Lono presented His Majesty a white linen shirt and a dagger—an instance of illiberality in every way discreditable to a god.

"On the 2d of February, at the desire of his commander, Captain King proposed to the priests to purchase for fuel the railing which surrounded the top of the temple of Lono! In this Cook manifested as little respect for the religion in the mythology of which he figured so conspicuously, as scruples in violating the divine precepts of his own. Indeed, throughout his voyages a spirit regardless of the rights and feelings of others, when his own were interested, is manifested, especially in his last cruise, which is a blot upon his memory."

Cook desecrated the holy places of the temple by storing supplies for his ships in them, and by using the level grounds within the enclosure as a general workshop for repairing his sails, etc.—ground which was so sacred that no common native dared to set his foot upon it. Ledyard, a Yankee sailor, who was with Cook, and whose journal is considered the most just and reliable account of this eventful period of the voyage, says two iron hatchets were offered for the temple railing, and when the sacrilegious proposition was refused by the priests with horror and indignation, it was torn down by order of Captain Cook and taken to the boats by the sailors, and the images which surmounted it removed and destroyed in the presence of the priests and chiefs.

The abused and insulted natives finally grew desperate under the indignities that were constantly being heaped upon them by men whose wants they had unselfishly relieved at the expense of their own impoverishment, and angered by some fresh baseness, they stoned a party of sailors and drove them to their boats. From this time onward Cook and the natives were alternately friendly and hostile until Sunday, the 14th, whose setting sun saw the circumnavigator a corpse.

Ledyard's account and that of the natives vary in no important particulars. A Kanaka, in revenge for a blow he had received at the hands of a sailor (the natives say he was flogged), stole a boat from one of the ships and broke it up to get the nails out of it. Cook determined to seize the King and remove him to his ship and keep him a prisoner until the boat was restored. By deception and smoothly-worded persuasion he got the aged monarch to the shore, but when they were about to enter the boat, a multitude of natives flocked to the place, and one raised a cry that their king was going to be taken away and killed. Great excitement ensued, and Cook's situation became perilous in the extreme. He had only a handful of marines and sailors with him, and the crowd of natives grew constantly larger and more clamorous every moment. Cook opened the hostilities himself. Hearing a native make threats, he had him pointed out, and fired on him with a blank cartridge. The man, finding himself unhurt, repeated his threats, and Cook fired again and wounded him mortally. A speedy retreat of the English party to the boats was now absolutely necessary; as soon as it was begun Cook was hit with a stone, and discovering who threw it, he shot the man dead. The officer in the boats observing the retreat, ordered the boats to fire; this occasioned Cook's guard to face about and fire also, and then the attack became general. Cook and Lieutenant Phillips were together a few paces in the rear of the guard, and perceiving a general fire without orders, quitted the King and ran to the shore to stop it; but not being able to make themselves heard, and being close pressed upon by the chiefs, they joined the guard, who fired as they retreated. Cook having at length reached the margin of the water, between the fire and the boats, waved with his hat for them to cease firing and come in; and while he was doing this, a chief stabbed him from behind with an iron dagger (procured in traffic with the sailors), just under the shoulder blade, and it passed quite through his body. Cook fell with his face in the water and immediately expired.

The native account says that after Cook had shot two men, he struck a stalwart chief with the flat of his sword, for some reason or other; the chief seized and pinioned Cook's arms in his powerful grip, and bent him backward over his knee (not meaning to hurt him, for it was not deemed possible to hurt the god Lono, but to keep him from doing further mischief) and this treatment giving him pain, he betrayed his mortal nature with a groan! It was his death warrant. The fraud which had served him so well was discovered at last. The natives shouted, "He groans!—he is not a god!" and instantly they fell upon him and killed him.

His flesh was stripped from the bones and burned (except nine pounds of it which were sent on board the ships). The heart was hung up in a native hut, where it was found and eaten by three children, who mistook it for the heart of a dog. One of these children grew to be a very old man, and died here in Honolulu a few years ago. A portion of Cook's bones were recovered and consigned to the deep by the officers of the ships.

Small blame should attach to the natives for the killing of Cook. They treated him well. In return, he abused them. He and his men inflicted bodily injury upon many of them at different times, and killed at least three of them before they offered any proportionate retaliation.

MARK TWAIN

20❀

KEALAKEKUA BAY (S. I.), 1866.

When I digressed from my personal narrative to write about Cook's death, I left myself, solitary, hungry, and dreary, smoking in the little warehouse at Kealakekua Bay. Brown was out somewhere gathering up a fresh lot of specimens, having already discarded those he dug out of the old lava flow during the afternoon. I soon went to look for him. He had returned to the great slab of lava upon which Cook stood when he was murdered, and was absorbed in maturing a plan for blasting it out and removing it to his home as a specimen. Deeply pained at the bare thought of such a sacrilege, I reprimanded him severely and at once removed him from the scene of temptation. We took a walk then, the rain having moderated considerably. We clambered over the surrounding lava field, through masses of weeds, and stood for a moment upon the doorstep of an ancient ruin—the house once occupied by the aged king of Hawaii—and I reminded Brown that that very stone step was the one across which Captain Cook drew the reluctant old king when he turned his footsteps for the last time toward his ship.

I checked a movement on Mr. Brown's part: "No," I said, "let it remain; seek specimens of a less hallowed nature than this historical stone."

We also strolled along the beach toward the precipice of Kealakekua, and gazed curiously at the semicircular holes high up in its face—graves, they are, of ancient kings and chiefs—and wondered how the natives ever managed to climb from the sea up the sheer wall and make those holes and deposit their packages of patrician bones in them.

Tramping about in the rear of the warehouse, we suddenly came upon another object of interest. It was a coconut stump, four or five feet high, and about a foot in diameter at the butt. It had lava boulders piled around its base to hold it up and keep it in its place, and it was entirely sheathed over, from top to bottom, with rough, discolored sheets of copper, such as ships' bottoms are coppered with. Each sheet had a rude inscription scratched upon it—with a nail, apparently—and in every case the execution was wretched. It was almost dark by this time, and the inscriptions would have been difficult to read even at noonday, but with patience and industry I finally got them all in my notebook. They read as follows:

Near this spot fell
CAPTAIN JAMES COOK,
The Distinguished Circumnavigator,
who Discovered these islands A.D. 1778.
His Majesty's Ship Imogene,
October 17, 1837.

Parties from H. M. Ship Vixen visited this spot Jan. 25, 1858.

This sheet and capping put on by Sparrowhawk, September 16, 1839, in order to preserve this monument to the memory of Cook.

Captain Montressor and officers of H.M.S. Calypso visited this spot the 18th of October, 1858.

This tree having fallen, was replaced on this spot by H. M. S. V. Cormorant, G. T. Gordon, Esq., Captain, who visited this bay May 18, 1846.

This bay was visited, July 4, 1843, by H. M. S. Carysfort, the Right Honorable Lord George Paulet, Captain, to whom, as the representative of Her Britannic Majesty Queen Victoria, these islands were ceded, February 25, 1843.

After Cook's murder, his second in command, on board the ship, opened fire upon the swarms of natives on the beach, and one of his cannon balls cut this coconut tree short off and left this monumental stump standing. It looked sad and lonely enough out there in the rainy twilight. But there is no other monument to Captain Cook. True, up on the mountain side we had passed by a large inclosure like an ample hogpen, built of lava blocks, which marks the spot where Cook's flesh was stripped from his bones and burned; but this is not properly a monument, since it was erected by the natives themselves, and less to do honor to the circumnavigator than for the sake of convenience in roasting him. A thing like a guideboard was elevated above this pen on a tall pole, and formerly there was an inscription upon it describing the memorable occurrence that had there taken place; but the sun and the wind have long ago so defaced it as to render it illegible.

"MUSIC SOOTHES THE SAD AND LONELY"

The sky grew overcast, and the night settled down gloomily. Brown and I went and sat on the little wooden pier, saying nothing, for we were tired and hungry and did not feel like talking. There was no wind; the drizzling, melancholy rain was still falling, and not a sound disturbed the brooding silence save the distant roar of the surf and the gentle washing of the wavelets against the rocks at our feet. We were very lonely. No sign of the vessel. She was still becalmed at sea, no doubt. After an hour of sentimental meditation, I bethought me of working upon the feelings of my comrade. The surroundings were in every way favorable to the experiment. I concluded to sing—partly because music so readily touches the tender emotions of the heart, and partly because the singing of pathetic ballads and such things is an art in which I have been said to excel. In a voice tremulous with feeling, I began:

" *'Mid pleasures and palaces though we may roam,*
   Be it ever so humble there's no place like home;
   H-o-m-e—ho-home—sweet, swe-he-he—"

My poor friend rose up slowly and came and stood before me and said:

"Now look a-here, Mark—it ain't no time, and it ain't no place, for you to be going on in that way. I'm hungry, and I'm tired and wet; and I ain't going to be put upon and aggravated when I'm so miserable. If you was to start in on any more yowling like that, I'd shove you overboard —I would, by geeminy."

"Poor vulgar creature," I said to myself, "he knows no

better. I have not the heart to blame him. How sad a lot is his, and how much he is to be pitied, in that his soul is dead to the heavenly charm of music. I cannot sing for this man; I cannot sing for him while he has that dangerous calm in his voice, at any rate."

HUNGER DRIVETH TO DESPERATE ENTERPRISES

We spent another hour in silence and in profound depression of spirits; it was so gloomy and so still, and so lonesome, with nothing human anywhere near save those bundles of dry kingly bones hidden in the face of the cliff. Finally Brown said it was hard to have to sit still and starve with plenty of delicious food and drink just beyond our reach—rich young coconuts! I said, "What an idiot you are not to have thought of it before. Get up and stir yourself; in five minutes we shall have a feast and be jolly and contented again!"

The thought was cheering in the last degree, and in a few moments we were in the grove of coco palms, and their ragged plumes were dimly visible through the wet haze, high above our heads. I embraced one of the smooth, slender trunks, with the thought of climbing it, but it looked very far to the top, and of course there were no knots or branches to assist the climber, and so I sighed and walked sorrowfully away.

"Thunder! what was that!"

It was only Brown. He had discharged a prodigious lava block at the top of a tree, and it fell back to the earth with a crash that tore up the dead silence of the place like an avalanche. As soon as I understood the nature of the case, I recognized the excellence of the idea. I said as much to Brown, and told him to fire another volley. I cannot throw lava blocks with any precision, never having been used to them, and therefore I apportioned our labor with that fact in view, and signified to Brown that he would only have to knock the coconuts down—I would pick them up myself.

Brown let drive with another boulder. It went singing through the air and just grazed a cluster of nuts hanging fifty feet above ground.

"Well done!" said I; "try it again."

He did so. The result was precisely the same.

"Well done again!" said I; "move your hindsight a shade to the left, and let her have it once more."

Brown sent another boulder hurling through the dingy air—too much elevation—it just passed over the coconut tuft.

"Steady, lad," said I; "you scatter too much. Now— one, two, fire!" and the next missile clove through the tuft and a couple of long, slender leaves came floating down to the earth. "Good!" I said, "depress your piece a line."

Brown paused and panted like an exhausted dog; then he wiped some perspiration from his face—a quart of it, he said—and discarded his coat, vest, and cravat. The next shot fell short. He said, "I'm letting down; them large boulders are monstrous responsible rocks to send up there, but they're rough on the arms."

He then sent a dozen smaller stones in quick succession after the fruit, and some of them struck in the right place, but the result was—nothing. I said he might stop and rest awhile.

"Oh, never mind," he said, "I don't care to take any advantage—I don't want to rest until you do. But it's singular to me how you always happen to divide up the work about the same way. I'm to knock 'em down, and you're to pick 'em up. I'm of the opinion that you're going to wear yourself down to just nothing but skin and bones on this trip, if you ain't more careful. Oh, don't mind about me resting—I can't be tired—I ain't hove only about eleven ton of rocks up into that liberty pole."

"Mr. Brown, I am surprised at you. This is mutiny."

"Oh, well, I don't care what it is—mutiny, sass, or what you please—I'm so hungry that I don't care for nothing."

It was on my lips to correct his loathsome grammar, but I considered the dire extremity he was in, and withheld the deserved reproof.

After some time spent in mutely longing for the coveted fruit, I suggested to Brown that if he would climb the tree I would hold his hat. His hunger was so great that he finally concluded to try it. His exercise had made him ravenous. But the experiment was not a success. With infinite labor and a great deal of awkwardly-constructed swearing, he managed to get up some thirty feet, but then he came to an uncommonly smooth place and began to slide back slowly but surely. He clasped the tree with his arms and legs, and tried to save himself, but he had got too much sternway, and the thing was impossible; he dragged for a few feet and then shot down like an arrow.

"It is tabu," he said sadly. "Let's go back to the pier. The transom to my trousers has all fetched away, and the legs of them are riddled to rags and ribbons. I wish I was drunk or dead or something—anything so as to be out of this misery."

I glanced over my shoulders, as we walked along, and observed that some of the clouds had parted and left a dim lighted doorway through to the skies beyond; in this place, as in an ebony frame, our majestic palm stood up and reared its graceful crest aloft; the slender stem was a clean, black line; the feathers of the plume—some erect, some projecting horizontally, some drooping a little and others hanging languidly down toward the earth—were all sharply cut against the smooth gray background.

"A beautiful, beautiful tree is the coco palm!" I said fervently.

"I don't see it," said Brown resentfully. "People that haven't clumb one are always driveling about how pretty it is. And when they make pictures of these hot countries they always shove one of the ragged things into the foreground. I don't see what there is about it that's handsome; it looks like a feather duster struck by lightning."

Perceiving that Brown's mutilated pantaloons were disturbing his gentle spirit, I said no more.

PROVIDENTIALLY SAVED FROM STARVATION

Toward midnight a native boy came down from the uplands to see if the *Boomerang* had got in yet, and we chartered him for subsistence service. For the sum of twelve and a half cents in coin he agreed to furnish coconuts enough for a dozen men at five minutes' notice. He disappeared in the murky atmosphere, and in a few seconds we saw a little black object, like a rat, running up our tall tree and pretty distinctly defined against the light place in the sky; it was our Kanaka, and he performed his contract without tearing his clothes—but then he had none on, except those he was born in. He brought five large nuts and tore the tough green husks off with his strong teeth, and thus prepared the fruit for use. We perceived then that it was about as well that we failed in our endeavors, as we never could have gnawed the husks off. I would have kept Brown trying, though, as long as he had any teeth. We punched the eyeholes out and drank the sweet (and at the same time pungent) milk of two of the nuts, and our hunger and thirst were satisfied. The boy broke them open and we ate some of the mushy, white paste inside for pastime, but we had no real need of it.

After a while a fine breeze sprang up and the schooner soon worked into the bay and cast anchor. The boat came ashore for us, and in a little while the clouds and the rain were gone. The moon was beaming tranquilly down on land and sea, and we two were stretched upon the deck sleeping the refreshing sleep and dreaming the happy dreams that are only vouchsafed to the weary and the innocent.

MARK TWAIN

21🏵

KEALAKEKUA BAY, JULY, 1866.

A FUNNY SCRAP OF HISTORY

In my last I spoke of the old coconut stump, all covered with copper plates bearing inscriptions commemorating the visits of various British naval commanders to Captain Cook's death place at Kealakekua Bay. The most magniloquent of these is that left by "the Right. Hon. Lord George Paulet, to whom, as the representative of Her Britannic Majesty Queen Victoria, the Sandwich Islands were ceded, February 25, 1843."

Lord George, if he is alive yet, would like to tear off that plate and destroy it, no doubt. He was fearfully snubbed by his government, shortly afterward, for his acts as Her Majesty's representative upon the occasion to which he refers with such manifest satisfaction.

A pestilent fellow by the name of Charlton had been Great Britain's consul at Honolulu for many years. He seems to have employed his time in sweating, fuming, and growling about everything and everybody; in acquiring property by devious and inscrutable ways; in blackguarding the Hawaiian Government and the missionaries; in scheming for the transfer of the islands to the British Crown; in getting the King drunk and laboring diligently to keep him so; in working to secure a foothold for the Catholic religion when its priests had been repeatedly forbidden by the King to settle in the country; in promptly raising thunder every time an opportunity offered, and in making himself prominently disagreeable and a shining nuisance at all times.

You will thus perceive that Charlton had a good deal of business on his hands. There was "a heap of trouble on the old man's mind."

He was sued in the Courts upon one occasion for a debt of long standing, amounting to three thousand pounds, and judgment rendered against him. This made him lively. He swore like the army in Flanders. But it was of no avail. The case was afterwards carefully examined twice—once by a commission of distinguished English gentlemen and once by the law officers of the British Crown—and the Hawaiian court's decision sustained in both instances. His property was attached, and one Skinner, a relative who had ten thousand dollars in bank, got ready to purchase it when it should be sold on execution. So far, so good.

Several other English residents had been worsted in lawsuits. They and Charlton became loud in their denunciation of what they termed a want of justice in the Hawaiian courts. The suits were all afterwards examined by the law officers of the British Crown, and the Hawaiian courts sustained, as in Charlton's case.

Charlton got disgusted, wrote a "sassy" letter to the King, and left suddenly for England, conferring his consulate, for the time being, upon a kindred spirit named Simpson, a bitter traducer of the Hawaiian Government—an officer whom the Government at once refused to recognize. Charlton left with Simpson a demand upon the Government for possession of a large and exceedingly valuable tract of land in Honolulu, alleged to have been transferred to him by a deed duly signed by a native gentleman, who had never owned the property, and whose character for probity was such that no one would believe he ever would have been guilty of such a proceeding. Charity compels us to presume that the versatile Charlton forged the deed. The boundaries, if specified, were vaguely defined; it contained no mention of a consideration for value received; it had been held in abeyance and unmentioned for twenty years, and its signer and witnesses were long since dead. It was a shaky instrument altogether.

On his way to England Charlton met my Lord George in a Queen's ship, and laid his grievances before him, and then went on. My lord sailed straight to Honolulu and began to make trouble. Under threats of bombarding the town, he compelled the King to make the questionable deed good to the person having charge of Charlton's property interests; demanded the reception of the new consul; demanded that all those suits—a great number—which had been decided adversely to Englishmen (including many which had even been settled by amicable arbitration between the parties) should be tried over again, and by juries composed entirely of Englishmen, although the written law provided that but half the panel should be English, and therefore, of course, the demand could not be complied with without a tyrannical assumption of power by the King; he stopped the seizure and sale of Charlton's property; he brought in a little bill (gotten up by the newly-created and promptly-emasculated consul, Simpson) for $117,000 and some odd change—enough to "bust" the Hawaiian exchequer two or three times over—to use a

popular missionary term—for all manner of imaginary
damages sustained by British subjects at divers and sundry
times, and among the items was one demanding three thousand dollars to indemnify Skinner for having kept his ten
thousand dollars lying idle for four months, expecting to
invest it in Charlton's property, and then not getting a
chance to do it on account of Lord George having stopped
the sale. An exceedingly nice party was Lord George, take
him all around.

For days and nights together the unhappy Kamehameha
III was in bitterest distress. He could not pay the bill, and
the law gave him no power to comply with the other de-
mands. He and his Ministers of State pleaded for mercy
—for time to remodel the laws to suit the emergency. But
Lord George refused steadfastly to accede to either request,
and finally, in tribulation and sorrow, the King told him
to take the Islands to do with them as he would; he knew
of no other way—his Government was too weak to main-
tain its rights against Great Britain.

And so Lord George took them and set up his government, and hauled down the royal Hawaiian ensign and
hoisted the English colors over the archipelago. And the sad
King notified his people of the event in a proclamation
which is touching in its simple eloquence:

> Where are you, chiefs, people, and commons from
> my ancestors, and people from foreign lands!
> Hear ye! I make known to you that I am in per-
> plexity by reason of difficulties into which I have been
> brought without cause; therefore I have given away
> the life of our land, hear ye! But my rule over you,
> my people, and your privileges will continue, for I

have hope that the life of the land will be restored when my conduct is justified.

KAMEHAMEHA III.

And then, I suppose, my Lord George Paulet, temporary King of the Sandwich Islands, went complacently skirmishing around his dominions in his ship, and feeding fat on glory—for we find him, four months later, visiting Kealakekua Bay and nailing *his* rusty sheet of copper to the memorial stump set up to glorify the great Cook—and imagining, no doubt, that his visit had conferred immortality upon a name which had only possessed celebrity before.

But my lord's happiness was not to last long. His superior officer, Rear Admiral Thomas, arrived at Honolulu a week or two afterward, and as soon as he understood the case he immediately showed the new government the door and restored Kamehameha to all his ancient powers and privileges. It was the 31st of July, 1843. There was immense rejoicing on Oahu that day. The Hawaiian flag was flung to the breeze. The King and as many of his people as could get into the great stone church went there to pray, and the balance got drunk. The 31st of July is Independence Day in the Sandwich Islands, and consequently in these times there are two grand holidays in the Islands in the month of July. The Americans celebrate the 4th with great pomp and circumstance, and the natives outdo them if they can, on the 31st—and the speeches disgorged upon both occasions are regularly inflicted in cold blood upon the people by the newspapers, that have a dreary fashion of coming out just a level week after one has forgotten any given circumstance they talk about.

A LUCRATIVE OFFICE

When I woke up on the schooner's deck in the morning, the sun was shining down right fervently, everybody was astir, and Brown was gone—gone in a canoe to Captain Cook's side of the bay, the captain said. I took a boat and landed on the opposite shore, at the port of entry. There was a house there—I mean a foreigner's house—and near it were some native grass huts. The collector of this port of entry not only enjoys the dignity of office, but has emoluments also. That makes it very nice, of course. He gets five dollars for boarding every foreign ship that stops there, and two dollars more for filling out certain blanks attesting such visit. As many as three foreign ships stop there in a single year, sometimes. Yet, notwithstanding this wild rush of business, the late collector of the port committed suicide several months ago. The foreign ships which visit this place are whalers in quest of water and potatoes. The present collector lives back somewhere—has a den up the mountain several thousand feet—but he comes down fast enough when a ship heaves in sight.

WASHOE MEN

I found two Washoe men at the house. But I was not surprised; I believe if a man were to go to perdition itself he would find Washoe men there, though not so thick, maybe, as in the other place.

THE HOLY PLACE

Two hundred yards from the house was the ruins of the pagan temple of Lono, so desecrated by Captain Cook when he was pretending to be that deity. Its low, rude walls look about as they did when he saw them, no doubt. In a coconut grove near at hand is a tree with a hole through its trunk, said to have been made by a cannon ball fired from one of the ships at a crowd of natives immediately after Cook's murder. It is a very good hole.

THE HERO OF THE SUNDAY SCHOOL BOOKS

The high chief cook of this temple—the priest who presided over it and roasted the human sacrifices—was uncle to Obookia, and at one time that youth was an apprentice priest under him. Obookia was a young native of fine mind, who, together with three other native boys, was taken to New England by the captain of a whale ship during the reign of Kamehameha I, and were the means of attracting the attention of the religious world to their country and putting it into their heads to send missionaries there. And this Obookia was the very same sensitive savage who sat down on the church steps and wept because his people did not have the Bible. That incident has been very elaborately painted in many a charming Sunday School book—aye, and told so plaintively and so tenderly that I have cried over it in Sunday School myself, on general principles, although at a time when I did not know much and could not understand why the people of the Sandwich Islands need care a cent about it as long as they did not know there was a Bible at all. This was the same Obookia—this was the very same old Obookia—so I reflected, and gazed upon the ruined temple with a new and absorbing interest. Here that gentle spirit worshiped; here he sought the better life, after his rude fashion; on this stone, perchance, he sat down with his sacred lasso, to wait for a chance to rope in some neighbor for the holy sacrifice; on this altar, possibly, he broiled his venerable grandfather, and presented the rare offering before the high priest, who may have said, "Well done, good and faithful servant." It filled me with emotion.

KANUI THE UNFORTUNATE

Obookia was converted and educated, and was to have returned to his native land with the first missionaries, had he lived. The other native youths made the voyage, and two of them did good service, but the third, Wm. Kanui, fell from grace afterward, for a time, and when the gold excitement broke out in California he journeyed thither and went to mining, although he was fifty years old. He succeeded pretty well, but the failure of Page, Bacon & Co. relieved him of six thousand dollars, and then, to all intents and purposes, he was a bankrupt community. Thus, after all his toils, all his privations, all his faithful endeavors to gather together a competence, the blighting hand of poverty was laid upon him in his old age and he had to go back to preaching again. One cannot but feel sad to contemplate such afflictions as these cast upon a creature so innocent and deserving.

And finally he died—died in Honolulu in 1864. The Rev. Mr. Damon's paper, referring—in the obituary notice —to Page-Bacon's unpaid certificates of deposit in the unhappy man's possession, observes that "he departed this life leaving the most substantial and gratifying evidence that he was prepared to die." And so he was, poor fellow, so he was. He was cleaned out, as you may say, and was prepared to go. He was all ready and prepared—Page-Bacon had attended to that for him. All he had to do was to shed his mortal coil. Then he was all right. Poor, poor old fellow. One's heart bleeds for him.

For some time after his bereavement in the matter of finances, he helped Rev. M. Rowell to carry on the Bethel Church in San Francisco and gave excellent satisfaction for a man who was so out of practice. Sleep in peace, poor tired soul!—you were out of luck many a time in your long, checkered life, but you are safe now where care and sorrow and trouble can never assail you any more.

TEMPLE TO THE RAIN GOD

Quite a broad tract of land near that port of entry, extending from the sea to the mountain top, was sacred to the god Lono in olden times—so sacred that if a common native set his sacrilegious foot upon it it was time for him to make his will, because his time was come. He might go around it by water, but he could not cross it. It was well sprinkled with pagan temples and stocked with awkward, homely idols carved out of logs of wood. There was a temple devoted to prayers for rain—and with rare sagacity it was placed at a point so well up on the mountain side that if you prayed there twenty-four times a day for rain you would be likely to get it every time. You would seldom get to your Amen before you would have to hoist your umbrella.

THE HOUSE BUILT BY THE DEAD MEN

And there was a large temple near at hand which was built in a single night, in the midst of storm and thunder and rain, by the ghastly hands of dead men! Tradition says that by the weird glare of the lightning a noiseless multitude of phantoms were seen at their strange labor far up the mountain side at dead of night—flitting hither and thither and bearing great lava-blocks clasped in their nerveless fingers—appearing and disappearing as the fitful lightning fell upon their pallid forms and faded away again. Even to this day, it is said, the natives hold this dread structure in awe and reverence, and will not pass by it in the night.

VENUS AT THE BATH

At noon I observed a bevy of nude native young ladies bathing in the sea, and went down to look at them. But with a prudery which seems to be characteristic of that sex everywhere, they all plunged in with a lying scream, and when they rose to the surface, they only just poked their heads out and showed no disposition to proceed any further in the same direction. I was naturally irritated by such conduct, and therefore I piled their clothes up on a boulder in the edge of the sea and sat down on them and kept the wenches in the water until they were pretty well used up. I had them in the door, as the missionaries say. I was comfortable, and I just let them beg. I thought I could freeze them out, maybe, but it was impracticable. I finally gave it up and went away, hoping that the rebuke I had given them would not be lost upon them. I went and undressed and went in myself. And then they went out. I never saw such singular perversity. Shortly a party of children of both sexes came floundering around me, and then I quit and left the Pacific Ocean in their possession.

THE SHAMELESS BROWN

I got uneasy about Brown finally, and as there were no canoes at hand, I got a horse whereon to ride three or four miles around to the other side of the bay and hunt him up. As I neared the end of the trip, and was riding down "the

Pathway of the Gods" toward the sea in the sweltering sun, I saw Brown toiling up the hill in the distance, with a heavy burden on his shoulder, and knew that canoes were scarce with him, too. I dismounted and sat down in the shade of a crag, and after a while—after numerous pauses to rest by the way—Brown arrived at last, fagged out and puffing like a steamboat, and gently eased his ponderous burden to the ground—the coconut stump all sheathed with copper memorials to the illustrious Captain Cook.

"Heavens and earth!" I said, "what are you going to do with that?"

"Going to do with it!—lemme blow a little—lemme blow —it's monstrous heavy, that log is; I'm most tired out— going to do with it! Why, I'm going to take her home for a specimen."

"You egregious ass! March straight back again and put it where you got it. Why, Brown, I am surprised at you— and hurt. I am grieved to think that a man who has lived so long in the atmosphere of refinement which surrounds me can be guilty of such vandalism as this. Reflect, Brown, and say if it be right—if it be manly—if it be generous—to lay desecrating hands upon this touching tribute of a great nation to her gallant dead? Why, Brown, the circumnavigator Cook labored all his life in the service of his country; with a fervid soul and a fearless spirit, he braved the dangers of the unknown seas and planted the banner of England far and wide over their beautiful island world. His works have shed a glory upon his native land which still lives in her history today; he laid down his faithful life in her service at last, and unforgetful of her son, she yet reveres his name and praises his deeds—and in token of her love, and in reward for the things he did for her, she had reared this monument to his memory—this symbol of a nation's gratitude—which you would defile with unsanctified hands. Restore it—go!"

"All right, if you say so; but I don't see no use of such a spread as you're making. I don't see nothing so very high-toned about this old rotten chunk. It's about the orneryest thing for a monument I've ever struck yet. If it suits Cook, though, all right; I wish him joy; but if I was planted under it, I'd highst it, if it was the last act of my life. Monument! it ain't fit for a dog—I can buy dead loads of just such for six bits. She puts this over Cook—but she put one over that foreigner—what was his name?—Prince Albert—that cost a million dollars—and what did *he* do? Why, he never done anything—never done anything but lead a gallus, comfortable life, at home and out of danger, and raise a large family for government to board at £300,-000 a year apiece. But with this fellow, you know, it was different. However, if you say the old stump's got to go down again, down she goes. As I said before, if it's your wishes, I've got nothing to say. Nothing only this—I've fetched her a mile or a mile and a half, and she weighs a hundred and fifty, I should judge, and if it would suit Cook just as well to have her planted up here instead of down there, it would be considerable of a favor to me."

I made him shoulder the monument and carry it back, nevertheless. His criticisms on the monument and its patron struck me, though, in spite of myself. The creature has got no sense, but his vaporings sound strangely plausible sometimes.

In due time we arrived at the port of entry once more.

MARK TWAIN

22🌸

KEALAKEKUA BAY, JULY, 1866.

THE ROMANTIC GOD LONO

I have been writing a good deal, of late, about the great god Lono and Captain Cook's personation of him. Now, while I am here in Lono's home, upon ground which his terrible feet have trodden in remote ages—unless these natives lie, and they would hardly do that, I suppose—I might as well tell who he was.

The idol the natives worshiped for him was a slender, unornamented staff twelve feet long. Unpoetical history says he was a favorite god on the island of Hawaii—a great king who had been deified for meritorious services—just our own fashion of rewarding heroes, with the difference that we would have made him a postmaster instead of a god, no doubt. In an angry moment he slew his wife, a goddess named Kaikilani Alii. Remorse of conscience drove him mad, and tradition presents us the singular spectacle of a god traveling "on the shoulder"; for in his gnawing grief he wandered about from place to place, boxing and wrestling with all whom he met. Of course this pastime soon lost its novelty, inasmuch as it must necessarily have been the case that when so powerful a deity sent a frail human opponent "to grass," he never came back any more. There-

243

fore, he instituted games called *makahiki,* and ordered that they should be held in his honor, and then sailed for foreign lands on a three-cornered raft, stating that he would return some day, and that was the last of Lono. He was never seen anymore; his raft got swamped, perhaps. But the people always expected his return, and they were easily led to accept Captain Cook as the restored god.

THE POETIC TRADITION

But there is another tradition which is rather more poetical than this bald historical one. Lono lived in considerable style up here on the hillside. His wife was very beautiful, and he was devoted to her. One day he overheard a stranger proposing an elopement to her, and without waiting to hear her reply he took the stranger's life and then upbraided Kaikilani so harshly that her sensitive nature was wounded to the quick. She went away in tears, and Lono began to repent of his hasty conduct almost before she was out of sight. He sat him down under a coconut tree to await her return, intending to receive her with such tokens of affection and contrition as should restore her confidence and drive all sorrow from her heart. But hour after hour winged its tardy flight and yet she did not come. The sun went down and left him desolate. His all-wise instincts may have warned him that the separation was final, but he hoped on, nevertheless, and when the darkness was heavy, he built a beacon fire at his door to guide the wanderer home again, if by any chance she had lost her way. But the night waxed and waned and brought another day, but not the goddess. Lono hurried forth and sought her far and wide, but found no trace of her. At night he set his beacon fire again and kept lone watch, but still she came not; and a new day found him a despairing, brokenhearted god. His misery could no longer brook suspense and solitude, and he set out to look for her. He told his sympathizing people he was going to search through all the island world for the lost light of his household, and he would never come back any more till he found her. The natives always implicitly believed that he was still pursuing his patient quest and that he would find his peerless spouse again some day, and come back; and so, for ages they waited and watched in trusting simplicity for his return. They gazed out wistfully over the sea at any strange appearance on its waters, thinking it might be their loved and lost protector. But Lono was to them as the rainbow-tinted future seen in happy visions of youth—for he never came.

Some of the old natives believed Cook was Lono to the day of their death; but many did not, for they could not understand how he could die if he was a god.

THE FIELD OF THE VANQUISHED GODS

Only a mile or so from Kealakekua Bay is a spot of historic interest—the place where the last battle was fought for idolatry. Of course we visited it, and came away as wise as most people do who go and gaze upon such mementoes of the past when in an unreflective mood.

While the first missionaries were on their way around the Horn, the idolatrous customs which had obtained in the Islands as far back as tradition reached were suddenly broken up. Old Kamehameha I was dead, and his son, Liholiho, the new King, was a free liver, a roystering, dissolute fellow, and hated the restraints of the ancient tabu.

His assistant in the Government, Kaahumanu, the Queen Dowager, was proud and high-spirited, and hated the tabu because it restricted the privileges of her sex and degraded all women very nearly to the level of brutes. So the case stood. Liholiho had half a mind to put his foot down, Kaahumanu had a whole mind to badger him into doing it, and whiskey did the rest. It was probably the first time whiskey ever prominently figured as an aid to civilization. Liholiho came up to Kailua as drunk as a piper, and attended a great feast; the determined Queen spurred his drunken courage up to a reckless pitch, and then, while all the multitude stared in blank dismay, he moved deliberately forward and sat down with the women! They saw him eat from the same vessel with them, and were appalled! Terrible moments drifted slowly by, and still the King ate, still he lived, still the lightnings of the insulted gods were withheld! Then conviction came like a revelation—the superstitions of a hundred generations passed from before the people like a cloud, and a shout went up, "The tabu is broken! the tabu is broken!"

Thus did King Liholiho and his dreadful whiskey preach the first sermon and prepare the way for the new gospel that was speeding southward over the waves of the Atlantic.

The tabu broken and destruction failing to follow the awful sacrilege, the people, with that childlike precipitancy which has always characterized them, jumped to the conclusion that their gods were a weak and wretched swindle, just as they formerly jumped to the conclusion that Captain Cook was no god, merely because he groaned, and promptly killed him without stopping to inquire whether a god might not groan as well as a man if it suited his pleasure

to do it; and satisfied that the idols were powerless to protect themselves, they went to work at once and pulled them
down—hacked them to pieces—applied the torch—annihilated them!

The pagan priests were furious. And well they might be;
they had held the fattest offices in the land, and now they
were beggared; they had been great—they had stood above
the chiefs—and now they were vagabonds. They raised a
revolt; they scared a number of people into joining their
standard, and Kekuokalani, an ambitious offshoot of royalty, was easily persuaded to become their leader.

In the first skirmish the idolaters triumphed over the
royal army sent against them, and full of confidence they
resolved to march upon Kailua. The King sent an envoy
to try and conciliate them, and came very near being an
envoy short by the operation; the savages not only refused
to listen to him, but wanted to kill him. So the King sent
his men forth under Major General Kalaimoku and the two
hosts met at Kuamoo. The battle was long and fierce—men
and women fighting side by side, as was the custom—and
when the day was done, the rebels were flying in every
direction in hopeless panic, and idolatry and the tabu were
dead in the land!

The royalists marched gaily home to Kailua glorifying
the new dispensation. "There is no power in the gods," said
they; "they are a vanity and a lie. The army with idols was
weak; the army without idols was strong and victorious!"

The nation was without a religion.

The missionary ship arrived in safety shortly afterward,
timed by providential exactness to meet the emergency,
and the gospel was planted as in a virgin soil.

CANOE VOYAGE

At noon, we hired a Kanaka to take us down to the ancient ruins at Honaunau in his canoe—price two dollars—
reasonable enough, for a sea voyage of eight miles, count-
ing both ways.

The native canoe is an irresponsible looking contrivance.
I cannot think of anything to liken it to but a boy's sled
runner hollowed out, and that does not quite convey the
correct idea. It is about fifteen feet long, high and pointed
at both ends, is a foot and a half or two feet deep, and so
narrow that if you wedged a fat man into it you might not
get him out again. It seems to sit right up on top of the
water like a duck, but it has an outrigger and does not
upset easily if you keep still. This outrigger is formed of
two long bent sticks, like plow handles, which project from
one side, and to the outer ends is bound a curved beam
composed of an extremely light wood, which skims along
the surface of the water and thus saves you from an upset
on that side, while the outrigger's weight is not so easily
lifted as to make an upset on the other side a thing to be
greatly feared. Still, until one gets used to sitting perched
upon this knife blade, he is apt to reason within himself
that it would be more comfortable if there were just an
outrigger or so on the other side also.

SLEEPY SCENERY

I had the bow seat, and Brown sat amidships and faced
the Kanaka, who occupied the stern of the craft and did
the paddling. With the first stroke the trim shell of a thing
shot out from the shore like an arrow. There was not
much to see. While we were on the shallow water of the

reef, it was pastime to look down into the limpid depths at the large bunches of branching coral—the unique shrubbery of the sea. We lost that, though, when we got out into the dead blue water of the deep. But we had the picture of the surf, then, dashing angrily against the cragbound shore and sending a foaming spray high into the air. There was interest in this beetling border, too, for it was honeycombed with quaint caves and arches and tunnels, and had a rude semblance of the dilapidated architecture of ruined keeps and castles rising out of the restless sea. When this novelty ceased to be a novelty, we had to turn our eyes shoreward and gaze at the long mountain with its rich green forests stretching up into the curtaining clouds, and at the specks of houses in rearward distance and the diminished schooner riding sleepily at anchor. And when these grew tiresome we dashed boldly into the midst of a school of huge, beastly porpoises engaged at their eternal game of arching over a wave and disappearing, and then doing it over again and keeping it up—always circling over, in that way, like so many well-submerged wheels. But the porpoises wheeled themselves away, and then we were thrown upon our own resources. It did not take many minutes to discover that the sun was blazing like a bonfire, and that the weather was of a melting temperature. It had a drowsing effect, too, and when Brown attempted to open a conversation, I let him close it again for lack of encouragement. I expected he would begin on the Kanaka, and he did:

"Fine day, John."

"Aole iki."

(I took that to mean "I don't know," and as equivalent to "I don't understand you.")

"Sorter sultry, though."

"Aole iki."

"You're right—at least I'll let it go at that, anyway. It makes you sweat considerable, don't it?"

"Aole iki."

"Right again, likely. You better take a bath when you get down here to Honaunau—you don't smell good, anyhow, and you can't sweat that way long without smelling worse."

"Aole iki."

"Oh, this ain't any use. This Injun don't seem to know anything but 'Owry ikky,' and the interest of that begins to let down after it's been said sixteen or seventeen times. I reckon I'll bail out a while for a change."

I expected he would upset the canoe, and he did. It was well enough to take the chances, though, because the sea had flung the blossom of a wave into the boat every now and then, until, as Brown said in a happy spirit of exaggeration, there was about as much water inside as there was outside. There was no peril about the upset, but there was a very great deal of discomfort. The author of the mischief thought there was compensation for it, however, in that there was a marked improvement in the Kanaka's smell afterwards.

THE RUINED CITY OF REFUGE

At the end of an hour we had made the four miles, and landed on a level point of land, upon which was a wide extent of old ruins, with many a tall coconut tree growing among them. Here was the ancient City of Refuge—a vast enclosure, whose stone walls were twenty feet thick at the base, and fifteen or twenty feet high; an oblong square, a thousand and forty feet one way, and a fraction under seven hundred the other. Within this enclosure, in early times, have been three rude temples; each was 210 feet long by one hundred wide, and thirteen high.

In those days, if a man killed another anywhere on the island, the relatives of the deceased were privileged to take the murderer's life; and then a chase for life and liberty began—the outlawed criminal flying through pathless forests and over mountain and plain, with his hopes fixed upon the protecting walls of the City of Refuge, and the avenger of blood following hotly after him! Sometimes the race was kept up to the very gates of the temple, and the panting pair sped through long files of excited natives, who watched the contest with flashing eye and dilated nostril, encouraging the hunted refugee with sharp, inspirited ejaculations, and sending up a ringing shout of exultation when the saving gates closed upon him and the cheated pursuer sank exhausted at the threshold. But sometimes the flying criminal fell under the hand of the avenger at the very door, when one more brave stride, one more brief second of time would have brought his feet upon the sacred ground and barred him against all harm. Where did these isolated pagans get this idea of a City of Refuge—this ancient Jewish custom?

This old sanctuary was sacred to all—even to rebels in arms and invading armies. Once within its walls, and confession made to the priest and absolution obtained, the wretch with a price on his head could go forth without fear or without danger—he was tabu, and to harm him was death. The routed rebels in the lost battle for idolatry fled to this place to claim sanctuary, and many were thus saved.

THE PLACE OF EXECUTION

Close to a corner of the great enclosure is a round structure of stone, some six or eight feet high, with a level top about ten or twelve feet in diameter. This was the place of execution. A high palisade of coconut piles shut out its cruel scenes from the vulgar multitude. Here criminals were killed, the flesh stripped from the bones and burned, and the bones secreted in holes in the body of the structure. If the man had been guilty of a high crime, the entire corpse was burned.

A STUDY FOR THE CURIOUS

The walls of the temple are a study. The same food for speculation that is offered the visitor to the Pyramids of Egypt he will find here—the mystery of how they were constructed by a people unacquainted with science and mechanics. The natives have no invention of their own for hoisting heavy weights, they had no beasts of burden, and they have never even shown any knowledge of the properties of the lever. Yet some of the lava blocks quarried out, brought over rough, broken ground, and built into this wall, six or seven feet from the ground, are of prodigious size and would weigh tons. How did they transport and how raise them?

Both the inner and outer surfaces of the walls present a smooth front and are very creditable specimens of masonry. The blocks are of all manner of shapes and sizes, but yet are fitted together with the neatest exactness. The gradual narrowing of the wall from the base upward is accurately preserved. No cement was used, but the edifice is firm and compact and is capable of resisting storm and decay for centuries. Who built this temple, and how was it built, and when, are mysteries that may never be unraveled.

THERE WERE GIANTS IN THOSE DAYS

Outside of these ancient walls lies a sort of coffin-shaped stone eleven feet four inches long and three feet square at the small end (it would weigh a few thousand pounds), which the high chief who held sway over this district many centuries ago brought hither on his shoulder one day to use as a lounge! This circumstance is established by the most reliable traditions. He used to lie down on it, in his indolent way, and keep an eye on his subjects at work for him and see that there was no "soldiering" done. And no doubt there was not any done to speak of, because he was a man of that sort of build that incites to attention to business on the part of an employe. He was fourteen or fifteen feet high. When he stretched himself at full length on his lounge, his legs hung down over the end, and when he snored, he woke the dead. These facts are all attested by irrefragable tradition.

Brown said: "I don't say anything against this Injun's inches, but I copper his judgment. He didn't know his own size. Because if he did, why didn't he fetch a rock that was long enough, while he was at it?"

KAAHUMANU'S ROCK

On the other side of the temple is a monstrous seven-ton rock, eleven feet long, seven feet wide, and three feet thick. It is raised a foot or a foot and a half above the ground, and rests upon half a dozen little stony pedestals.

The same old fourteen-footer brought it down from the mountain, merely for fun (he had his own notions about fun, and they were marked by a quaint originality, as well), and propped it up as we find it now and as others may find it at a century hence, for it would take a score of horses to budge it from its position. They say that fifty or sixty years ago the proud Queen Kaahumanu used to fly to this rock for safety, whenever she had been making trouble with her fierce husband, and hide under it until his wrath was appeased. But these Kanakas will lie, and this statement is one of their ablest efforts—for Kaahumanu was six feet high— she was bulky—she was built like an ox—and she could no more have squeezed under that rock than she could have passed between the cylinders of a sugar mill. What could she gain by it, even if she succeeded? To be chased and abused by her savage husband could not be otherwise than humiliating to her high spirit, yet it could never make her feel so flat as an hour's repose under that rock would.

SCIENCE AMONG BARBARIANS

We walked a mile over a raised macadamized road of uniform width; a road paved with flat stones and exhibiting in its every detail a considerable degree of engineering skill. Some say that wise old pagan Kamehameha I planned and built it, but others say it was built so long before his time that the knowledge of who constructed it has passed out of the traditions. In either case, however, as the handiwork of an untaught and degraded race it is a thing of pleasing interest. The stones are worn and smooth, and pushed apart in places, so that the road has the exact appearance of those ancient paved highways leading out of Rome which one sees in pictures.

A PETRIFIED NIAGARA

The object of our tramp was to visit a great natural curiosity at the base of the foothills—a congealed cascade of lava. Some old forgotten volcanic eruption sent its broad river of fire down the mountainside here, and it poured down in a great torrent from an overhanging bluff some fifty feet high to the ground below. The flaming torrent cooled in the winds from the sea, and remains there today, all seamed and frothed and rippled—a petrified Niagara. It is very picturesque, and withal so natural that one might almost imagine it still flowed. A smaller stream trickled over the cliff and built up an isolated pyramid about thirty feet high, which has the resemblance of a mass of large gnarled and knotted vines and roots and stems intricately twisted and woven together.

NATURE'S MINING ACHIEVEMENTS

We passed in behind the cascade and the pyramid, and found the bluff pierced by several cavernous tunnels, whose crooked courses we followed about fifty feet, but with no notable result, save that we made a discovery that may be of high interest to men of science. We discovered that the darkness in there was singularly like the darkness observable in other particularly dark places—exactly like it, I thought. I am borne out in this opinion by my comrade, who said he did not believe there was any difference, but if there was, he judged it was in favor of this darkness here.

Two of these winding tunnels stand as proof of Nature's mining abilities. Their floors are level, they are seven feet wide, and their roofs are gently arched. Their height is not uniform, however. We passed through one a hundred feet long, which leads through a spur of the hill and opens out well up in the sheer wall of a precipice whose foot rests in the waves of the sea. It is a commodious tunnel, except that there are occasionally places in it where one must stoop to pass under. The roof is lava, of course, and is thickly studded with little lavapointed icicles an inch long, which hardened as they dripped. They project as closely together as the iron teeth of a corn sheller, and if one will stand up straight and walk any distance there, he can get his hair combed free of charge.

Brown tried to hurry me away from this vicinity by saying that if the expected land breeze sprang up while we were absent, the *Boomerang* would be obliged to put to sea without waiting for us; but I did not care; I knew she would land our saddles and shirt collars at Kau, and we could sail in the superior schooner *Emmeline* [*Emeline*], Captain Crane, which would be entirely to my liking. Wherefore we proceeded to ransack the country for further notable curiosities.

MARK TWAIN

23 ❀

THE HIGH CHIEF OF SUGARDOM

I have visited Haleakala, Kilauea, Wailuku Valley, the Petrified Cataracts, the Pathway of the Great Hog God— in a word, I have visited all the principal wonders of the island, and now I come to speak of one which, in its importance to America, surpasses them all. A land which produces six, eight, ten, twelve, yea, even thirteen thousand pounds of sugar to the acre on unmanured soil! There are precious few acres of unmanured ground in Louisiana— none at all, perhaps—which will yield 2,500 pounds of sugar; there is not an unmanured acre under cultivation in the Sandwich Islands which yields less. This country is the king of the sugar world, as far as astonishing productiveness is concerned. Heretofore the Mauritius has held this high place. Commodore Perry, in his report on the Mauritius, says:

"Before the introduction of guano into Mauritius the product of sugar on that island was from 2,000 to 2,500 pounds to the acre; but the increase since the application of this fertilizer has been so extraordinary as to be scarcely credible. In ordinary seasons the product has been from 6,000 to 7,000 pounds, and under peculiarly favorable circumstances it has even reached 8,000 pounds to the acre."

It was "scarcely credible." Guano has not been used in the Sandwich Islands at all, yet the sugar crop of Maui averages over 6,000 pounds straight through, all the time, for every acre cultivated. Last year the average was 7,000 pounds per acre on the Ulupalakua plantation; this year the "plant" crop on the Wailuku plantation averages 8,000. Portions of the Waikapu, Wailuku, Waihee, Ulupalakua, and many other plantations have yielded over 11,000 pounds to the acre, and twenty acres on the fourth named averaged the enormous yield of 13,000 pounds per acre one season! These things are "scarcely credible," but they are true, nevertheless.

By late Patent Office reports it appears that the average sugar yield per acre throughout the world ranges from 500 to 1,000 pounds. The average in the Sandwich Islands, lumping good, bad, and indifferent, is 5,000 pounds per acre.

PROGRESS OF THE ISLAND'S PRODUCTION

The cultivation of sugar in the Islands dates back fourteen years; its cultivation as an actual business dates back only four years. This year the aggregate yield is 27 million pounds. The cultivation of sugar in Louisiana dates back one hundred and fifteen years; its cultivation as an actual business dates back just one hundred years. When it had been a business forty years, there were a hundred plantations in Louisiana—ten years later there were one hundred and fifty on the Mississippi, and the aggregate yield was only 10 million pounds; a few years later it reached 25 million. Compare that with the 27 million yield of *twenty-nine* small plantations in the Sandwich Islands. The sugar history of the islands may be compressed into a very small table. Aggregate yield of pounds for:

1852	730,000	1861	2,567,498
1856	554,805	1862	3,005,603
1857	700,556	1863	5,292,121
1858	1,204,061	1864	10,414,441
1859	1,826,620	1865	15,318,097
1860	1,444,271	1866	27,050,000

The exports of molasses during the entire year of 1865 amounted to half a million gallons—only a little more than was exported during the first six months of the present year.

The following table gives the yield in pounds of the twenty-nine principal plantations for the present year:

ISLAND OF HAWAII

Harto	150,000	Kauiki	1,600,000
Kohala	2,000,000	Hoonsing	600,000
Onomea	1,200,000	Paukau	600,000
Metcalf's	1,200,000		

ISLAND OF MAUI

Makee	1,800,000	Hobron	1,200,000
Haua	600,000	Haiku	800,000
Waikapu	1,000,000	East Maui	800,000
Wailuku	2,400,000	C. & Turton	1,000,000
Bailey & Son	400,000	Lahaina Sugar Co.	1,200,000
Lewers	2,000,000	Bal and Adams	700,000

ISLAND OF KAUAI

Princeville	2,000,000	Koloa	700,000
Lihue	700,000	Waipoa	300,000

ISLAND OF OAHU

Kauahai	200,000	Story & Co.	200,000
Wilder	600,000	Halawa	400,000
Kaalia	400,000	Wailua	300,000

Total 27,050,000

When all the cane lands in the Islands are under full cultivation, they will produce over 250,000,000 pounds of sugar annually.

COMPARATIVE

In Louisiana, sugar planters paid from $20 to $200 an acre for land, $500 to $1,000 apiece for Negroes, $50,000 to $100,000 for stock, mills, etc., raised 1,000 to 1,500 pounds of sugar to the acre, sold it for 5 and 6¢—and got rich.

In the Islands wild sugar land is worth from $1 to $20 an acre, mills and stock cost about the same as in Louisiana. The hire of each laborer is $100 a year—just about what it used to cost to board and clothe and doctor a Negro—but there is no original outlay of $500 to $1,000 for the purchase of the laborer, or $50 to $100 annual interest to be paid on the sum so laid out. The price of sugar is double what it was in Louisiana, and the actual net profit to the planter, notwithstanding high freights and high duties, is also double.

In Louisiana, it cost not less than $180,000 to purchase and stock with Negroes, mill, animals, etc., a plantation of 300 acres, and its crop would yield $30,000 (allowing each acre to produce 2,000 pounds to the acre—which it wouldn't do). Deduct $60,000 outlay for Negroes and half the cost of the land, $10,000, and the same plantation in the Islands would cost $110,000 and be ready for business.

Its crop would yield 6,000 pounds to the acre and sell for $180,000 in San Francisco. If the planters of Louisiana have done well, surely those of the Islands ought.

When the production of a staple steadily increases and capital sticks to it and shows confidence in it, it is fair to presume that investments in it are considered secure and profitable. In 1839, '40, and '41, the yield in Louisiana ranged along in the neighborhood of 100 million pounds annually—price, 4, 5 and 6¢ a pound. In 1852, '53, and '54, her yearly yield fluctuated between 350 million and 500 million pounds—market price, 3½ to 5 cents. Thus, 1,000 to 1,500 pounds to the acre, at 3½ to 6¢, was so encouraging as to more than quadruple Louisiana's sugar production in less than thirty years. Six or eight thousand pounds to the acre, at 10 to 15¢ a pound, has encouraged the extravagant advance in the Islands from 3 million pounds to 27 million, annual yield, in four years. Against this argument in favor of the security and productiveness of capital invested there, no logic can prevail.

MORE FIGURES

They have a bad system in the Sandwich Islands, whereby the planter has to ship twice and pay broker's commissions as often. This must change some day. The sugar pays a duty of three cents a pound when it enters San Francisco, and of course this comes out of the planter's pocket also. This year the Lewers (or Waihee), Wailuku, Ulupalakua, Princeville, and Kohala plantations will each pay the United States about $60,000 in coin for duties alone; and the Waikapu, Onomea, Metcalf's, and several other plantations whose names I could mention will each pay about half as much. The following bill of expenses will show the processes by which the planter's profits are diminished. The estimate was made in the island of Maui, in June, when sugar had been falling and had got down to $210 to $220 a ton in San Francisco:

ON A TON OF SUGAR

Barreling	$16.00
Drayage from mill	1.00
Shipping to Honolulu	3.00
Brokerage in Honolulu	2.50
Freight to San Francisco	6.00
United States duty	60.00
Drayage in San Francisco	1.00
Brokerage in San Francisco	11.00
	$100.50
Gross sale	210.00
Remainder	$109.50

And out of that $109.50 must come about sixty percent for plantation expenses and interest on the original outlay for land, mill, stock, etc.

The following estimate was made when sugar was worth a cent a pound more. It shows the business done the present year with three hundred acres, on a plantation which cost considerably under $90,000 for its stock, mill, lands, and everything complete. The land was purchased unimproved, at an insignificant price. The present year's crop was 1,000 tons of sugar:

Gross yield		$240,000
Plantation expenses	$ 60,000	
Freight, duties, etc., etc.	120,000	
Interest on original outlay	10,000	
Total disbursement		$190,000
Net profit		$ 50,000

There is more than one plantation in the islands which is worth, with all its appurtenances, $250,000, and will produce a $260,000 crop next year—perhaps this—and yield a profit of $70,000, after deducting all expenses of cultivating, shipping and disposal in San Francisco, and interest.

One of the best plantations in the Islands, though not one of the largest, by any means, cost, with its appurtenances, $100,000. All bills were promptly paid and no debts allowed to accrue and breed interest. The consequence was, that three years after the first plow disturbed its virgin soil, it had paid for itself and added a dividend of $20,000.

ADVANTAGES

In Louisiana they take off one plant and two ratoon crops usually before replanting, and so they do in the Islands, as a general thing, though some think the ratoons would run several years longer without disadvantage. The sugar crop in Louisiana is never sure—in the Islands, when favorably situated for irrigation, it never fails. In the former it must be immediately cut upon the first suspicion of a frost, whether it is mature or not—in the latter there is no frost, and the planter may cut it when it suits his convenience; it will stand several months after ripening without deteriorating. Not much of the cane of the species that tassel is cultivated, but even tassel cane can remain in the field four months after maturing without deteriorating.

In Louisiana the cane must always be cut before the frost comes, but in the Islands it may be cut whenever it is ripe —any day in the year. Consequently, the mills can take their time and grind comfortably along in all seasons, whereby the putting on of large extra forces and the employment of mills of immense capacity on small plantations to rush off a threatened crop and grind it is avoided. Louisiana has only five or six weeks to get her crop in, and so the juice is generally green and the sugar necessarily inferior to that of the Islands.

The fuel chiefly used to make steam is the dry crushed cane which has passed through the mill. It is called "trash." It is mixed with hard wood, and the two combined make a very hot fire.

On the low ground of West Maui plant cane matures in from eighteen to twenty months, and ratoons ripen in from fifteen to eighteen months. At Ulupalakua, whose lowest cane lands are two thousand feet, and its highest 3,500 feet, above sea level, plant cane requires all the way from twenty-two months to three years to ripen, according to elevation. One may see there plant cane that is just sprouting, cane that is half grown, cane that is full-grown, and first, second, and third ratoons—all on the same plantation. At all seasons of the year there is cane ready for the mill, and labor in no department of sugar cultivation and manufacture need ever stop. A thousand acres are in cane, and from two hundred to three hundred of it are taken off yearly, yielding from eight hundred to one thousand tons of sugar. This plantation being high up in the neighborhood of the clouds, depends upon the frequent rains for irrigation, but forty thousand barrels of water are kept in cisterns for mill purposes, use of stock, etc., to be ready for emergencies. The West Maui plantations are all liberally irrigated from unfailing mountain streams.

In the hot neighborhood of Lahaina cane matures in nine or ten months, and a year is the average for the islands of Hawaii, Oahu, and Kauai.

SPECIMEN OF A HAWAIIAN MILL

The sugar works of the Lewers plantation (formerly known as the Waihee plantation) are considered the model in the Islands, in the matter of cost, extent, completeness, and efficiency. They make as fine an appearance as any between Baton Rouge and New Orleans and are doubtless as perfect in their appliances. The main building is some two hundred feet long and about forty wide (perhaps more) and proportionally high. Its walls are of stone masonry and very thick. It has a stately chimney that might answer for a shot tower. Being painted snow white, the mill building and the tall chimney stand out in strong contrast with the surrounding bright green cane fields. A long, elevated flume in front, and a laboring overshot wheel of large diameter; at one side a broad inclosure peopled with coolies spreading "trash" to dry; half a dozen Kanakas feeding cane to the whirling cylinders of the mill and a noisy procession of their countrymen driving cartloads of the material to their vicinity and dumping it—these things give the place a businesslike aspect which is novel in the slumbering Sandwich Islands. The neighboring offices of the proprietor, the dwelling of the superintendent, the store, blacksmith shop, quarters for white employes, native huts and a row of frame quarters for Chinese coolies, make Waihee a village of very respectable pretensions. The employes of the mill and plantation, with their families, number 350 persons, perhaps.

Within the commodious mill building I have described, are four long rows of iron vats (coolers), about twenty-five in a row, occupying almost the whole of the great floor, and with railways between the rows which are traversed by cars which convey the cooked sugar in a liquid state to the vats to be cooled. Each vat is about six feet long, three and a half or four feet wide, and about two feet deep, and is able to contain an amount of sweetness equivalent to thirteen young women—in unpoetical figures, fourteen hundred pounds.

In the center is a small machine called a grinder—an exceedingly useful contrivance, and the only one I have seen in the Islands. When the sugar in the coolers becomes grained and hardened, it has many hard lumps in it which it is difficult to reduce in the centrifugals, and this service the grinder performs. It is simply two swiftly-revolving iron cylinders, placed close together, and after the grained sugar has passed between them, lumps before are lumps no longer.

Close to the grinder are six centrifugals—small metallic tubs, whose sides are pierced with a few thousand pinholes to the square inch. The nasty-looking grained sugar—it is about half black molasses, and looks like an inferior quality of mud—is dumped in, to the amount of a bushel; the tub is set to spinning around at the rate of ten or twelve hundred revolutions a minute—the mud begins to retreat from the center and cling to the sides—and in about three minutes the bottom is as clean as a dinner plate; the sides are packed with a coating two or three inches thick of beautiful light straw-colored sugar ready for the table, and all the disagreeable molasses has been expressed through the innumerable pinholes by the frightful velocity of the machine.

At the upper end of the apartment are several five-hundred-gallon steam clarifiers, which receive the raw juice from the mill (which is a large machine on the same principle as the grinder, between whose cylinders the canes are squeezed dry of their juice) and cleanse it of its impurities.

Then it passes through pipes to the "train"—a row of great iron kettles, where it is well boiled and kept in constant motion.

The Weitzel pan receives the cane juice next, and completes the evaporation of the water from it. A revolving wheel paddles it into ceaseless motion here. This pan is heated by steam.

The persecuted juice goes hence to the "vacuum pan"—a very costly contrivance which is little used in the Islands. It is a huge iron globe, capable of containing several hundred gallons. The virtues claimed for it are that it will boil the juice at half the temperature required by the ordinary open "concentrator" and that consequently the sugar will cool and grain quicker; that the sugar can even be grained in the pan, if necessary, and transferred at once to the centrifugals, instead of lingering in the coolers from four to seven days, as is the case in other mills; and lastly, that it will make almost first quality sugar out of first molasses. The vacuum pan boils at a temperature of 140 to 160 degrees—the common open concentrator at 230 to 260. The juice is soon cooked and ready for the coolers, where it remains the best part of a day; then it passes through the grinder and from thence through the centrifugals. The perfected sugar is discharged through chutes into bins in the basement, and the expressed molasses sent back to be wrought into sugar or barreled for market. A cooper shop on the premises prepares the kegs to receive the sugar, and an ingenious affair alongside the bins packs the article in them. It is a large auger set in a framework and worked by a screw; its blades resemble those of a propeller, and after being lowered into the empty barrel, it works upward as the sugar is shoveled in, packing it smoothly as it comes. Three Kanakas are required to tend it, and it does the work of six or seven. It packs four hundred kegs in a day; a man's full day's work by the customary pounding process with a maul, is sixty. This is the only machine for packing I have heard of in the Islands.

I have seen the cane cut in the fields; hauled to the works; squeezed through the mill; transferred to the clarifiers; thence to the train; thence to the Weitzel pan; thence to the vacuum pan; thence to the coolers; thence to the grinder; thence to the centrifugals; thence, as sugar, to the bins below; thence to the packer; thence to the artist who branded the quality and weight and the plantation's name upon the kegs, and thence to the schooner riding at anchor a mile and a half away—I have frequently seen this whole process gone through with in two days, and yet I do not consider myself competent to make sugar.

Steam is used for half the machinery, and water power for the other half. The proprietor has just completed, at a cost of less than $7,000, a broad and deep ditch, four miles long, which carries an abundant stream of clear water along the base of the rear hills and full length of his plantation. It can be used to irrigate not only the 530 acres now in cane, but will add 210 more that were never susceptible of cultivation before—which addition is equivalent to adding $120,000 to the gross yield of the concern—that much, at any rate; the land produces the ordinary average—three tons to the acre.

I have described the Lewers mill as well as I could, and the same description will answer, in the main, for the Wailuku, Waikapu, Ulupalakua, and all the other mills I have visited. No two mills are just alike, and yet no two are sufficiently unlike to render it worthwhile for a man to describe both.

The plantations I have named are all situated on the island of Maui. Perhaps a few acres of plant cane on either of them have fallen short of three tons this year, or any year, and choice pieces of ground on the Ulupalakua, Waikapu, and Wailuku have yielded double that amount per acre. This plant cane averages about equally clear through —say three to three and a half tons per acre—except in the case of the Wailuku, which reached an average of four tons this year. One twenty-acre lot on this plantation produced ten thousand pounds of sugar to the acre, and one eleven-acre lot eleven thousand pounds per acre. I take the figures from the official account books of the superintendent. The mill was turning out 200,000 pounds of excellent sugar a month when I was there.

MOLASSES

I have said nothing about molasses. They work some of it over and reduce it to sugar, and each planter ships a few thousand dollars' worth of it, and (as at Ulupalakua) feeds the third quality to his hogs, if he has any. Formerly inferior molasses was always thrown away, but here, lately, an enlightened spirit of progress has moved the Government to allow the erection of three distilleries, I am told, and hereafter it will be made into whiskey. (That remark will be shuddered at in some quarters. But I don't care. Ever since I have been a missionary to these islands I have been snubbed and kept down by the other missionaries, and so I will just bring our calling into disrepute occasionally by that sort of dreadful remarks. It makes me feel better.)

MONOPOLY

A San Francisco refinery company once contracted for all the sugar crop of the Islands for a year, to be taken directly from the coolers by its agent and paid for at the rate of about seven or seven and a half cents a pound, I think it was. This saved the planters a great deal of trouble and some expense, but they lost confidence and broke up the arrangement. It would have been a profitable thing for all parties if it could have been continued, and I think the planters would like to give some responsible man the sole control of the sugar market of the Pacific Coast on similar terms.

LABOR

The principal labor used on the plantations is that of Kanaka men and women—six dollars to eight dollars a month and find them, or eight to ten dollars and let them find themselves. The contract with the laborer is in writing, and the law rigidly compels compliance with it; if the man shirks a day's work and absents himself, he has to work two days for it when his time is out. If he gets unmanageable and disobedient, he is condemned to work on the reef for a season, at twenty-five cents a day. If he is in debt to the planter for such purchases as clothing and provisions, however, when his time expires, the obligation is canceled —the planter has no recourse at law.

The sugar product is rapidly augmenting every year, and day by day the Kanaka race is passing away. Cheap labor had to be procured by some means or other, and so the Government sends to China for coolies and farms them out to the planters at $5 a month each for five years, the planter to feed them and furnish them with clothing. The Hawaiian agent fell into the hands of Chinese sharpers, who showed him some superb coolie samples and then loaded his ships with the scurviest lot of pirates that ever went unhung. Some of them were cripples, some were lunatics, some afflicted with incurable diseases, and nearly all were intractable, full of fight, and animated by the spirit of the very devil. However, the planters managed to tone them down and now they like them very well. Their former trade of cutting throats on the China seas has made them uncommonly handy at cutting cane. They are steady, industrious workers when properly watched. If the Hawaiian agent had been possessed of a reasonable amount of business tact, he could have got experienced rice and sugar cultivators—peaceable, obedient men and women—for the same salaries that must be paid to these villains, and done them a real service by giving them good homes and kind treatment in place of the wretchedness and brutality they experience in their native land. Some of the women are being educated as house servants, and I observe that they do not put on airs, and "sass" their masters and mistresses, and give daily notice to quit, and try to boss the whole concern, as the tribe do in California.

COOLIES FOR CALIFORNIA

You will have coolie labor in California some day. It is already forcing its superior claims upon the attention of your great mining, manufacturing, and public improvement corporations. You will not always go on paying $80 and $100 a month for labor which you can hire for $5. The sooner California adopts coolie labor the better it will be for her. It cheapens no labor of men's hands save the hard-

est and most exhausting drudgery—drudgery which neither intelligence nor education are required to fit a man for
—drudgery which all white men abhor and are glad to
escape from. You may take note of the fact that to adopt
coolie labor could work small hardship to the men who
now do the drudgery, for every shipload of coolies received
there and put to work would so create labor—would permit men to open so many mines they cannot afford to
work now, and begin so many improvements they dare not
think of at present—that all the best class of the working
population who might be emancipated from the pick and
shovel by that shipload would find easier and more profitable employment in superintending and overseeing the
coolies. It will be more profitable, as you will readily admit,
to the great mining companies of California and Nevada
to pay 300 Chinamen an aggregate of $1,500 a month—or
five times the amount, if you think it more just—than to
pay 300 white men $30,000 a month. Especially when the
white men would desert in a body every time a new mining
region was discovered, but the Chinamen would have to
stay until their contracts were worked out.

People are always hatching fine schemes for inducing
Eastern capital to the Pacific Coast. Yonder in China are
the capitalists you want—and under your own soil is a
bank that will not dishonor their checks. The mine purchased for a song by Eastern capital would pour its stream
of wealth past your door and empty it in New York. You
would be little the richer for that. There are hundreds of
men in California who are sitting on their quartz leads,
watching them year after year, and hoping for the day
when they will pay—and growing gray all the time—
hoping for a cheapening of labor that will enable them to

work the mine or warrant another man in buying it—who would soon be capitalists if coolie labor were adopted.

The Mission Woolen Mill Company take California wool and weave from it fabrics of all descriptions, which they challenge all America to surpass, and sell at prices which defy all foreign competition. The secret is in their cheap Chinese labor. With white labor substituted the mills would have to stop.

The Pacific Railroad Company employ a few thousand Chinamen at about thirty dollars a month, and have white men to oversee them. They pronounce it the cheapest, the best, and most quiet, peaceable, and faithful labor they have tried.

Some of the heaviest mining corporations in the state have it in contemplation to employ Chinese labor. Give this labor to California for a few years, and she would have fifty mines opened where she has one now—a dozen factories in operation where there is one now—a thousand tons of farm produce raised where there are a hundred now—leagues of railroad where she has miles today, and a population commensurate with her high and advancing prosperity.

With the Pacific Railroad creeping slowly but surely toward her over mountain and desert and preparing to link her with the East, and with the China mail steamers about to throw open to her the vast trade of our opulent coastline stretching from the Amoor [Amur] River to the equator, what state in the Union has so splendid a future before her as California? Not one, perhaps. She should awake and be ready to join her home prosperity to these tides of commerce that are so soon to sweep toward her from the east and the west.

To America it has been vouchsafed to materialize the vision, and realize the dream of centuries, of the enthusiasts of the Old World. We have found the true Northwest Passage—we have found the true and only direct route to the bursting coffers of "Ormus and of Ind"—to the enchanted land whose mere drippings, in the ages that are gone, enriched and aggrandized ancient Venice, first, then Portugal, Holland, and in our own time, England—and each in succession they longed and sought for the fountainhead of this vast Oriental wealth, and sought in vain. The path was hidden to them, but we have found it over the waves of the Pacific, and American enterprise will penetrate to the heart and center of its hoarded treasures, its imperial affluence. The gateway of this path is the Golden Gate of San Francisco; its depot, its distributing house, is California; her customers are the nations of the earth; her transportation wagons will be the freight cars of the Pacific Railroad, and they will take up these Indian treasures at San Francisco and flash them across the continent and the vessels of the Pacific Mail Steamship Company will deliver them in Europe fifteen days sooner than Europe could convey them thither by any route of her own she could devise.

California has got the world where it must pay tribute to her. She is about to be appointed to preside over almost the exclusive trade of 450,000,000 people—the almost exclusive trade of the most opulent land on earth. It is the land where the fabled Aladdin's lamp lies buried—and she is the new Aladdin who shall seize it from its obscurity and summon the genie and command him to crown her with power and greatness, and bring to her feet the hoarded treasures of the earth!

I may have wandered away from my original subject a little, but it is no matter—I keep thinking about the new subject, and I must have wandered into it eventually anyhow.

MARK TWAIN

24🌸

A NOTABLE DISCOVERY

Leaving the caves and tunnels, we returned to the road
and started in a general direction toward Honaunau, but
were presently attracted by a number of holes in a bluff
not more than three or four hundred yards from the place
we had just left. We concluded to go up and examine them.
Our native boatman, who had faithfully followed us thus
far, and who must have been bearing the chief part of the
heat and burden of the day, from the amount of perspiring
he was doing, looked a little discouraged, I thought, and
therefore we signified to him, in elaborate pantomime, that
he might sit down and wait till we came back. We scram-
bled through a tangle of weeds which concealed great beds
of black and wrinkled lava, and finally reached the low
bluff. But the holes were just high enough to be out of
reach. I bent a little below the lower one and ordered
Brown to mount my shoulders and enter it. He said he
could hold me easier than I could hold him, and I said he
was afraid to go in that dark cavern alone. He used some
seditious language of small consequence and then climbed
up and crawled in. I suppose the fellow felt a little nervous,
for he paused up there on his hands and knees and peered

into the darkness for some minutes with nothing of him
visible in the face of the precipice but his broad boot soles
and a portion of his person which a casual acquaintance
might not have recognized at a cursory glance. Then he
and his boot soles slowly disappeared. I waited a minute in
a state of lively curiosity; another minute with flagging
curiosity as regarded the cave, but with a newborn attention to the pelting sun; another long minute with no curiosity at all—I leaned drowsily against the wall. And about
this time the investigator backed suddenly out of the hole
and crushed me to the earth. We rolled down the slight
declivity and brought up in a sitting posture face to face.
I looked astonished, maybe, but he looked terrified.

"It's one of them infernal old ancient graveyards!" he
said.

"No? This is why the superstitious Kanaka stayed behind
then?"

"Yes, likely. I suppose you didn't know that bone yard
was there, else you'd have gone in yourself, instead of me.
Certainly you would—oh, of course."

"Yes, you are right—but how is it in there, Brown?
Compose yourself, lad—what did you find?"

"Oh, it's easy enough to talk, but I'm not going to prospect any more of them holes, not if I know myself, I ain't,
and I think I do; it ain't right, anyway, to be stirring up a
dead man that's done his work and earned his rest, and
besides it ain't comfortable."

"But what did you see, Brown—what did you see?"

"I didn't see anything, at first—I only felt. It was dark
as the inside of a whale in there, and I crawled about fifteen
feet and then fetched up against something that was wood
with my nose and skinned the end of it a little where you

notice it's bloody. I felt of it with my hand, and judged it to be a canoe, and reached in and took out something and backed out till it was light enough, and then I found it was a withered hand of one of them rusty old kings. And so I laid it down and come out."

"Yes, you did 'come out'—and you 'come out' in something of a hurry, too. Give me a light."

I climbed in and put the relic back into the canoe, with its fellows, and I trust the spirit of the deceased, if it was hovering near, was satisfied with this mute apology for our unintentional sacrilege.

And thus another item of patiently acquired knowledge grew shaky. We had learned, early, that the bones of great chiefs were hidden, like those of Kamehameha the Great; the information was accepted until we learned that it was etiquette to convey them to the volcano and cast them into the lakes of fire; that was relied on till we discovered that the legitimate receptacle for them was the holes in the precipice of Kealakekua; but now found that the walls of the City of Refuge contain orifices in which the bones of the great chiefs are deposited, and lo! here were more in this distant bluff!—and bones of great chiefs, too—all bones of great chiefs. The fact is, there is a lie out somewhere.

FREE-AND-EASY FASHIONS OF NATIVE WOMEN

Tired and overheated, we plodded back to the ruined temple. We were blistered on face and hands, our clothes were saturated with perspiration and we were burning with thirst. Brown ran the last hundred yards, and without waiting to take off anything but his coat and boots jumped into the sea, bringing up in the midst of a party of native girls who were bathing. They scampered out, with a modesty which was not altogether genuine, I suspect, and ran, seizing their clothes as they went. He said they were very handsomely formed girls. I did not notice, particularly.

These creatures are bathing about half their time, I think. If a man were to see a nude woman bathing at noonday in the States, he would be apt to think she was very little better than she ought to be, and proceed to favor her with an impudent stare. But the case is somewhat different here. The thing is so common that the white residents pass carelessly by, and pay no more attention to it than if the rollicking wenches were so many cattle. Within the confines of even so populous a place as Honolulu, and in the very center of the sultry city of Lahaina, the women bathe in the brooks at all hours of the day. They are only particular about getting undressed safely, and in this science they all follow the same fashion. They stoop down, snatch the single garment over the head, and spring in. They will do this with great confidence within thirty steps of a man. Finical highfliers wear bathing dresses, but, of course, that is an affectation of modesty born of the high civilization to which the natives have attained, and is confined to a limited number.

Many of the native women are prettily formed, but they have a noticeable peculiarity as to shape—they are almost as narrow through the hips as men are.

EXIT "BOOMERANG"

As we expected, there was no schooner *Boomerang* at Kealakekua when we got back there, but the *Emmeline* [*Emeline*] was riding quietly at anchor in the same spot so lately occupied by our vessel, and that suited us much better. We waited until the land breeze served, and then put to sea. The land breeze begins to blow soon after the sun sets and the earth has commenced cooling; the sea breeze rushes inland in the morning as soon as the sun has begun to heat the earth again.

TRANQUIL SCENERY

All day we sailed along within three to six miles of the shore. The view in that direction was very fine. We were running parallel with a long mountain that apparently had neither beginning nor end. It rose with a regular swell from the sea till its forests diminished to velvety shrubbery and were lost in the clouds. If there were any peaks we could not see them. The white mists hung their fringed banners down and hid everything above a certain well-defined altitude. The mountainside, with its sharply marked patches of trees; the smooth green spaces and avenues between them; a little white habitation nestling here and there; a tapering church spire or two thrust upward through the dense foliage; and a bright and cheerful sunlight over all —slanted up abreast of us like a vast picture, framed in between ocean and clouds. It was marked and lined and tinted like a map. So distinctly visible was every door and window in one of the white dwellings, that it was hard to believe it was two or three miles from our ship and two thousand feet above the level of the sea. Yet it was—and it was several thousand feet below the top of the mountain, also.

INHERENT UNSELFISHNESS OF THE NATIVES

The night closed down dark and stormy. The sea ran tolerably high and the little vessel tossed about like a cork.

About nine or ten o'clock we saw a torch glimmering on the distant shore, and presently we saw another coming toward us from the same spot; every moment or so we could see it flash from the top of a wave and then sink out of sight again. From the speed it made I knew it must be one of those fleet native canoes. I watched it with some anxiety, because I wondered what desperate extremity could drive a man out on such a night and on such a sea to play with his life—for I did not believe a canoe could live long in such rough water. I was on the forecastle. Pretty soon I began to think maybe the fellow stood some chance; shortly I almost believed he would make the trip, though his light was shooting up and down dangerously; in another minute he darted across our bow and I caught the glare from his torch in my face. I sprang aft then to get out of him his dire and dreadful news. . . .

It was a swindle. It was one of those simple natives risking his life to bring the captain a present of half a dozen chickens.

"He has got an ax to grind." I spoke in that uncharitable spirit of the civilized world which suspects all men's motives—which cannot conceive of an unselfish thought wrought into an unselfish deed by any man whatsoever, be he pagan or Christian.

"None at all," said the captain; "he expects nothing in return—wouldn't take a cent if I offered it—wouldn't thank me for it, anyway. It's the same instinct that made them load Captain Cook's ships with provisions. They think it is all right—they don't want any return. They will bring us plenty of such presents before we get to Kau."

I saw that the Kanaka was starting over the side again. I said:

"Call him back and give him a drink anyhow; he is wet —and dry also, maybe."

"Pison him with that Jamaica rum down below," said Brown.

"It can't be done—five hundred dollars fine to give or sell liquor to a native."

The captain walked forward then to give some orders, and Brown took the Kanaka downstairs and "pisoned" him. He was delighted with a species of rum which Brown had tried by mistake for claret during the day, and had afterwards made his will, under the conviction that he could not survive it.

They are a strange race, anyhow, these natives. They are amazingly unselfish and hospitable. To the wayfarer who visits them they freely offer their houses, food, beds, and often their wives and daughters. If a Kanaka who has starved two days gets hold of a dollar, he will spend it for poi, and then bring in his friends to help him devour it. When a Kanaka lights his pipe, he only takes one or two whiffs and then passes it around from one neighbor to another until it is exhausted. The example of white selfishness does not affect their native unselfishness any more than the example of white virtue does their native licentiousness. Both traits are born in them—are in their blood and bones, and cannot be educated out.

IN DISTRESS

By midnight we had got to within four miles of the place we were to stop at—Kau—but to reach it we must weather a point which was always hard to get around on account of contrary winds.

The ship was put about and we were soon standing far

out to sea. I went to bed. The vessel was pitching so fearfully an hour afterward that it woke me up. Directly the
captain came down, looking greatly distressed, and said:

"Slip on your clothes quick and go up and see to your
friend. It has been storming like everything for fifteen or
twenty minutes, and I thought at first he was only seasick
and could not throw up, but now he appears to be out of
his head. He lies there on the deck and moans and says,
'Poetry—poetry—oh, me.' It is all he says. What the devil
should he say that for? Hurry!"

Before the speech was half over I was plunging about
the cabin with the rolling of the ship, and struggling fran-
tically to get into my clothes. But the last sentence or two
banished my fears and soothed me. I understood the case.

I was soon on deck in the midst of the darkness and the
whistling winds, and with assistance groped my way to the
sufferer. I told him I had nothing but some verses built out
of alternate lines from the "Burial of Sir John Moore" and
the "Destruction of the [*sic*] Sennacherib," and proceeded
to recite them:

THE BURIAL OF SIR JOHN MOORE

And Other Parties, Subsequently to the Destruction
of the Sennacherib.

The Assyrian came down like the wolf on the fold,
The turf with our bayonets turning,
And his cohorts were gleaming in purple and gold,
And our lanterns dimly burning.

And the tents were all silent, the banners alone,
When the clock told the hour for retiring—

The lances unlifted, the trumpet unblown,
  Though the foe were sullenly firing.

And the might of the Gentile, unsmote by the sword,
  As his corse to the ramparts we hurried,
Hath melted like snow in the glance of the Lord,
  O'er the grave where our hero we buried.

For the Angel of Death spread his wings on the blast,
  And smoothed down his lonely pillow,
And breathed in the face of the foe as he passed—
  And we far away on the billow!

And the eyes of the sleepers waxed deadly and chill,
  As we bitterly thought on the morrow,
And their hearts but once heaved and forever grew still,
  But we spake not a word of sorrow!

And there lay the steed, with his nostril all wide,
  In the grave where a Briton hath laid him,
And the widows of Ashur are loud in their wail,
  And o'er his cold ashes upbraid him.

And there lay the rider, distorted and pale,
  From the field of his fame fresh and gory,
With the dew on his brow and the rust on his mail—
  So we left him alone in his glory!

"It is enough. God bless you!" said Brown, and threw up
everything he had eaten for three days.

KAU AND WAIOHINU

All day the next day we fought that treacherous point—
always in sight of it but never able to get around it. At
night we tacked out forty or fifty miles, and the following
day at noon we made it and came in and anchored.

We went ashore in the first boat and landed in the midst of a black, rough, lava solitude, and got horses and started to Waiohinu, six miles distant. The road was good, and our surroundings fast improved. We were soon among green groves and flowers and occasional plains of grass. There are a dozen houses at Waiohinu, and they have got sound roofs, which is well, because the place is tolerably high up on the mountainside and it rains there pretty much all the time. The name means "sparkling water," and refers to a beautiful mountain stream there, but they ought to divide up and let it refer to the rain also.

A sugar plantation has been started at Waiohinu, and 150 acres planted, a year ago, but the altitude ranges from 1,800 to 2,500 feet above sea level, and it is thought it will take another year for the cane to mature.

We had an abundance of mangoes, papayas, and bananas here, but the pride of the islands, the most delicious fruit known to men, cherimoya, was not in season. It has a soft pulp, like a papaw, and is eaten with a spoon. The papaya looks like a small squash, and tastes like a papaw.

In this rainy spot trees and flowers flourish luxuriantly, and three of those trees—two mangoes and an orange— will live in my memory as the greenest, freshest, and most beautiful I ever saw—and withal, the stateliest and most graceful. One of those mangoes stood in the middle of a large grassy yard, lord of the domain and incorruptible sentinel against the sunshine. When one passed within the compass of its broad arms and its impenetrable foliage he was safe from the pitiless glare of the sun—the protecting shade fell everywhere like a somber darkness.

In some places on the Islands where the mango refused to bear fruit, a remedy suggested by the *Scientific Ameri-*

can has been tried with success. It consists in boring a hole in the trunk of the tree, filling the same with gunpowder and plugging it up. Perhaps it might be worthwhile to try it on other fruit trees.

THE CISTERN TREE

Speaking of trees reminds me that a species of large-bodied tree grows along the road below Waiohinu whose crotch is said to contain tanks of fresh water at all times; the natives suck it out through a hollow weed, which always grows near. As no other water exists in that wild neighborhood, within a space of some miles in circumference, it is considered to be a special invention of Providence for the behoof of the natives. I would rather accept the story than the deduction, because the latter is so manifestly but hastily conceived and erroneous. If the happiness of the natives had been the object, the tanks would have been filled with whiskey.

KAU INDEPENDENCE—JUDICIAL SAGACITY

The natives of the district of Kau have always dwelt apart from their fellow islanders—cut off from them by a desolate stretch of lava on one side and a mountain on the other—and they have ever shown a spirit and an independence not elsewhere to be found in Hawaii-nei. They are not thoroughly tamed yet, nor civilized or Christianized. Kau was the last district on the island that submitted to Kamehameha I. Two heaps of stones near the roadside mark where they killed two of the early kings of Hawaii. On both occasions these monarchs were trying to put down rebellion. They used to make their local chiefs very uncomfortable sometimes, and ten years ago, in playful mood, they made two tax collectors flee for their lives.

Most natives lie some, but these lie a good deal. They still believe in the ancient superstitions of the race, and believe in the Great Shark God and pray each other to death. When sworn by the Great Shark God, they are afraid to speak anything but the truth; but when sworn on the Bible in court, they proceed to soar into flights of fancy lying that make the inventions of Munchausen seem poor and trifling in comparison.

They worship idols in secret, and swindle the wayfaring stranger.

Some of the native judges and justices of the peace of the Kau district have been rare specimens of judicial sagacity. One of them considered that all the fines for adultery (thirty dollars for each offense) properly belonged to himself. He also considered himself a part of the Government, and that if he committed that crime himself it was the same as if the Government committed it, and, of course, it was the duty of the Government to pay the fine. Consequently, whenever he had collected a good deal of money from other court revenues, he used to set to work and keep on convicting himself of adultery until he had absorbed all the money on hand in paying the fines.

The adultery law has been so amended that each party to the offense is now fined thirty dollars; and I would remark, in passing, that if the crime were invariably detected and the fines collected, the revenues of the Hawaiian Government would probably exceed those of the United States. I trust the observation will not be considered in the light of an insinuation, however.

An old native judge at Hilo once acquitted all the parties

to a suit and then discovering, as he supposed, that he had no further hold on them and thus was out of pocket, he condemned the witnesses to pay the costs!

A Kau judge, whose two years' commission had expired, redated it himself and went on doing business as complacently as ever. He said it didn't make any difference—he could write as good a hand as the King could.

THE PROCESSION MOVETH AGAIN

Brown bought a horse from a native at Waiohinu for twelve dollars, but happening to think of the horse-jockeying propensities of the race, he removed the saddle and found that the creature needed "half-soling," as he expressed it. Recent hard riding had polished most of the hide off his back. He bought another and the animal went dead lame before we got to the great volcano, forty miles away. I bought a reckless little mule for fifteen dollars, and I wish I had him yet. One mule is worth a dozen horses for a mountain journey in the Islands.

The first eighteen miles of the road lay mostly down by the sea, and was pretty well sprinkled with native houses. The animals stopped at all of them—a habit they had early acquired; natives stop a few minutes at every shanty they come to, to swap gossip, and we were forced to do likewise —but we did it under protest.

Brown's horse jogged along well enough for sixteen or seventeen miles, but then he came down to a walk and refused to improve on it. We had to stop and intrude upon a gentleman who was not expecting us, and who I thought did not want us, either, but he entertained us handsomely, nevertheless, and has my hearty thanks for his kindness.

We looked at the ruddy glow cast upon the clouds above the volcano, only twenty miles away, now (the fires had become unusually active a few days before) for awhile after supper, and then went to bed and to sleep without rocking.

We stopped a few miles further on, the next morning, to hire a guide, but happily were saved the nuisance of traveling with a savage we could not talk with. The proprietor and another gentleman intended to go to the volcano the next day, and they said they would go at once if we would stop and take lunch. We signed the contract, of course. It was the usual style. We had found none but pleasant people on the island, from the time we landed at Kailua.

To get through the last twenty miles, guides are indispensable. The whole country is given up to cattle ranching, and is crossed and recrossed by a riddle of "bull paths" which is hopelessly beyond solution by a stranger.

IN FAIRYLAND

Portions of that little journey bloomed with beauty. Occasionally we entered small basins walled in with low cliffs, carpeted with greenest grass, and studded with shrubs and small trees whose foliage shone with an emerald brilliancy. One species, called the *mamona* [mamani], with its bright color, its delicate locust leaf, so free from decay or blemish of any kind, and its graceful shape, chained the eye with a sort of fascination. The rich verdant hue of these fairy parks was relieved and varied by the splendid carmine tassels of the ohia tree. Nothing was lacking but the fairies themselves.

THE KINGDOM OF DESOLATION

As we trotted up the almost imperceptible ascent and neared the volcano, the features of the country changed. We came upon a long dreary desert of black, swollen, twisted, corrugated billows of lava—blank and dismal desolation! Stony hillocks heaved up, all seamed with cracked wrinkles and broken open from center to circumference in a dozen places, as if from an explosion beneath. There had been terrible commotion here once, when these dead waves were seething fire; but now all was motionless and silent—it was a petrified sea! The narrow spaces between the upheavals were partly filled with volcanic sand, and through it we plodded laboriously. The invincible ohia struggled for a footing even in this desert waste, and achieved it—towering above the billows here and there, with trunks flattened like spears of grass in the crevices from which they sprang.

We came at last to torn and ragged deserts of scorched and blistered lava—to plains and patches of dull gray ashes —to the summit of the mountain, and these tokens warned us that we were nearing the palace of the dread goddess Pele, the crater of Kilauea.

MARK TWAIN

25✿

VOLCANO HOUSE, JUNE 3d—MIDNIGHT.

THE GREAT VOLCANO OF KILAUEA

I suppose no man ever saw Niagara for the first time without feeling disappointed. I suppose no man ever saw it the fifth time without wondering how he could ever have been so blind and stupid as to find any excuse for disappointment in the first place. I suppose that any one of nature's most celebrated wonders will always look rather insignificant to a visitor at first, but on a better acquaintance will swell and stretch out and spread abroad, until it finally grows clear beyond his grasp—becomes too stupendous for his comprehension. I know that a large house will seem to grow larger the longer one lives in it, and I also know that a woman who looks criminally homely at a first glance will often so improve upon acquaintance as to become really beautiful before the month is out.

I was disappointed when I saw the great volcano of Kilauea (Ke-low-way-ah) today for the first time. It is a comfort to me to know that I fully expected to be disappointed, however, and so, in one sense at least, I was not disappointed.

As we "raised" the summit of the mountain and began to canter along the edge of the crater, I heard Brown exclaim, "There's smoke, by George!" (poor infant—as if it

were the most surprising thing in the world to see smoke
issuing from a volcano), and I turned my head in the opposite direction and began to crowd my imagination down.
When I thought I had got it reduced to about the proper
degree, I resolutely faced about and came to a dead halt.
"Disappointed, anyhow!" I said to myself. "Only a considerable hole in the ground—nothing to Haleakala—a wide,
level, black plain in the bottom of it, and a few little sput-
tering jets of fire occupying a place about as large as an
ordinary potato patch, up in one corner—no smoke to
amount to anything. And these 'tremendous' perpendicular
walls they talk about, that inclose the crater! they don't
amount to a great deal, either; it is a large cellar—nothing
more—and precious little fire in it, too." So I soliloquized.
But as I gazed, the "cellar" insensibly grew. I was glad of
that, albeit I expected it. I am passably good at judging of
heights and distances, and I fell to measuring the diameter
of the crater. After considerable deliberation I was obliged
to confess that it was rather over three miles, though it was
hard to believe it at first. It was growing on me, and tolerably fast. And when I came to guess at the clean, solid,
perpendicular walls that fenced in the basin, I had to acknowledge that they were from six hundred to eight hundred feet high, and in one or two places even a thousand,
though at a careless glance they did not seem more than
two or three hundred. The reason the walls looked so low
is because the basin inclosed is so large. The place looked a
little larger and a little deeper every five minutes, by the
watch. And still it was unquestionably small; there was no
getting around that. About this time I saw an object which
helped to increase the size of the crater. It was a house
perched on the extreme edge of the wall, at the far end of

the basin, two miles and a half away; it looked like a martin box under the eaves of a cathedral! That wall appeared immensely higher after that than it did before.

I reflected that night was the proper time to view a volcano, and Brown, with one of those eruptions of homely wisdom which rouse the admiration of strangers, but which custom has enabled me to contemplate calmly, said five o'clock was the proper time for dinner, and therefore we spurred up the animals and trotted along the brink of the crater for about the distance it is from the Lick House, in San Francisco, to the Mission, and then found ourselves at the Volcano House.

On the way we passed close to fissures several feet wide and about as deep as the sea, no doubt, and out of some of them steam was issuing. It would be suicidal to attempt to travel about there at night. As we approached the lookout house I have before spoken of as being perched on the wall, we saw some objects ahead which I took for the brilliant white plant called the "silver sword," but they proved to be "buoys"—pyramids of stones painted white, so as to be visible at night, and set up at intervals to mark the path to the lookout house and guard unaccustomed feet from wandering into the abundant chasms that line the way.

By the path it is half a mile from the Volcano House to the lookout house. After a hearty supper we waited until it was thoroughly dark and then started to the crater. The first glance in that direction revealed a scene of wild beauty. There was a heavy fog over the crater and it was splendidly illuminated by the glare from the fires below. The illumination was two miles wide and a mile high, perhaps; and if you ever, on a dark night and at a distance, beheld the light from thirty or forty blocks of distant

buildings all on fire at once, reflected strongly against overhanging clouds, you can form a fair idea of what this
looked like.

THE VISION OF HELL AND ITS ANGELS

Arrived at the little thatched lookout house, we rested
our elbows on the railing in front and looked abroad over
the wide crater and down over the sheer precipice at the
seething fires beneath us. The view was a startling improvement on my daylight experience. I turned to see the effect
on the balance of the company and found the reddest-
faced set of men I almost ever saw. In the strong light every
countenance glowed like red-hot iron, every shoulder was
suffused with crimson and shaded rearward into dingy,
shapeless obscurity! The place below looked like the infernal regions and these men like half-cooled devils just come
up on a furlough.

I turned my eyes upon the volcano again. The "cellar"
was tolerably well lighted up. For a mile and a half in front
of us and half a mile on either side, the floor of the abyss
was magnificently illuminated; beyond these limits the
mists hung down their gauzy curtains and cast a deceptive
gloom over all that made the twinkling fires in the remote
corners of the crater seem countless leagues removed—
made them seem like the campfires of a great army far
away. Here was room for the imagination to work! You
could imagine those lights the width of a continent away
—and that hidden under the intervening darkness were
hills, and winding rivers, and weary wastes of plain and
desert—and even then the tremendous vista stretched on
and on and on!—to the fires and far beyond! You could
not compass it—it was the idea of eternity made tangible

—and the longest end of it made visible to the naked eye!

The greater part of the vast floor of the desert under us was as black as ink, and apparently smooth and level; but over a mile square of it was ringed and streaked and striped with a thousand branching streams of liquid and gorgeously brilliant fire! It looked like a colossal railroad map of the State of Massachusetts done in chain lightning on a midnight sky. Imagine it—imagine a coal-black sky shivered into a tangled network of angry fire!

Here and there were gleaming holes twenty feet in diameter, broken in the dark crust, and in them the melted lava —the color a dazzling white just tinged with yellow—was boiling and surging furiously; and from these holes branched numberless bright torrents in many directions, like the "spokes" of a lady's fan, and kept a tolerably straight course for a while and then swept round in huge rainbow curves, or made a long succession of sharp worm-fence angles, which looked precisely like the fiercest jagged lightning. These streams met other streams, and they mingled with and crossed and recrossed each other in every conceivable direction, like skate tracks on a popular skating ground. Sometimes streams twenty or thirty feet wide flowed from the holes to some distance without dividing— and through the opera glasses we could see that they ran down small, steep hills and were genuine cataracts of fire, white at their source, but soon cooling and turning to the richest red, grained with alternate lines of black and gold. Every now and then masses of the dark crust broke away and floated slowly down these streams like rafts down a river. Occasionally the molten lava flowing under the superincumbent crust broke through—split a dazzling streak, from five hundred to a thousand feet long, like a sudden

flash of lightning, and then acre after acre of the cold lava
parted into fragments, turned up edgewise like cakes of ice
when a great river breaks up, plunged downward and were
swallowed in the crimson caldron. Then the wide expanse
of the "thaw" maintained a ruddy glow for a while, but
shortly cooled and became black and level again. During a
"thaw," every dismembered cake was marked by a glittering white border which was superbly shaded inwards by
aurora-borealis rays, which were a flaming yellow where
they joined the white border, and from thence toward their
points tapered into glowing crimson, then into a rich, pale
carmine, and finally into a faint blush that held its own
a moment and then dimmed and turned black. Some of the
streams preferred to mingle together in a tangle of fan-
tastic circles, and then they looked something like the confusion of ropes one sees on a ship's deck when she had just
taken in sail and dropped anchor—provided one can imagine those ropes on fire.

Through the glasses, the little fountains scattered about
looked very beautiful. They boiled, and coughed, and
spluttered, and discharged sprays of stringy red fire—of
about the consistency of mush, for instance—from ten to
fifteen feet into the air, along with a shower of brilliant
white sparks—a quaint and unnatural mingling of gouts
of blood and snowflakes!

We had circles and serpents and streaks of lightning all
twined and wreathed and tied together, without a break
throughout an area more than a mile square (that amount
of ground was covered, though it was not strictly
"square"), and it was with a feeling of placid exultation
that we reflected that many years had elapsed since any
visitor had seen such a splendid display—since any visitor

had seen anything more than the now snubbed and insignificant "North" and "South" lakes in action. We had been reading old files of Hawaiian newspapers and the "Record Book" at the Volcano House, and were posted.

I could see the North Lake lying out on the black floor away off in the outer edge of our panorama, and knitted to it by a web work of lava streams. In its individual capacity it looked very little more respectable than a school-house on fire. True, it was about nine hundred feet long and two or three hundred wide, but then, under the present circumstances, it necessarily appeared rather insignificant, and besides it was so distant from us. We heard a week ago that the volcano was getting on a heavier spree than it had indulged in for many years, and I am glad we arrived just at the right moment to see it under full blast.

I forgot to say that the noise made by the bubbling lava is not great, heard as we heard it from our lofty perch. It makes three distinct sounds—a rushing, a hissing, and a coughing or puffing sound; and if you stand on the brink and close your eyes it is no trick at all to imagine that you are sweeping down a river on a large low-pressure steamer, and that you hear the hissing of the steam about her boilers, the puffing from her escape pipes, and the churning rush of the water abaft her wheels. The smell of sulphur is strong, but not unpleasant to a sinner.

THE PILLAR OF FIRE

We left the lookout house at ten o'clock in a half-cooked condition, because of the heat from Pele's furnaces, and wrapping up in blankets (for the night was cold) returned to the hotel. After we got out in the dark we had another fine spectacle. A colossal column of cloud towered to a great height in the air immediately above the crater, and the outer swell of every one of its vast folds was dyed with a rich crimson luster, which was subdued to a pale rose tint in the depressions between. It glowed like a muffled torch and stretched upward to a dizzy height toward the zenith. I thought it just possible that its like had not been seen since the children of Israel wandered on their long march through the desert so many centuries ago over a path illuminated by the mysterious "pillar of fire." And I was sure that I now had a vivid conception of what the majestic "pillar of fire" was like, which almost amounted to a revelation.

ACCOMMODATIONS FOR MAN AND BEAST

It is only at very long intervals that I mention in a letter matters which properly pertain to the advertising columns, but in this case it seems to me that to leave out the fact that there is a neat, roomy, well-furnished, and well-kept hotel at the volcano, would be to remain silent upon a point of the very highest importance to anyone who may desire to visit the place. The surprise of finding a good hotel in such an outlandish spot startled me considerably more than the volcano did. The house is new—built three or four months ago—and the table is good. One could not easily starve here even if the meats and groceries were to give out, for large tracts of land in the vicinity are well paved with excellent strawberries. One can have as abundant a supply as he chooses to call for. There has never heretofore been anything in this locality for the accommodation of travellers but a crazy old native grass hut, scanty fare, hard beds of matting, and a Chinese cook.

MARK TWAIN